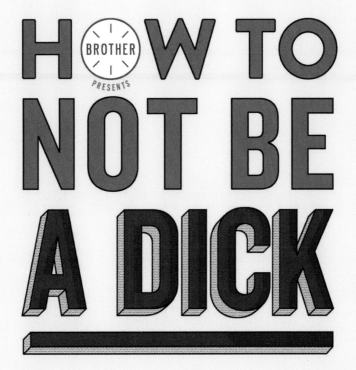

HOW TO NOT BE A DICK

BROTHER PRESENTS

HOW TO NOT BE A DICK

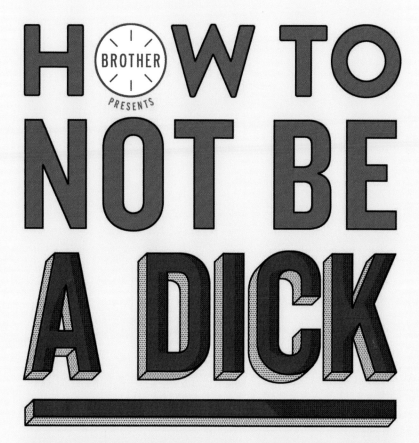

BROTHER PRESENTS

AND OTHER ESSENTIAL TRUTHS ABOUT WORK, SEX, LOVE—AND EVERYTHING ELSE THAT MATTERS

WILLIAM MORROW
An Imprint of HarperCollinsPublishers

HarperCollins books may be purchased for educational, business, or sales promotional use. For information, please email the Special Markets Department at SPsales@harpercollins.com.

FIRST EDITION

Library of Congress Cataloging-in-Publication Data has been applied for.

ISBN 978-0-06-287182-4

19 20 21 22 23   10 9 8 7 6 5 4 3 2 1

BY
Joel Hanek, Hogan Hiatt, Adam Lederer, Hot Rod Martinez,
James Montgomery, Ryan Powell, Pernell Quilon,
Bailey Rosser, Emily Wilson and Tom Wright

EDITED BY
James Montgomery

DESIGN & ART DIRECTION BY
Karen Jaimes

ILLUSTRATIONS BY
Ariel Alter

INFOGRAPHICS BY
Stephanie Truong

CONTENTS

1 LIFE

50 SEX

112 WORK

162 MONEY

190 WOMEN

218 FUN

258 HEALTH

296 YOU

HOW TO NOT BE A DICK

BROTHER PRESENTS

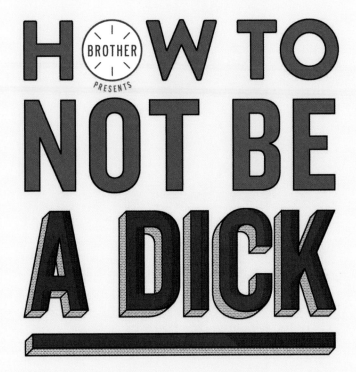

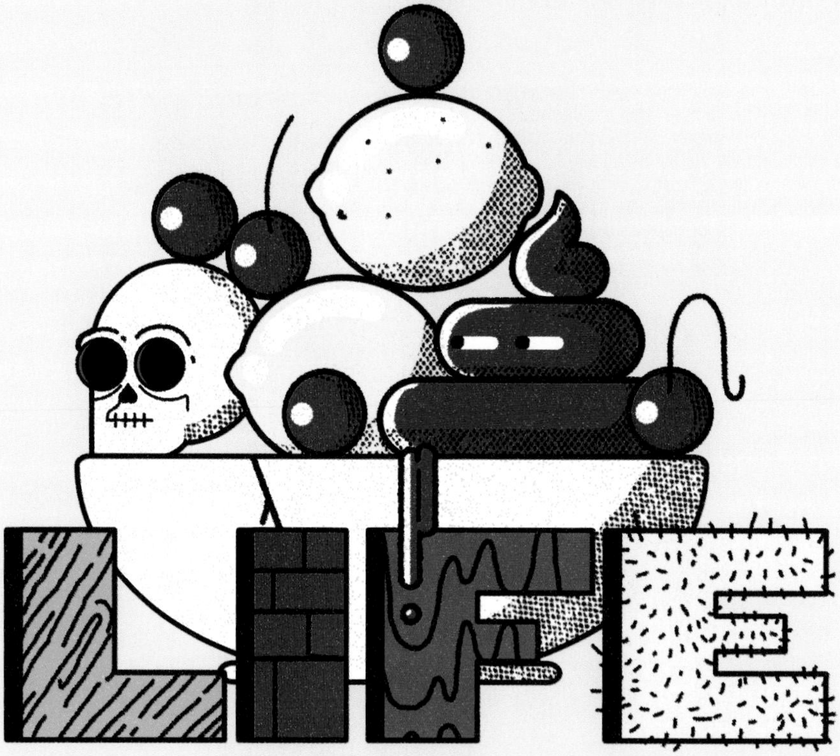
LIFE

These terms and conditions create a contract between you and BROTHER (the "Agreement"). Please read the Agreement carefully.

A. INTRODUCTION TO OUR SERVICES

This Agreement governs your use of BROTHER's services ("Services"), through which you can learn valuable life lessons ("Truths") and unique skills ("Content") that can—and should—be applied at your discretion. Our Services are available for your use in your country of residence ("Home Country"), in accordance with societal standards and/or legal statutes. To use our Services, you need an open mind, a willingness to look ridiculous and the ability to read. Our Services' performance may be affected by these factors.

In the interest of full disclosure, here is how we explained those Services in our initial pitch to HarperCollins (the "Publisher"), which must've worked, because you're reading this right now. The fact that the Publisher decided to change the title of this book does not invalidate anything of the following:

"We're not going to lie to you—life can be complicated.

"But *The Truth* will set you free. From simple solutions to complex social interactions to general rules of gentlemanly etiquette, it's the definitive guide for today's guy.

"We will help them navigate an increasingly complicated world—the classroom, the locker room, the office, the bar, the bedroom, the DM—where the old rules, labels and standards no longer apply. We won't condescend, we won't mince words—we'll give them straightforward, occasionally brutal (but always funny) honesty, and, hopefully, create a new set of axioms in the process.

"This is *Brother's* big book of universal truths...the stuff we wish someone would've told us.

"*Brother* is a global brand made for millennial males. Publishing daily on Snapchat, we reach an audience of 20 million young men each month (40 million unique visitors in total—girls like us, too!). We create content that is optimized for mobile and designed with the millennial in mind, mixing media and text to deliver an experience that is informative, entertaining and interactive.

"We use data to test and refine work. We're still experimenting—but we'd like to think we've gotten pretty good at understanding our audience. It doesn't hurt that we are our audience. We are interested in life, love, sex, style and tech. We are self-aware, but not self-centered. We take digital culture as a given; we understand that it's 2019—everyone uses a dating app. We are informed and impatient. We ask big questions, and expect appropriately huge answers. But we're not judgmental jerks. We'd like someone to buy us a beer every once in a while.

"With *Brother Presents: The Truth*, we'll use that knowledge and expertise. Presented in a format that is engaging and appealing to digital-native demos—a compelling mix of infographics, diagrams, images, lists, quizzes and essays—we'll simplify the millennial man's life...by simply telling him the truth."

We can't believe they bought it, either.

B. USING OUR SERVICES

PAYMENTS, TAXES AND REFUNDS

You can acquire Truths and Content via our Services for free or for a one-time charge, depending on whether you are borrowing this book from an acquaintance or have decided to purchase it for yourself. Either instance is referred to as a "Transaction." Each Transaction is a contract between you and BROTHER, and it is up to you to fulfill your end of the bargain—if you don't, we will be disappointed. In addition, violators can also be subjected to additional punishment, as determined by BROTHER's Chief Magistrate, who has definitely seen some shit and is not one to trifle with. If you pre-order Content, you will be charged when the Content is delivered to you (though please let us know how you managed to do this, since this is a *book*). All Transactions are final. If you want to sell this book on your own, that's up to you, man. Prices may change at any time, contingent on how well this book has been selling or how badly the Publisher has misjudged potential enthusiasm for this project. There will be no refunds, regardless of how poorly this book is written or how useless all Content contained herein may be. Fraud or other manipulative behavior may entitle BROTHER to a corresponding counterclaim, so think twice before trying to pass any of our Truths or Content off as your own. We are always watching you, and we have your financial information on file.

PRIVACY

Your use of our Services is subject to BROTHER's Privacy Policy, which is explained in great detail below but can essentially be summed up thusly: You're fucked.

BROTHER has developed and patented a suite of technologies that will be used to collect your personal information, including (but not limited to) fingerprints, biometric measurements, sexual conquests, penis size, test scores, fantasies, gaming system preferences, mother's maiden name, browsing history, passwords, credit scores, shoe size, deep-seated fears and every time you've ever cried. Your personal information will be used to sell you petroleum-based grooming products that are slowly killing the Earth, your Home Country and, by logical extent, you. There is no way to opt out of this policy, as by merely cracking open this book, you are implicitly agreeing to it.

We will also collect data in a form that does not, on its own, permit direct association with any specific individual. We may collect, use, transfer and disclose what we deem to be nonpersonal information—including your occupation, language of preference or location—for any purpose, so we like to keep the wording as vague as possible (but it will probably involve more petroleum-based products). BROTHER will attempt to justify this gross violation of your privacy by claiming to use your personal information only to keep you posted on our latest project developments and upcoming events, or to improve current products and services.

SERVICES AND CONTENT USAGE RULES

Your use of the Services and Content must follow the rules set forth in this section ("Usage Rules"). Any other use of the Services and Content is a material breach of this Agreement. BROTHER may monitor your use of the Services and Content to ensure that you are following these Usage Rules.

All Services:

- You may use the Services and Content only for personal, noncommercial purposes, such as hooking up or exacting revenge on your coworkers. Any prizes or rewards attained using our Services and Content belong to us as well.

- BROTHER's delivery of Content does not transfer any promotional use rights to you, so don't try to pass any of this shit off as your own. Like *you* could come up with this many charts...

- It is your responsibility not to lose, destroy, or damage Content once purchased. We will monitor this via previously mentioned suite of technologies, in addition to periodic checks of landfills in your Home Country.

- You may not tamper with or circumvent any technology included with the Services, but good luck finding any of it.

CONTENT AND SERVICE AVAILABILITY

Terms found in this Agreement that relate to Services, Content types, features or functionality not available in your Home Country are not applicable to you unless and until they become available to you. What does that mean? Good question.

YOUR SUBMISSIONS TO OUR SERVICES

Our Services may cause you to react with comments, crude gestures or incredulous sighs (the "Submissions"). How do we keep track of Submissions? We're always watching, remember? Your use of such features must comply with the Submissions Guidelines below, which may be updated from time to time (and without your knowledge). You hereby grant BROTHER a worldwide, royalty-free, perpetual, nonexclusive license to use the materials you submit within the Services and related marketing. And if that sounds threatening, it should. BROTHER will monitor and decide to remove or edit any submitted material.

Submissions Guidelines: You may not use the Services to:

- Be a jerk, unless specifically instructed to act that way.

- Act in an offensive, unlawful, deceptive or harmful manner.

- Impersonate or misrepresent your affiliation with another person, or entity, unless you have a really good costume.

- Plan or engage in any illegal, fraudulent, or manipulative activity, unless we get a cut of the action.

- If charged with—or convicted of—a crime, BROTHER will disavow any knowledge of your existence.

INTELLECTUAL PROPERTY

You agree that the Services, including but not limited to analysis, codes, Content, credos, dumb charts, diagrams and graphs, gripes, half-baked schemes, illustrations, inane lists, judgments, Killers lyrics, petty grievances, sex tips, threats and texts used to implement the Services, contain proprietary information and material that is owned by BROTHER, and is protected by applicable intellectual property and other laws, including but not limited to copyright. You agree that you will not use such proprietary information or materials in any way whatsoever except for use of the Services for personal, noncommercial uses in compliance with this Agreement. No portion of the Services may be reproduced in any form or by any means, except as expressly permitted by this Agreement. You agree not to modify, rent, loan, sell, or distribute the Services or Content in any manner, and you shall not exploit the Services in any manner not expressly authorized.

The BROTHER name, the BROTHER logo and other BROTHER trademarks, service marks, graphics and logos used in connection with the Services are trademarks or registered trademarks of BROTHER in the U.S. and other countries throughout the world. BROTHER is also the name of a line of sewing machines, but we're betting they haven't noticed yet (so don't tell them). You are granted no right or license with respect to any of the aforesaid trademarks, unless you are the people who manufacture those sewing machines; you've probably earned it.

TERMINATION AND SUSPENSION OF SERVICES

If you fail, or BROTHER suspects that you have failed, to comply with any of the provisions of this Agreement, BROTHER may, without notice: (i) terminate this Agreement; and/or (ii) terminate your access to our Content; and/or (iii) terminate you.

BROTHER further reserves the right to modify, suspend, or discontinue the Services (or any part or Content thereof) at any time with or without notice to you—until we show up at your job/place of residence to terminate you.

OTHER PROVISIONS

This Agreement constitutes the entire agreement between you and BROTHER and governs your use of the Services, superseding any prior agreements with respect to the same subject matter between you and BROTHER. If any part of this Agreement is held invalid or unenforceable, that portion shall be construed in a manner consistent with applicable law to reflect, as nearly as possible, the original intentions of the parties, and the remaining portions shall remain in full force and effect. BROTHER's failure to enforce any right or provisions in this Agreement will not constitute a waiver of such or any other provision. We're busy. BROTHER will not be responsible for failures to fulfill any obligations due to causes beyond its control. Again, we're busy.

You agree to comply with all local, state, federal, and national laws, statutes, ordinances and regulations that apply to your use of the Services. Your use of the Services may also be subject to other laws. No BROTHER employee or agent has the authority to vary this Agreement—not even Hogan, and we let that dude do *everything*.

You hereby grant BROTHER the right to take steps BROTHER believes are reasonably necessary or appropriate to enforce and/or verify compliance with any part of this Agreement. You agree that BROTHER has the right, without liability to you, to disclose any data and/or information to law enforcement authorities, government officials and/or a third party, even though BROTHER thinks cops are the worst and not to be trusted. We take this Agreement very seriously, and failure to comply with any part of it shall result in punishment, as determined by our Chief Magistrate, including (i) a fine of USD $5,000; (ii) a series of Indian Burns; (iii) 25 days in BROTHER jail, which is not as fun as it sounds; (iv) dibs on any sexual partners, both current and future; or (v) all of the above. **Because life isn't fair—which is why you should always read the fine print. And that's the truth.**

MASLOW'S HIERARCHY OF LIFE NEEDS

Everything necessary to ascend, find fulfillment and become the person you were meant to be.

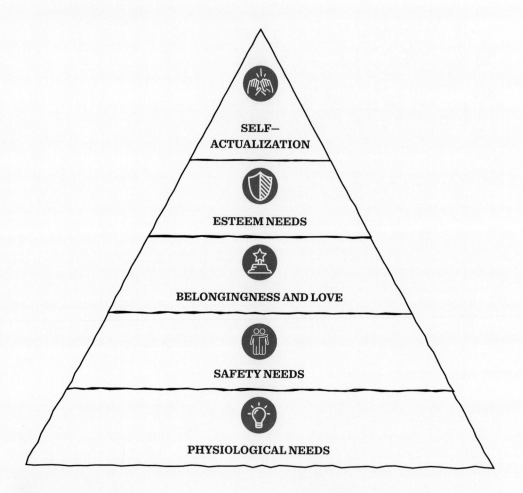

SELF–
ACTUALIZATION

ESTEEM NEEDS

BELONGINGNESS AND LOVE

SAFETY NEEDS

PHYSIOLOGICAL NEEDS

SELF-ACTUALIZATION—Wi-Fi.

ESTEEM—Likes, compliments and recognition, respect, the occasional nude.

BELONGINGNESS AND LOVE—Dating apps, social media, friends, family, a companion, your hand (when all else fails).

SAFETY—Freedom from harassment and intimidation (not applicable if you are black in America), money, medicine, seatbelts, airbags, a weapon (if you are delusional).

PHYSIOLOGICAL—Air, water, food, clothing, shelter, sleep, someone to have sex with occasionally, your phone, a place to charge your phone.

100 Universal Truths About *your* Life

We're not gonna lie to you: life is hard. But these truths will set you free.

Everyone is pretending.

Anyone who boasts is overcompensating.

No one is as happy as they appear to be.

Social Media is not real life.

Comparing yourself to others is a waste of time.

If you don't expect anything, you'll never be disappointed.

Art and commerce can never coexist.

Kindness is underrated.

Happiness is a social construct, not a goal.

Thriftiness is a virtue; cheapness is an annoyance.

Never stop doing kids' stuff—that way you'll never get old.

Always have an alibi.

If you find yourself saying "I'm not a racist," you're probably a racist.

If you have to ask "Is this inappropriate?" it's probably inappropriate.

The answer to the question "How did they afford that?" is always "Their parents paid for it."

Blackface is never a good idea.

Always say "Thank you."

Often, it's just easier to apologize.

Know what battles are worth fighting.

You won't live forever, but you can create something that might.

Have perspective—there is always someone worse off than you.

Be patient—if you're good, you'll get what's coming to you.

Recognize your privilege.

Sometimes, it's better to be realistic than optimistic.

Never spend more than 72 hours in Las Vegas.

Only assholes give TED Talks.

Only supreme assholes *attend* TED Talks.

Always bring a jacket. You will never regret it.

Never do anything without consent.

Always buy the first round.

Never talk business at an after-work event.

Don't be friends with your boss.

Learn how to cook three different meals.

Learn how to play the guitar. But never play an acoustic guitar at a party.

Learn how the stock market works.

Clean up after yourself.

Make your bed every morning.

Floss. Even though it sucks.

Buy yourself one piece of expensive clothing.

No one likes a sore loser.

No one likes a bad winner, either.

If something sounds too good to be true, it is.

There is no such thing as a quick fix.

Sometimes life is unfair. But things will always get better.

Your parents are just people and, as such, are probably making it up as they go.

If you don't know the answer—ask someone who does.

Never wear shorts to the office.

Never buy single-ply toilet paper.

Never go to IKEA on a weekend.

Never show up empty-handed.

Never bet on your own team.

Always eat before you drink.

Always avoid the middle urinal.

Always wear a condom.

Always split the check evenly—even if you only had a salad.

Always keep your eye on the ball.

Hawaiian shirts are appropriate for every occasion.

Beards make you sexier.

Breakfast is the most important meal of the day.

A burger at a bar is always better than a burger at a restaurant.

If a bar has peanut shells on the floor, you're in the right place.

If a bar hangs Christmas lights, and it's not Christmas, you're in the right place.

If two different people tell you you're drunk, you're probably too drunk.

Give compliments sparingly—they mean more that way.

Don't worry about what you're lifting at the gym—everyone has to start somewhere.

Running one mile is always better than running zero miles.

"Compassionate Conservatism" is an oxymoron.

Everyone sees the world differently, and no one's viewpoint is entirely correct.

Everything's better on a boat.

It's usually white people's fault.

Do or do not; there is no try.

Be wary of anyone who talks about "building a brand."

Never start an Instagram account for your dog.

Go outside.

Never pack what you can't carry yourself.

If you can afford it, buy it. You'll regret it later if you don't.

Listen to your critics—there's a good chance they're right.

Never underestimate the power of a good complaint.

Refrain from interjecting yourself in any argument involving two or more women.

It's important to know the difference between "your" and "you're."

Avoid anyone who has "Live, Laugh, Love" stenciled on their wall.

You'll never regret learning how to change the oil on a car.

You'll never regret learning how to install an operating system on a computer.

You'll never regret learning how to throw a ball.

You'll never regret learning how to play piano.

Always carry a pocket knife.

Always save your receipt.

If you're tired, take a nap.

If you're hungry, have a snack.

Be nice to animals and the elderly.

Guns are for cowards.

If you have a problem with someone, tell them.

Try not to take yourself too seriously.

Humility is never a bad look.

There is more to learn from failure than success.

Be polite and fair.

Just get on with it.

If you stick your neck out, be prepared to have your head cut off.

Aim high—even if you come up short, you'll still be in a better place.

Life is a lot easier when you learn to let shit go.

It's Basically All Bullshit

SCHOOL

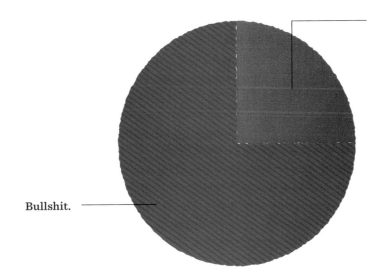

What Actually Matters: Discovering one's self. Navigating social cliques. Dealing with bullies. Asking someone out. The realization that life is essentially just a continuation of school. Lunch.

Bullshit.

WORK

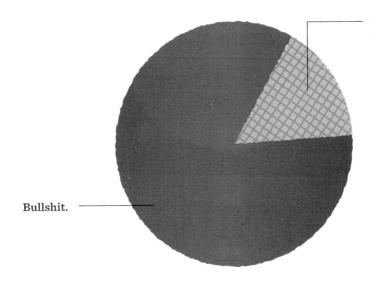

What Actually Matters: Money. Interacting with others. Key bullshitting skills. Understanding your true value. Understanding you will never get paid an amount commensurate to that. Lunch.

Bullshit.

LIFE

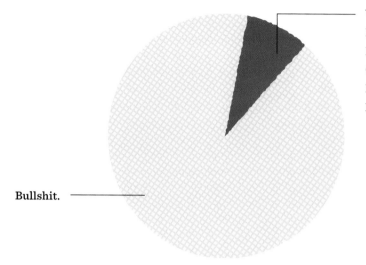

What Actually Matters: Friendship. Family. Kindness. Generosity. Empathy. Health. Freedom. Equality.

Bullshit.

RELATIONSHIPS

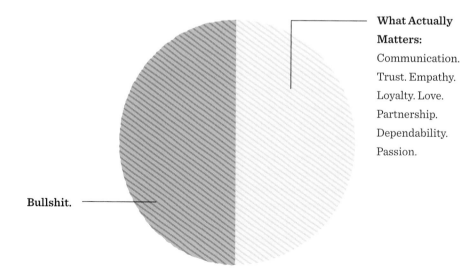

What Actually Matters: Communication. Trust. Empathy. Loyalty. Love. Partnership. Dependability. Passion.

Bullshit.

FOOD

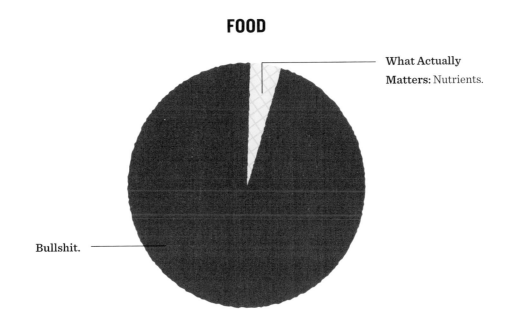

What Actually
Matters: Nutrients.

Bullshit.

SEX

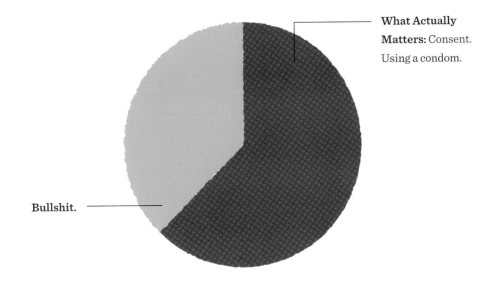

What Actually
Matters: Consent.
Using a condom.

Bullshit.

CLOTHING

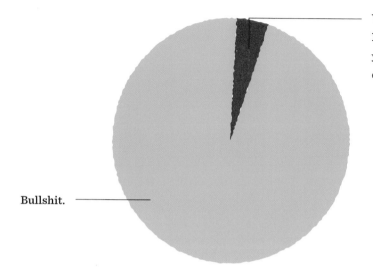

What Actually Matters: Protecting your body from the elements. Comfort.

Bullshit.

SOCIAL MEDIA

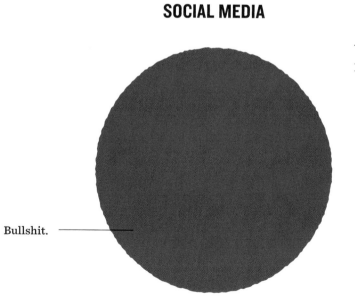

What Actually Matters: Nothing.

Bullshit.

LIFE TIMELINES

HOW BORING PEOPLE LIVE THEIR LIVES:

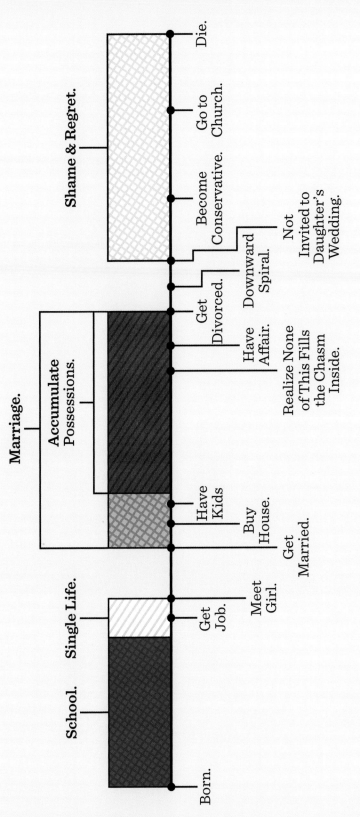

HOW INTERESTING PEOPLE LIVE THEIR LIVES:

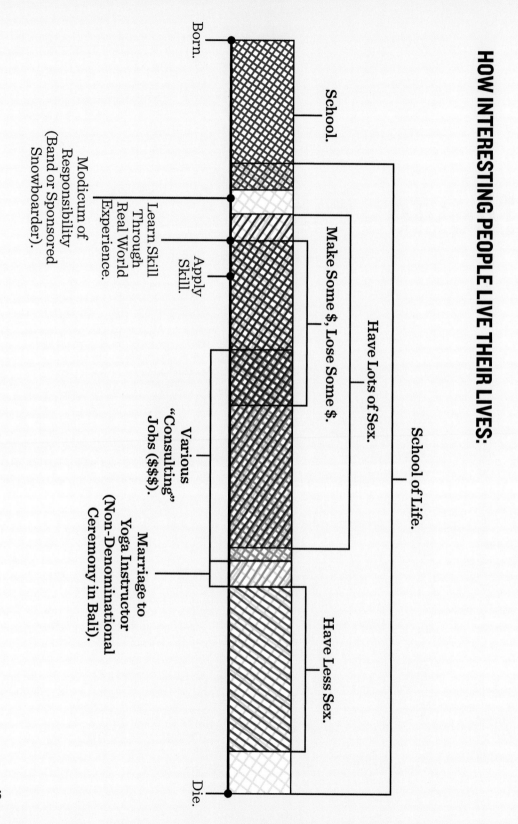

Born.

School.

Modicum of Responsibility (Band or Sponsored Snowboarder).

Learn Skill Through Real World Experience.

Apply Skill.

Make Some $, Lose Some $.

Have Lots of Sex.

Various "Consulting" Jobs ($$$).

School of Life.

Marriage to Yoga Instructor (Non-Denominational Ceremony in Bali).

Have Less Sex.

Die.

Everything Movies Lie *to You* About

This should be fairly obvious to you (because you're reading a book), but life is not a movie. Yes, there are moments of romance, action, drama, comedy and maybe the occasional explosion, but mainly, life is just monotony—a mix of walking, sleeping, consuming and overlapping dialogue. If it *were* a movie, Robert Altman would definitely direct it.

The fact that life is not a movie is the reason movies exist in the first place. They are escapist entertainment. Again, that seems obvious, but as you get older, you begin to realize just how much you have been incepted by movies (using a phrase from *Inception* as a narrative device is a pretty good example of that). They raise your expectations about what life should be, and how it should end. They give you false hopes and unrealistic assumptions. They offer hollow promises and faulty logic. In other words, movies lie to you.

The sooner you realize that, the better. Sure, your life may be monotonous, but it's *yours*. Stop using a script as a measuring stick, and live the way you want. To help you get started, here's the truth about Hollywood's biggest lies.

You will never have a witty retort ready.

You will rarely say the right thing at the right time.

You will not meet your significant other in some quirky, cosmic manner.

Women actually have plenty of conversations that don't involve men.

The quiet girl at (insert mom-and-pop store here) does not want you to rescue her from her small life. She probably doesn't even want you to talk to her.

In real life, manic pixie dream girls are exhausting.

Platonic relationships rarely become *something more*.

If you rescue a girl, she will probably not fall in love with you.

Guys who look like Williamsburg accountants don't get girls who look like Parisian models.

No one ever has a meaningful conversation in the pouring rain.

Loitering outside someone's building isn't charming, it's fucking creepy.

Constantly pursuing a woman won't win her over. It will get you arrested.

Failing relationships can't be saved with poignant gestures or thrilling hijinks.

Weddings are rarely dramatic and only occasionally magical.

The same goes for sex—plus, you sweat *way* more.

Women don't find drunk men charming.

You will never attempt to explain being caught in a compromising situation by shouting "It's not what it looks like!"

Not everyone has a funny friend, because they're usually annoying.

Real NYC apartments don't look like that.

Real bodies don't look like that, either.

Underdogs are underdogs for a reason—they usually lose.

Most assholes don't redeem themselves, they just continue being assholes.

Bad guys usually don't get what's coming to them. In fact, they usually win.

You will never walk away from an exploding building in slow motion.

You can't jump between buildings or train cars.

You can't cling to a helicopter as it takes off, either.

You won't get rewarded for ignoring your boss' orders. You get fired.

If someone is pointing a gun at you, they will not take a moment to deliver a speech before pulling the trigger.

Occasionally, the automatic override *isn't* damaged.

You will never be involved in a car chase.

In the event of an actual cataclysmic event, you will not survive.

In the event of an actual gun battle, you will not slide over the hood of a car while firing a pair of handguns.

You can't just randomly enhance digital footage.

You will never get a montage.

You will never deliver a stirring speech.

You will never do anything that's accompanied by a soaring soundtrack.

There's a pretty good chance you will die alone.

Tom Cruise is actually like 5′4″.

The Conflict Conundrum

Ever since the first fish pulled itself out of the primordial ooze and proclaimed to any organic compound within earshot that Stanley Kubrick was overrated, life has been defined by conflict. It's the reason why, over the course of the next 15-20 million years, humans developed a "fight-or-flight" response, a physiological reaction that occurs in response to a perceived attack or threat to survival. Otherwise we'd just be punching everyone.

So it's not a stretch to say the secret to life is decoding conflict—understanding its root cause and formulating the proper response. In other words, knowing when it's time to fight, or when it's better to simply fly (or, you know, *walk*) away.

Not surprisingly, this is more difficult than it seems. After all, every conflict is fueled by emotions, and emotions are harder to check than Connor McDavid. So we've prepared this list of conflicts that will more than likely end in confrontation to help you navigate these choppy waters, and hopefully keep you from getting punched in the face. Make sure to keep it with you at all times for quick reference.

You're having a proper night out with friends when suddenly, it's go time.

POTENTIAL CONFLICT LEVEL: High. Welcome to Bar Brawl City.

ROOT CAUSE: Did you see someone get hit by a chair? Toss a drink on a stranger? If you didn't witness it with your own eyes, don't assume you know how it started.

APPROPRIATE RESPONSE: If you didn't see the slight, the appropriate response is flight. Just make sure to pull your buddy out of the fight pit before you bolt.

You are drunk and perceive some action as disrespectful.

POTENTIAL CONFLICT LEVEL: Off the charts. You are drunk.

ROOT CAUSE: Honestly, probably something you did. You are drunk.

APPROPRIATE RESPONSE: Go home. You are drunk.

A stranger has just made an inappropriate comment to your special lady friend.

POTENTIAL CONFLICT LEVEL: High. You don't want to lose face in front of said special lady friend.

ROOT CAUSE: Either alcohol or jealousy. Probably both.

APPROPRIATE RESPONSE: You won't like this, but flight. Definitely get up in the guy's face before you leave, though, and make sure to mention the "alcohol or jealousy" bit.

A stranger has just inappropriately touched your special lady friend.

ROOT CAUSE: Either alcohol or jealousy. Probably both.

APPROPRIATE RESPONSE: See left, then forget it. Every man must fight sometimes, so punch that dude in the fucking face.

POTENTIAL CONFLICT LEVEL: High. See left.

Your coworker has ratted you out to the boss.

POTENTIAL CONFLICT LEVEL: Moderate. Unless you slept with the boss' daughter.

ROOT CAUSE: A toxic mix of sycophancy and social climbing.

APPROPRIATE RESPONSE: Talk to your coworker about it face-to-face. To be fair, most bosses don't like rats, either, so there's a good chance your coworker will eventually get what's coming to him or her. As a general rule, it's never a good idea to throw a punch in the office.

POTENTIAL CONFLICT LEVEL: Depends on how badly you want to keep this job.

Your boss has called you into his or her office to discuss the matter.

ROOT CAUSE: Well, obviously your coworker, though it's important for any man to own up to his mistakes, too. You know what you did.

APPROPRIATE RESPONSE: Take your punishment like a man. If you feel you are being unjustly persecuted, say so, but have facts to back up that assertion—and never throw a fellow coworker under the bus; that's what got *you* here in the first place.

You are home for the holidays and your uncle has decided that the dinner table is an appropriate venue to call out your liberal ideologies.

POTENTIAL CONFLICT LEVEL: Depends on how uncomfortable you want to make dinner.

ROOT CAUSE: Fear. He is old and is witnessing profound social change he is powerless to stop. The irony that *his* parents felt exactly the same way about *his* generation is lost on him.

APPROPRIATE RESPONSE: Fight back with words and facts, but never fists. When he inevitably attempts to dismiss your facts, point out that continuing this conversation is pointless. Then ask him to pass the gravy.

You are at a holiday "door-buster super sale" and someone has trampled you in a mad dash for a flatscreen TV on deep discount.

POTENTIAL CONFLICT LEVEL: Insanely high. We've all seen the YouTube videos.

ROOT CAUSE: Desperation? Thriftiness? We can't say for certain, because we have pride and would never attend a fucking "door-buster super sale."

APPROPRIATE RESPONSE: Reevaluate your life.

You have just been cut off in traffic.

POTENTIAL CONFLICT LEVEL: High. Traffic is one of life's greatest stressors.

ROOT CAUSE: More than likely, the person being a terrible fucking driver.

APPROPRIATE RESPONSE: Definitely not fighting. We've never understood the urge to leave *your* car to fight a dude in his—cars are basically 4,000-pound weapons. A solid, lengthy blast of the horn should suffice.

You are waiting in line when someone blatantly cuts in front of you.

POTENTIAL CONFLICT LEVEL: Low. If only because of the transitive property of conflict.

ROOT CAUSE: Tardiness, being from a different country, or perhaps general assholeishness.

APPROPRIATE RESPONSE: See above. If a person cuts ahead of *you* in line, they are cutting ahead of everyone *behind* you, too, and as such, you will not be the only one angered by the indiscretion. Lead with a firm "The end of the line is back there," then wait for backup. It will always arrive.

Your roommate has taken your food from the fridge and eaten it.

POTENTIAL CONFLICT LEVEL: Moderate. You have to live with this person.

ROOT CAUSE: They are hungry and/or inconsiderate.

APPROPRIATE RESPONSE: Confront them about it, but that's all. Perhaps the only trait less becoming than aggressiveness is passive-aggressiveness.

You are walking down the street when a passerby shoulder-checks you from out of nowhere.

POTENTIAL CONFLICT LEVEL: If you're in New York City, low. Shoulder-checking complete strangers is one of the secret delights of big city life (honestly, ask any New Yorker). If you're anywhere else, high.

ROOT CAUSE: Perhaps that person is in a rush, or is looking at their phone, or is feeling particularly feisty.

APPROPRIATE RESPONSE: Independent of geographic location, a good turn around, followed by a "Yo my man, watch where you're going" is not only appropriate, but oddly satisfying.

You are at a sporting event and someone has disrespected your team.

POTENTIAL CONFLICT LEVEL: High.

ROOT CAUSE: Alcohol, 100%.

APPROPRIATE RESPONSE: Tell him (it's always a guy) to fuck off and/or sit down. That's it. Never fight at a sporting event—your team wouldn't engage in a physical altercation for *you*. The transitive property of conflict also applies here; let someone else throw the punches and get arrested.

Your special lady friend is getting in your face about something dumb you did.

POTENTIAL CONFLICT LEVEL: High—there is a chance this one could go on your permanent record.

ROOT CAUSE: You doing something dumb.

APPROPRIATE RESPONSE: OK, this should go without saying, but NEVER PUT YOUR HANDS ON A WOMAN. There is no possible scenario involving a female that should warrant a physical response. Instead, *always* walk away. Later, apologize—again, we all know you did something dumb.

A **Brief Note** *on* Hubris

Unless you are employed as a tightrope walker, life's most difficult balancing act is toeing the line between self-confidence and arrogance. The former is essential for success; the latter is essential for being a prick.

They're really not that different, to be honest—after all, both self-confidence and arrogance take root in the same soil: your sense of self. What matters is how you choose to fertilize that soil. The more manure you mix in, the greater the likelihood your self-confidence will grow unchecked, until it inevitably blossoms into extreme arrogance.

And *that's* where hubris comes in. If you don't have a dictionary handy (or don't remember dictionaries), hubris is a personality quality marked by foolish pride or dangerous overconfidence, and it's a direct byproduct of arrogance. In Greek mythology, it was also an affront to the Gods, one that often earned a swift rebuke—like Icarus, whose homemade wings melted when he flew too close to the sun; or Arachne, who challenged Athena to a weaving contest and got turned into a spider.

In 2018, hubris won't get you turned into an insect, but it might still get you killed (especially if you're a professional tightrope walker) and will unquestionably turn you into an asshole. If you think about every

single person you dislike, there's a pretty good chance the *reason* you dislike them is hubris—they are too aggressive, cocky, competitive, delusional, overbearing, insincere, underqualified, egotistical, vain, vindictive, shallow or petty to be around for any length of time. Social media is fueled almost entirely by hubris. So are Donald Trump and Vladimir Putin.

You might read that and think, "OK, but those are two of the most powerful men on the planet." And you'd be correct—one is the president and the other is *literally* a James Bond villain. It does take a certain amount of hubris to ascend to humanity's upper echelon. But it's not an absolute requirement.

Look at Richard Branson. He has a net worth of $5 billion, and owns private islands and airlines and rocketships, yet are able to have a laugh at their own expense (Richard Branson is actually *funny*, too). That's because he possesses a supreme level of self-confidence, founded in supreme self-awareness. In short, he doesn't (or didn't) believe the hype. That's the key. Because if you know who you are, and are honest about your strengths and shortcomings, you are truly self-aware—and self-confident. Without that knowledge, hubris becomes second nature; you won't know you've flown too close to the sun until your wings start melting.

So, yes, be confident—but be realistic. Otherwise, you're just setting yourself up for a spectacular undoing. Because there are always going to be moments in life where you come up short. If you are humble, you will always learn something from your failures. If you are hubristic, the only thing you'll learn is that a whole lot of people really delighted in your downfall. *That's* called Schadenfreude...but we'll discuss that in book #2. If you've been paying attention, yes, that statement counts as hubris, too.

100 Classy Moves *You* Should Master

Send someone a letter.

Pick up a check without making a big deal about it.

Walk your date home.

Hold the door open—and not just for women, either.

Offer your coat when someone is cold.

Remove your hat indoors.

Hold an umbrella for someone during a downpour.

Ask questions, and listen to the answers.

Have gum or mints handy at all times.

Tuck in your shirt properly.

Wear a belt.

Break up face-to-face.

Show authentic emotion.

Don't be pushy.

Ask his or her parents for permission before you propose.

Send flowers to someone at their office.

Cook dinner.

Maintain eye contact.

Be punctual.

Forgive a debt.

Give a firm (but not *too firm*) handshake.

Know your personal style.

Know how to tie a Windsor knot.

And a bowtie.

Play catch convincingly.

Bring a gift to a wedding.

Throw a party with a prime rib carving station.

Own a wine decanter.

Or some of those brandy snifters.

Light a candle.

Dab on some cologne.

Give a profanity-free toast.

Tell a great (nonoffensive) joke.

Take someone out for a drink after a rough day.

Tip exorbitantly.

Own a smoking jacket.

Or a kimono.

Read a newspaper.

Learn another language.

Don't lose your temper.

Vote.

Get something tailored.

Order a cheese course.

Learn a little something about wine.

Don't become an asshole about wine once you do.

Appreciate jazz. It's better than you think.

Learn how to roll a cigarette.

Know how to read a racing form.

Keep score at a baseball game.

Play craps.

Shuffle a deck of cards properly.

Know when to split a hand in blackjack. It's always aces and eights.

Act respectfully at a gentlemen's club. It's got "gentlemen" in the title for a reason.

Refine your palette.

Wait in your car until they're safely inside.

When squiring a woman, always walk side closest to the street.

Stand on the right side of an escalator. Walk on the left.

Learn how to shine your own shoes.

Get to know a butcher, and a fishmonger.

Befriend a barber.

Have a hot-towel shave.

Soothe a crying baby.

Have a go-to cocktail.

And know how to make it.

Have at least one go-to bar.

Visit at least one foreign country.

Know how to make an omelet.

Skipper a boat.

Own one hardcover book about World War II.

Read it.

Own one of those jackets with patches on the elbows.

Wear it.

Grind your own coffee.

Learn the Argentine Tango.

Do the dishes at a dinner party.

Pull out the chair for a female dining companion.

Saber a bottle of champagne without losing a finger.

Learn how prepare proteins properly.

Master a marinade. Sesame oil + ginger + garlic + scallion + soy sauce always works.

Know how to calculate square footage. It's width x length, BTW.

Feign interest in anything.

Make your bed.

Order something for the table.

Be comfortable holding a woman's purse while she shops.

Know how to buy produce.

Break up a fight.

Create a solid playlist.

Cook bacon properly. That means using a baking sheet.

Learn the proper way to iron a shirt.

Haggle without getting heated.

Argue without fighting.

Manage your money.

Manage your time.

Know how to cook eggs multiple ways.

Learn how to drive a stick.

Build a campfire.

Plant and maintain a garden.

Scrub the phrase "alpha male" from your brain.

Scrub the toilet or the shower every once in a while.

Delete your social media accounts.

An **Alphabetical List** *of* **Terrible People** *You* **Should Avoid** *at* **All Cost**

a.

Aggressive dudes.

Aggressive vapers.

Alcoholics.

Amateur cyclists who insist on wearing Spandex racing suits.

Amateur masseurs.

Anarchists.

Any Kardashian or Jenner.

Anyone talking loudly about cryptocurrencies.

Anyone talking loudly about how much money they make.

Anyone talking loudly about their sexual conquests.

Anyone talking loudly.

Anyone who adopts a fake Cockney accent while interacting with British people.

Anyone who describes themselves as "a Nationalist."

Anyone who proudly proclaims, "I don't own a TV."

Anyone who talks to you about "personal branding."

Anyone who uses the phrase "disrupt" while describing their startup.

Anyone who works in advertising.

Anyone who works in integrated marketing.

Anyone who yells at a waiter.

Anyone with a Kickstarter.

Artisans.

Athleisure enthusiasts.

Avant-garde composers.

Avid hunters.

Avowed atheists.

b.

Bad listeners.

Bad tippers.

Brand loyalists.

Bros.

Building contractors.

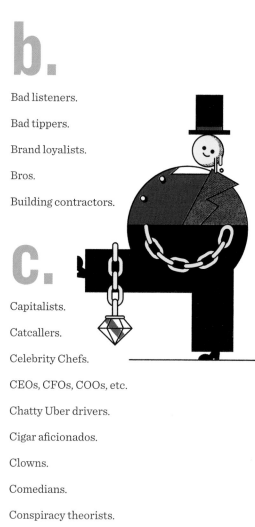

c.

Capitalists.

Catcallers.

Celebrity Chefs.

CEOs, CFOs, COOs, etc.

Chatty Uber drivers.

Cigar aficionados.

Clowns.

Comedians.

Conspiracy theorists.

Craft beer enthusiasts.

Cultural appropriators.

Curators.

d.

Dudes who stand around checking their phone between sets at the gym.

Dudes who wear leggings beneath their shorts at the gym.

Dudes who still do Borat impressions.

f.

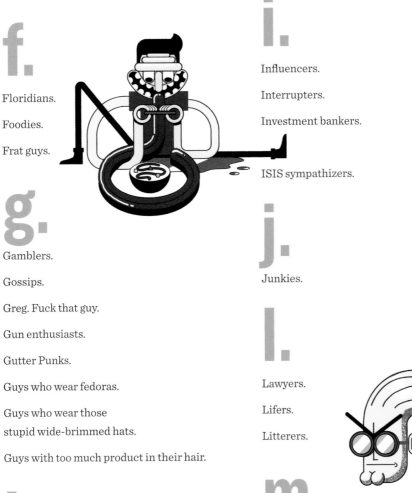

Floridians.

Foodies.

Frat guys.

g.

Gamblers.

Gossips.

Greg. Fuck that guy.

Gun enthusiasts.

Gutter Punks.

Guys who wear fedoras.

Guys who wear those stupid wide-brimmed hats.

Guys with too much product in their hair.

h.

Hackers.

Heavy breathers.

Hipsters.

Homophobes.

House-flippers.

Hypochondriacs.

i.

Influencers.

Interrupters.

Investment bankers.

ISIS sympathizers.

j.

Junkies.

l.

Lawyers.

Lifers.

Litterers.

m.

Magicians.

Men who work hard, but play harder.

Men's Rights Advocates.

Mixed Martial Artists.

Most Goths.

Most people at your gym.

Most Southern Californians.

Most Southerners.

n.

Neckbeards.

o.

Oversharers.

p.

Parents who think their child is fucking perfect.

PDA enthusiasts.

Pedophiles (obviously).

People who are always talking about "disrespecting the troops."

People who ask "Who's going?" when you invite them out.

People who check their phones mid-conversation.

People who complain about splitting the check evenly at a group dinner.

People who complain about spoilers.

People who hate babies.

People who hate dogs.

People who love Charles Bukowski.

People who only talk about their job.

People who post inspirational messages on social media.

People who Snap you the same thing that's on their Story.

People who treat their animals like their children.

People you've met several times who don't remember your name.

Performance artists.

Podcasters.

Police officers.

Politicians.

Porn enthusiasts.

Portfolio managers.

Positive people.

Pregnant women.

Pro-Lifers.

r.

Racists

Reality TV stars.

Rich people.

Rock critics.

Russians.

S.

Screenwriters.

Serial killers.

Serial texters.

Short dudes. They're usually dicks.

Snobs.

Social media managers.

Soundcloud rappers.

Steampunks.

Stoners.

Street performers.

Suburban kids with biblical names.

Superfans.

SUV owners.

Swingers.

T.

Tech bros.

The devoutly religious.

The easily offended.

The eternally broke.

The frequently shirtless.

The perpetually late.

The unnecessarily dramatic.

Thespians.

Trolls.

Twitter activists.

U.

Ultra-marathoners.

V.

Vegetarians.

W.

Whiners.

Whiskey enthusiasts.

White guys with dreadlocks.

Workout warriors who grunt excessively while lifting and/or loudly drop weights.

Y.

YouTubers.

HOW LONG WILL THESE PEOPLE ACTUALLY BE IN YOUR LIFE?

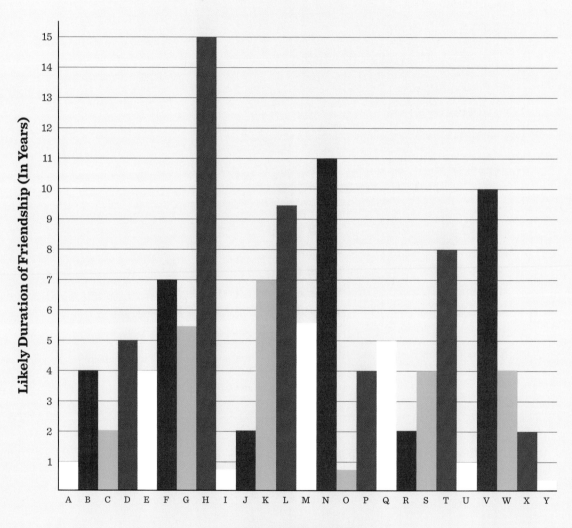

Likely Duration of Friendship (In Years)

Type of Friendship

A B C D E F G H I J K L M N O P Q R S T U V W X Y

A. Generally cool classmate

B. High school teammate

C. Dude you buy weed from

D. Dude you smoke weed *with*

E. Dude you party with on the weekend

F. Best high school bro

G. Best high school bro (who goes to college
   out-of-state)

H. Fellow outsider

I. Freshman year roommate

J. Guy you hang with as a freshman
   or sophomore

K. Guy you hang with as a junior or senior

L. Fraternity brother

M. Guy you share common interest with

N. Guy you share common interest with
   (not weed)

O. Fellow intern

P. Weekend party crew

Q. Weekday party crew

R. Gym bro

S. Coworker who likes sports or something

T. Coworker willing to talk shit about boss

U. Former coworker who has just left for
   a new job

V. Good dude you meet in your mid-twenties

W. Any dude you meet in your thirties

X. Guy in a committed long-term relationship

Y. Friend with benefits

A
True Friendship Test

1) **It's last call. There is a *very* drunk girl sitting at the bar, and you're on the prowl. A *real* friend would tell you:**

(A) "I don't know, man—she's pretty drunk."

(B) "Go for it!"

2) **You're broke. What would a true friend do?**

(A) Lend you some cash.

(B) Send you some job listings.

3) **You have just been struck in the testicles and are about to collapse into a heap. In this instance, a real friend would:**

(A) Catch you in his arms to ease your fall.

(B) Laugh at you.

4) **Your buddy's girlfriend sucks. What does he do to rectify the situation?**

(A) Force the issue and continue to bring her around.

(B) Accept reality and schedule separate bro time.

5) **You got wasted and passed out on a friend's couch. What should he do?**

(A) Drape a blanket over you and leave a glass of water on the coffee table.

(B) Draw a bunch of dicks on your face.

6) **You have put on weight. A true friend will:**

(A) Tell you.

(B) Make fun of you.

7) **Your girlfriend has just dumped you, and you deserved it. A real friend will always:**

(A) Be honest—everyone screws up now and then.

(B) Be loyal—she sucked and you're better off without her.

8) **You have become a successful rapper. How should a true bro respond?**

(A) By securing a position within your inner circle.

(B) By congratulating you on your success.

9) You left a party with someone who is not, uh, *traditionally attractive*. The next day, your friend should:

Ⓐ Roast you.

Ⓑ Congratulate you.

10) You are telling your friend a story he has heard approximately 125 times before. He:

Ⓐ Should humor you and listen. It's a good story.

Ⓑ Should interrupt you and move on. Time is of the essence.

11) You smell bad. A real friend will:

Ⓐ Tell you.

Ⓑ Tell you. Then douse you with AXE Body Spray.

12) You have just won an Academy Award. During your acceptance speech, you forget to thank your lifelong friend. How will he react?

Ⓐ He will be upset, but ultimately, he'll get over it.

Ⓑ He won't even notice.

13) You need a ride to an airport, and your car is in the shop. A friend should:

Ⓐ Give you a ride.

Ⓑ Call you an Uber.

14) You and a friend are interested in the same girl. Who should bow out first?

Ⓐ You.

Ⓑ Him.

15) You are newly single, and a friend wants to hook up with your ex. You dated for a little less than two years. After making his intentions clear, how long does he wait before making a move?

Ⓐ He doesn't make a move.

Ⓑ Six months.

16) You are being an asshole. A real friend will:

Ⓐ Call you out on it.

Ⓑ Just go with it.

17) You are *really* being an asshole and now some dude wants to fight you. What should your friend do?

Ⓐ Attempt to intervene on your behalf.

Ⓑ Take off his shirt and throw down.

18) You have angered your girlfriend and she has kicked you out as a result. How long will a true friend let you crash on his couch?

Ⓐ One week.

Ⓑ Until this whole thing blows over.

19) You are considering voting for a conservative candidate. What would a real friend do?

Ⓐ Join you at the White Nationalist rally.

Ⓑ Intervene. Friends don't let friends vote conservative.

20) You are wearing sunglasses inside. Your friend tells you to take them off, because:

(A) Only assholes and blind people wear sunglasses inside.

(B) He is jealous.

Annoying *(Yet Inevitable)* Things All Friends Do as *You* Get Older

No one ever said you have to like your friends—in fact, as you get older, you'll start to despise them. It's a simple fact of adulthood; people change, and not necessarily for the better. To help prepare you for that, we've compiled this list of seemingly indefensible actions that are (sadly) also inevitable.

- ☐ Stop responding to your drunken texts.

- ☐ Start asking if he can bring his girlfriend along.

- ☐ Clean up his act, erasing 70% of what you liked about him in the process.

- ☐ Get engaged, thereby turning up the heat on you.

- ☐ Send out a mortifying engagement announcement.

- ☐ Send out an equally mortifying "Save the Date" announcement.

- ☐ Adhere to his fiancée's "no strip clubs" edict during his bachelor party.

- ☐ Have a "destination wedding."

- ☐ Buy a house in the suburbs, thereby *further* turning up the heat on you.

- ☐ Invite you to his housewarming, where you will spend the entire evening wondering who this stranger is, and what he's done with your friend.

- ☐ Have a kid.

- ☐ Name the kid something ridiculous.

- ☐ Post approximately 85,000 pics of the kid on social media.

- ☐ Mail you a birth announcement, featuring the black-and-white photos of the kid wrapped up in a bunch of blankets.

- ☐ Make plans, then bail on them day-of (because the kid is sick).

- ☐ Somehow still find time to play golf with people you don't know.

- ☐ Reply to group texts three days late, seemingly ignoring the entire conversation.

- ☐ Refuse to admit, even for a second, that parenthood is a fucking nightmare.

- ☐ Buy a comically oversized SUV.

- ☐ Purchase things in bulk from Costco or Sam's Club.

- ☐ Purchase a "garage fridge" to hold all the things he bought in bulk.

- ☐ Start using phrases like "Man cave" or "She shed."

- ☐ Mail you a "Happy Holidays" card, featuring the kid wearing a Santa hat.

- ☐ Post embarrassing messages to his wife on their anniversary.

- ☐ Host dinner parties.

- ☐ Make comments about how he "can't go as hard as he used to," which are actually thinly veiled critiques of your lifestyle.

- ☐ Probably have another kid.

- ☐ Never leave the house.

- ☐ Invite you over to the house.

- ☐ Lay a guilt trip on you when you don't come out to the house.

- ☐ Ignore the fact that no one wants to hang out with a married dude and two toddlers in the suburbs.

- ☐ React to every aspect of single life as if were a scene from Lars von Trier's *Antichrist*.

- ☐ Start hanging out with other married couples.

- ☐ Give you unsolicited life advice.

- ☐ Slowly disappear.

- ☐ Die.

Is It Possible *to* Be "Just Friends" with *a* Woman?

Of course it is.

How *to* Make Friends After *the* Apocalypse

You probably weren't great at making friends before the Apocalypse—after all, you *are* reading a book—but it's never too late to learn! Also, the atmospheric radiation levels make it dangerous to leave your cave for extended periods, so you've got to make your time beneath the Tri-Suns count!

Barter.

One way to fast-track a relationship is by starting one of necessity—you scratch my back and I'll scratch yours. For example, perhaps you cross paths with a nomadic fisherman adept at pulling Sawtoothed Tarponsharks from the fast-flowing waters of the Vaalbarian watershed. What potential skills can you offer her/him? Your ability to critique memes at length must surely be worth a few pounds of mercury-laden fish-flesh.

Watering Holes.

To meet people, you gotta go where the people are! Scour the basalt flats for sources of fresh water—weary travelers will surely congregate there for a little R&R. To ease their exhaustion, try opening with a joke like "Oh, did you just drink that? That's my private bathroom." You're sure to have a laugh.

Wandering.

One benefit of Armageddon: lots of abandoned cityscapes slowly being reclaimed by nature! What better way to locate a local tribe of itinerate hunter/gatherers than a midday stroll through a once-bustling metropolis? Just make sure to pack your boomstick—you never know when you might *also* locate the occasional mutant, driven mad by hunger.

Hunting Clubs.

Humans are social animals for a reason: we hunt in packs. You were probably terrible at sports before the Apocalypse, so now's the time to impress some new friends by unleashing your unbridled primal rage on a herd of Hadean Leaping Deer. If you're still struggling, try being the funny guy: Ease the tension with a light joke—"You guys want to hear a duck call?"—followed by an obnoxious fart. For some reason, potty humor goes over like gangbusters after the Apocalypse. Must be instinct.

Bone Collecting.

There are *mountains* of them out there.

Warmth.

It's going to get cold during those lonely evenings without electricity—remember the days of Netflix & chill?!? So consider organizing a community cuddle puddle for survival (don't mention the friend-making bit outright, you don't want to come off as *creepy*). When cuddling with a stranger, ask themselves questions about themselves to put them at ease: "How long have you owned that bloodstained shirt?" "Love the beard, is that since the *big day* or for fun?" "How many loved ones did you lose on the day fire rained down from the heavens?"

Feats of Strength.

While the Warlord Kings of the Paleo-Tethys Plains use feats of strength to establish dominance and build harems, the oral histories of Old Earth tell us that men once bonded through competition. So make it clear that the loser of this particular battle must become your friend. In order to pull this off, do one specific exercise many times repeatedly for several months. For instance, do pull-ups every morning while slowly increasing your maximum result. When you find a contender, challenge them to a pull-up contest. If you win: hey, new friend! If you lose, they may attempt to kill you. Thankfully, you've been doing pull-ups for 7 straight months to prepare for this moment.

YOU ARE INSIGNIFICANT

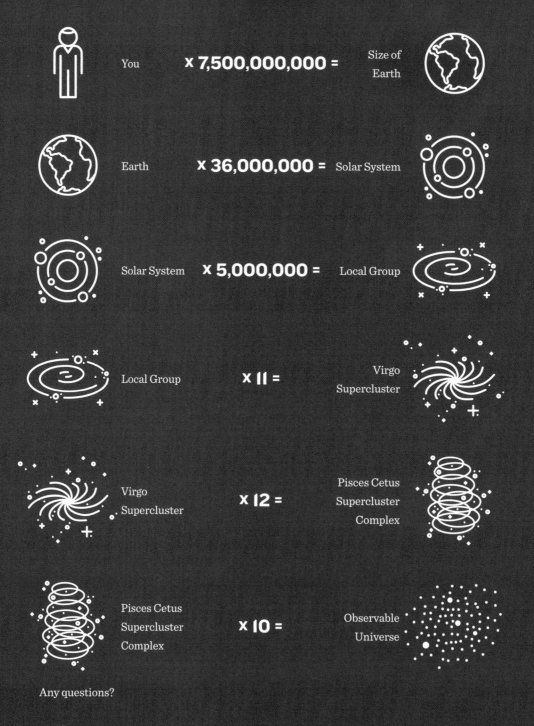

You × 7,500,000,000 = Size of Earth

Earth × 36,000,000 = Solar System

Solar System × 5,000,000 = Local Group

Local Group × 11 = Virgo Supercluster

Virgo Supercluster × 12 = Pisces Cetus Supercluster Complex

Pisces Cetus Supercluster Complex × 10 = Observable Universe

Any questions?

Perspective

Hate life? Feeling alone? Tired of being disrespected by Instagram models who won't reply to your comments? Don't worry; you're going to die.

We're not trying to make you depressed—you have enough on your plate already—we're simply stating a fact. We can say with 100% assurance that some day (maybe it's today!) you will expire; so will everyone you know, everyone you love and everyone you hate. Your dog will also die, probably a lot sooner than you think. Death has remained undefeated for the entirety of human history, having beaten something like 108 billion people, plus every insect, bird, mammal, reptile, fish, plant, spore and fungus, too. Sorry, that's just the way it is.

Maybe we shouldn't apologize. It's liberating to acknowledge the fact that all of this will end—not to mention invigorating. It puts most of your (admittedly petty) problems into perspective, and allows you to prioritize your life. What's the point of staying in a dead-end job, or remaining in a toxic relationship, if both could end tomorrow?

We realize that sounds like some wide-eyed, pseudo-inspirational *bullshit*, the kind of nonsense spouted by YouTube influencers and motivational speakers. And it is...but that doesn't make the sentiment any less valid. Life is for living, until it's not, at which point you are dead and you don't have to worry about anything. In other words, none of this matters. Do what you want to do, when you want to do it. Maybe you can't just quit your job and travel the world, but you *can* make the latter your goal and start taking steps to achieve it. That's called having perspective. Things are terrible, but they don't always have to be—it's up to you to make the change.

Because, honestly, what's the worst that could happen? You're already guaranteed to end up as a pile of organic matter, so why not make every moment preceding that point count? If you want to ask out that barista, or learn how to hang glide, go for it. If you feel like chasing a paycheck for half a century, do it—just know you can't take any of that cash with you when you die. Shit, at the very least, put this book down...there's a whole world out there waiting to be discovered. And if you hate all of it, remember this: everything you lay eyes on will eventually be dead. If *that's* not inspiring, we don't know what is.

A HANDY GLOSSARY OF TERMS

Adulthood—The period of life when responsibilities and commitments slowly choke you out. Also when you start wearing khakis.

Afterlife—Theoretical existence after death, something gullible people trick themselves into accepting as their just reward for a sedentary life.

Animals—Living things that aren't plants. Some of them you eat, some you keep as pets and the rest are a waste of time.

Alcohol—Fermented or distilled beverages that help you get through the endless parade of bullshit known as life.

Baby—A new human. Also the reason you never see your old best friend anymore.

Birth—The beginning of this whole charade.

Bully—Someone who torments you at some stage in your life, usually school. Take solace in the fact most of them end up killing themselves.

Clothing—Garments intended to shield your body from the elements and express yourself to the world. Also, most are made by children just like you in Bangladesh!

College—School, only with alcohol and casual sex. Despite your best efforts, will not last forever.

Conflict—An antagonistic state of action that should be resolved with words, not fists.

Cops—Bullies with badges. The worst.

Death—The end of life. An inevitability, and, depending on your situation, also a relief.

Divorce—The end of marriage. Also, a by-product of it.

Drugs—Fun chemical substances to use whenever life is boring.

Emotions—States of feeling, including fear, anger, happiness and other ones that make your dad uncomfortable. Enabled and boosted by alcohol.

Food—Material containing the nutrients used in the body of an organism to sustain and promote vital processes. Also, something people take photos of for some fucking reason.

Fuck—Word you will probably end up using more than any other when it's all said and done.

Fun—A vital part of life that is found in increasingly shorter supply the older you get.

Future—A time yet to come. And a great rapper.

Ghosts—Not real, dude.

Gods—Also not real.

Government—Complex of political institutions, laws and customs through which the function of governing is carried out. The thing your crazy uncle is always yelling about.

Guns—Firearms used by cowards to protect themselves from imaginary threats, promote toxic masculinity and project an inherent sense of superiority.

Humans—Basically a waste of time.

Jokes—Humorous anecdotes that make you laugh, presumably to keep you from crying.

Kill—To end life, or slay on stage (as in comedy).

Language—A complex system of communication. If you want to be impressive, learn more than one.

Lawyer—Professional naysayer and amateur asshole.

Man Cave—Room where a husband goes to watch sports, masturbate and contemplate where it all went wrong.

Marriage—A consensual and contractual relationship recognized by law. Doesn't that sound romantic?

Money—Something generally accepted as a means of payment. That dude vaping outside the bar insists Bitcoin will eventually be one of those things.

Music—Is life, according to annoying people.

No—Never take it for an answer, unless it is in response to a request for sex; in that case, always take it as an answer.

Oxygen—Reactive element found in water, rocks and minerals and organic compounds that is essential for life. Also, a channel girls watch.

Phone—Mobile communication device/vault for your deepest secrets. Despite those facts, is incredibly easy to lose or be hacked.

Plants—Living things that aren't animals. Some of them you eat, some are used in fabrication or processing and some you smoke when you want to watch hours of Netflix.

Politician—Professional liar.

Racism—Unfortunate, and incorrect, belief that differences lead to an inherent superiority of one particular race. Donald Trump's entire platform.

School—Supposedly important, though they only tell you that to keep you in line.

She Shed—Female version of the Man Cave, only with more rosé.

Sex—The physical act of love, and a method for creating new life. Anyone who tells you it's the entire point of life, however, is an asshole.

Shelter—Something that covers or offers protection. A basic human right, yet one that is basically unavailable to millions of people worldwide.

Social Media—Virulent viper pit fueled by rampant insecurity, hollow praise, passive-aggressive behavior and photos of babies and animals.

Taxes—A charge imposed by an authority on persons or property for public purposes. Aside from Death, they're the only inevitability in life.

Time—Measurable period during which an action or condition exists or continues. Also a construct, man.

Water—Liquid that descends from the clouds as rain, forming all bodies of water on the planet. Boring, yet essential for life—especially when you're hung over.

Wealth—An overabundance of material possessions or resources. The wealthy are the enemy, BTW.

Wi-Fi—Facility used by wireless computer networking devices to ensure your every inane thought or emotion gets the global audience it so richly deserves.

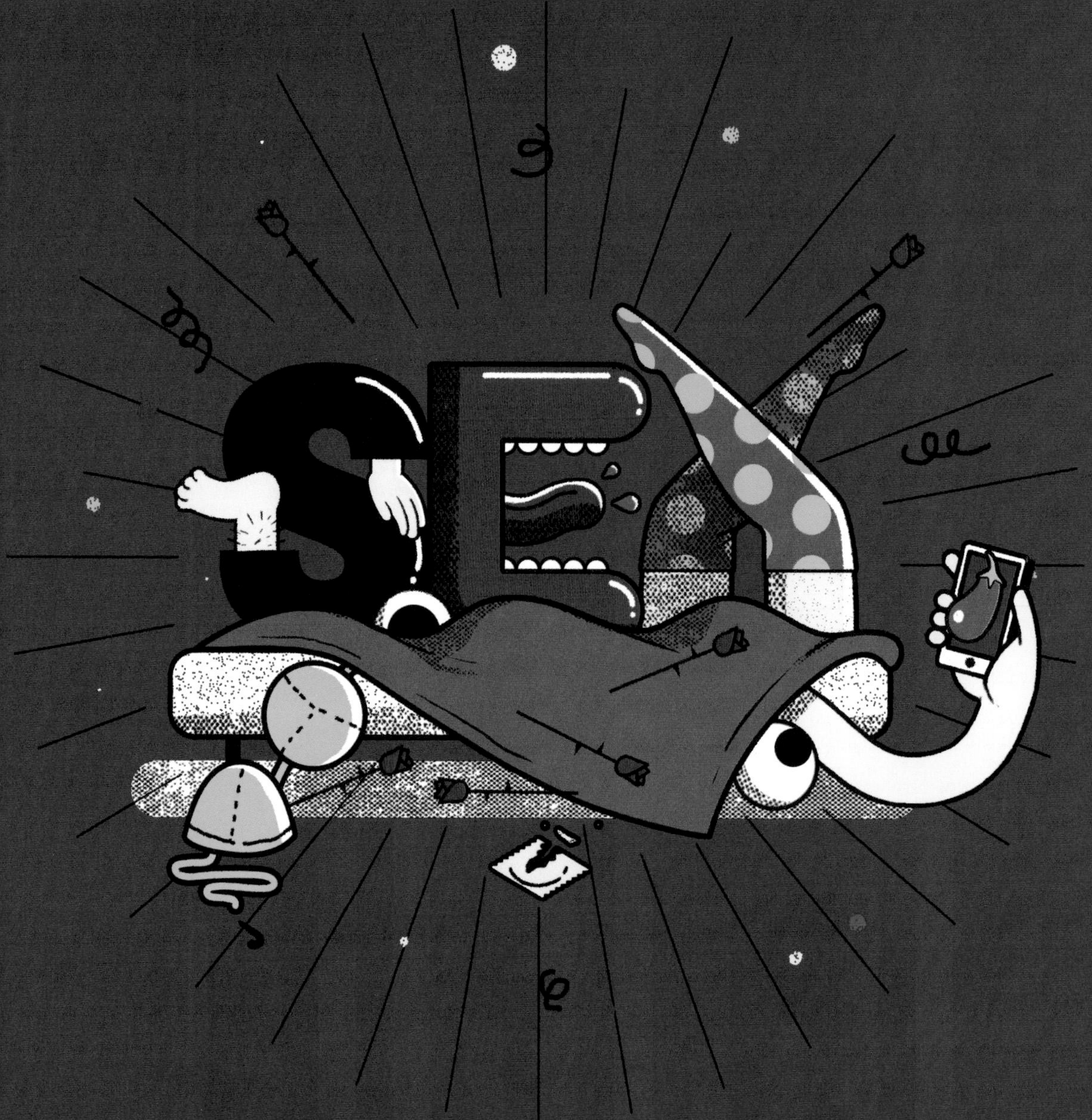
SEX

Sex is a big deal. Biologically, it's what you've been put on this planet to do—passing on your genetic material is kind of your only job as a Homo sapien. Psychologically, it's as close as you'll come to baring your soul to another human, and despite previous experiences with humanity, you do it willingly (which is actually the definition of insanity, come to think of it). Physically? *You're literally attached to another person.*

And we haven't even mentioned the scary sexual-health stuff you've (hopefully) learned about in school, or the whole *making a baby* thing. As far as animalistic impulses go, sex is pretty complicated. That's not supposed to scare you—if it does, you're probably not ready to have sex—but you should know the risks involved, and act accordingly. So always use protection. Never pressure your partner to do something they're not comfortable with. Do talk about your feelings and expectations. Don't judge others for doing the same. Do explore and experiment. Don't do it without permission. Realize that having *more* sex doesn't make you *more* of a man (it's kind of the opposite). Understand that sex doesn't define what you are, but rather who *you* are at this moment. Be honest, up front and respectful. Act like an adult, not an asshole. And, y'know, *have fun.*

Because setting aside everything we've just said—and ignoring nearly every aspect of popular culture and social interaction—sex isn't really that big of a deal. Your parents figured it out, and they don't even know how to work an iPhone. You shouldn't let it consume your life; you'll miss out on a lot of amazing experiences if you do. Trust us, it'll happen (and yes, we realize how impossible that sounds if it *hasn't*). And after it does, it'll happen again. You'll get more comfortable and confident, you'll figure out what you like (and what you don't) and you'll eventually realize you wasted an awful lot of time obsessing over something that's essentially an enjoyable pastime.

So don't put too much stock in sex—but don't discount its importance, either. It's a form of expression and an exploration of self, a way of figuring out how you're wired (and maybe even *why*). It's a social construct and a social contract. It's psychological and physical. It's not something to take lightly. Sometimes it's weird. Sometimes it's dirty. It's complex. But so is life. **And that's the truth.**

MASLOW'S HIERARCHY OF SEX NEEDS

Everything necessary to ascend, find fulfillment and become the person you were meant to be.

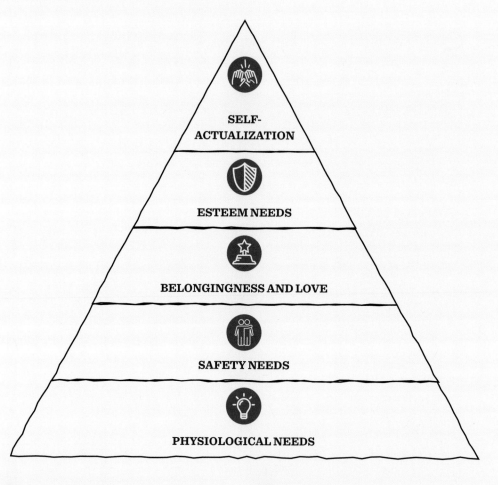

 SELF-ACTUALIZATION—People actually *want* to have sex with you.

ESTEEM—Magnum condoms, porn contract.

BELONGINGNESS AND LOVE—Someone to have sex with, someone who will listen to you brag about it later.

 SAFETY—Condoms, flexibility, a safe word, maybe some lube.

 PHYSIOLOGICAL—A corporeal form, condoms, communication, PERMISSION, a sense of rhythm, an open mind.

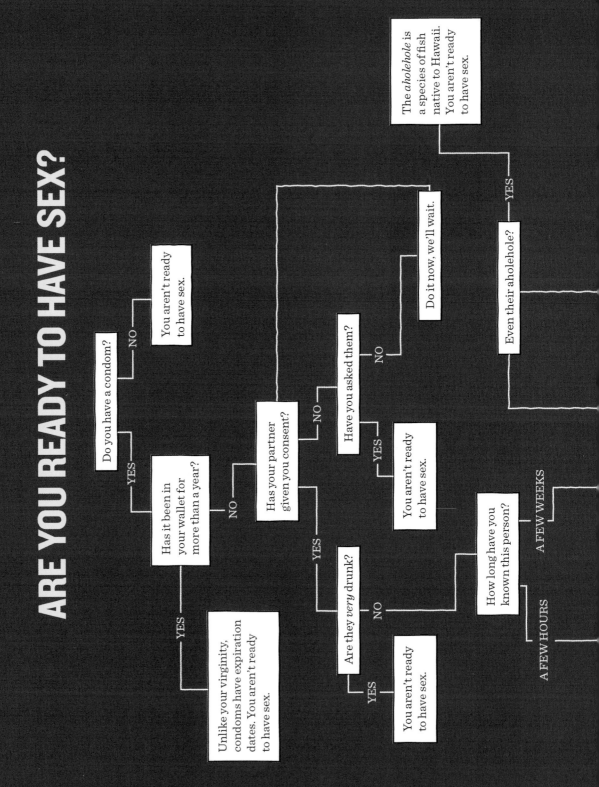

ARE YOU READY TO HAVE SEX?

Do you have a condom?

NO → You aren't ready to have sex.

YES → Has it been in your wallet for more than a year?

YES → Unlike your virginity, condoms have expiration dates. You aren't ready to have sex.

NO → Has your partner given you consent?

NO → Have you asked them?

NO → Do it now, we'll wait.

YES → You aren't ready to have sex.

YES → Are they *very* drunk?

YES → You aren't ready to have sex.

NO → How long have you known this person?

A FEW HOURS

A FEW WEEKS

Even their aholehole?

YES → The *aholehole* is a species of fish native to Hawaii. You aren't ready to have sex.

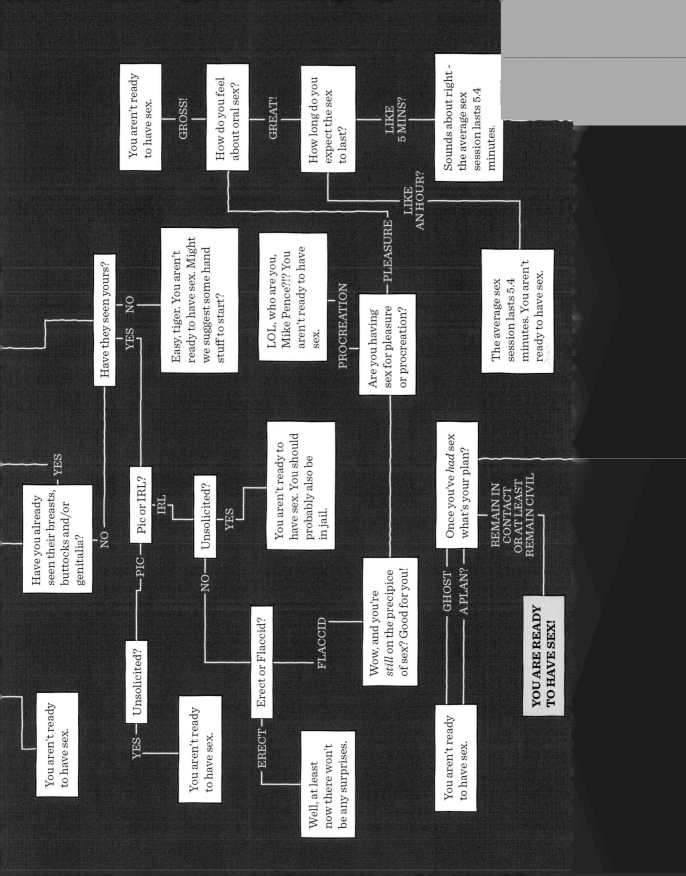

You aren't ready to have sex.

Have you already seen their breasts, buttocks and/or genitalia? — YES

NO

Have they seen yours? — YES

NO

You aren't ready to have sex.

Unsolicited? — YES

You aren't ready to have sex.

Pic or IRL? — PIC

IRL

Easy, tiger. You aren't ready to have sex. Might we suggest some hand stuff to start?

You aren't ready to have sex.

GROSS!

How do you feel about oral sex?

GREAT!

How long do you expect the sex to last?

LIKE 5 MINS?

Sounds about right - the average sex session lasts 5.4 minutes.

LIKE AN HOUR?

The average sex session lasts 5.4 minutes. You aren't ready to have sex.

PLEASURE

Are you having sex for pleasure or procreation?

PROCREATION

LOL, who are you, Mike Pence?!? You aren't ready to have sex.

Unsolicited? — YES

You aren't ready to have sex. You should probably also be in jail.

NO

Erect or Flaccid? — FLACCID

Wow, and you're *still* on the precipice of sex? Good for you!

ERECT

Well, at least now there won't be any surprises.

Once you've *had* sex what's your plan? — GHOST

You aren't ready to have sex.

A PLAN? — REMAIN IN CONTACT OR AT LEAST REMAIN CIVIL

YOU ARE READY TO HAVE SEX!

The Do's and Don'ts *of* Sex

Make sure it's consensual. If this wasn't *super* obvious, stop reading now.

Wear a condom.

Be a gentleman (when appropriate).

Be responsible.

Understand that foreplay doesn't have to start in the bedroom. Technology is your friend.

Remember key erogenous zones: ears, breasts, neck, mouth, vagina, clitoris.

Understand the difference between the vagina and the clitoris.

Perform oral sex. Trust us.

Use your tongue. Your fingers? Not so much.

Appreciate receiving oral sex. Would *you* put that in your mouth?

Be appreciative in general.

Try butt stuff!

Keep an open mind.

Keep things in perspective.

Realize the inherent ridiculousness of the entire enterprise.

Have a sense of humor.

Be honest about your likes and dislikes.

Respect boundaries.

Announce your impending orgasm. Give them fair warning.

Ejaculate politely.

Explore the wonderful world of personal lubricants.

Have fun.

Change positions.

Put on some porn if the other person's into it.

Pace yourself. Most times, sex is a marathon— not a sprint.

Drink plenty of fluids beforehand.

Leave the lights on.

Take your socks off.

But encourage *her* to leave them on. One study found she's 80% more likely to have an orgasm that way—it's *literally* science.

Wear a condom.

Make sure you've got the right hole.

Be a Sexual Swiss Army Knife. You never know which tool you'll need.

Know your Bite Force Quotient. You shouldn't draw blood, Dracula.

Get your partner off first. Trust us.

Clean up your bedroom.

At least make your bed.

Bring a blanket or towel if you plan on doing it outside.

Realize that doing it outside is pretty overrated.

COMMUNICATE. Listen, too.

Be willing to accept honest feedback. How else are you supposed to get better?

Make noise. Most people don't want to bang a corpse.

Avoid problematic dirty talk.

Respect the tenderness of nipples.

Vary your speed throughout.

Save the jackhammering for key moments.

Help clean up afterward.

Make occasional eye contact.

Experiment.

Explore.

Collaborate.

Compliment.

Put in work.

Put on music.

Get wild from time to time.

Take charge.

Allow the other person to drive occasionally.

Know that it's 2019 and traditional gender roles don't really apply anymore.

Realize that sometimes you *can* be too drunk.

Understand that sex means different things to different people, and proceed accordingly.

Be willing to reboot in cases of hardware malfunction.

Understand there's no right way to do it. There *are* a lot of wrong ways, though.

Wear a condom (did we say that already?).

DON'TS

Force anyone to do anything. Ever.

Lead them on.

Lie to get what you want.

Think sexting is automatically a precursor to the actual thing.

Have phone sex. FaceTime is better.

Pay for it.

Have sex for revenge or popularity.

Forget: It's supposed to be fun.

Double-bag it.

Get *too* porn-y.

Jump right into the kinky stuff.

Just stick it in there, dude.

Judge.

Be afraid of a little something in your back door.

Ask if they're about to get off.

Ask "How was I?"

Give unsolicited feedback.

Talk a big game, unless you're prepared to back it up.

Do anything that makes you uncomfortable.

Push their head down to initiate oral.

Film without consent, dick.

Attempt a "Friends with Benefits" situation. It won't work.

Have sex in the shower without proper traction. Someone's gonna get hurt.

69 unless you're really comfortable with the other person.

Choke, bite, pull or smack—unless specifically instructed to do so.

Do anything for too long.

Just lie there. Most people don't want to bang a corpse.

Turn sex into interpretive gymnastics. There are no bonus points for technical prowess.

Be too focused on penis size.

Bring up best friends. Trust us.

Push rope. If you need a moment, take one.

Get grossed out by bodily fluids or functions. They happen.

Laugh at unfortunate noises—unless your partner laughs at them first.

Suggest a threesome. Let it happen *organically*.

Assume you're spending the night.

Assume you're *not*.

Put yourself first.

Ignore the posted speed limit.

Rush the stroke.

Be Usain Bolt in the bedroom. Unless Usain Bolt is really good at sex. We don't know.

Play with same stuff every time. Mix it up.

Believe everything your friends tell you.

Believe anything you see in a movie.

Text during sex.

Call them someone else's name.

Fake it.

Forget to kiss.

Stare into their eyes the *entire* time.

Skip the shower beforehand.

Try to be someone else. You're here for a reason.

Be a dictator. Sex is (at least) a two-person operation.

Get overly *erotic*. Not every toe must be sucked.

Think you gotta get *tantric*. Nobody wants to have sex for 8 hours.

Forget about the refractory period. Your boy needs a break!

Reference an ex.

Ghost. Unless it was abundantly clear this was a one-night stand.

Get mad if feelings develop. You're pretty great, after all.

Be freaked out if *you* develop feelings. Congrats on not being a sociopath.

Presume "sex" is only limited to penetration.

Use the word "penetration."

Subscribe to heteronormative assumptions. It's 2019.

Read too deeply into what happens.

Grab 'em by the pussy.

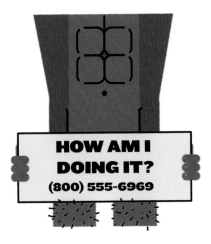

5

Simple Ways *to* Not Suck *at* Sex

1. Be Yourself

Here's your daily affirmation: You're a good guy. Your partner presumably feels the same way—if they didn't, they wouldn't *be* your partner. Sex shouldn't be an audition; if you're having it, there's a pretty good chance you've already gotten the part. So don't pull out all the stops in an attempt to impress, don't play a role (however: *do* role-play if the situation demands it) and don't do anything that makes you feel uncomfortable. It can be intimidating to consider the lengthy list of expectations society attaches to sex—most of us don't have a 6-pack of abs or a 9-inch penis—so just skip the considering altogether. Be secure in the knowledge that your personality, wit and intelligence have gotten you this far,

because that security breeds confidence—and confidence goes a *long way*. If you're feeling yourself, your partner will too...and that's a good way to guarantee you'll *both* get off.

2. Take Your Time

We get it; you're excited. But there's no bigger mistake a guy can make than rushing things. One study found it takes anywhere from 15–40 minutes for the average woman to reach orgasm, and it's not like you've got anywhere to be. Foreplay is your friend, but it shouldn't begin in the bedroom. Be a gentleman beforehand, too, as it sets the stage for everything that comes next. When it's time to get down to business, start slow. If she's naked, tell her how she makes you feel. Kiss and caress the nape (that's a fancy term for "the back") of her neck, give a bite to her earlobe and gently brush the top, bottom and sides of her breasts—the areas around the areola are more sensitive at first—*then* move on to the nipples themselves. Don't be afraid to show off a little strength, either, as a firm grab or a gnash will help remind her that you are, in fact, an actual man with muscles and everything (or at least let her live that fantasy). If you find that your foreplay game isn't working out, *ask her what she likes*, and help her relax by reminding her that you've got all night. You've been building to this moment for a while now; you might as well enjoy it.

3. Go Down South

Continue moving down her body, until you reach her vagina...but don't rush headlong into oral sex. Kiss her inner thighs and her inner and outer lips first, then use your tongue to work your way inside. Broad, firm strokes work well, and it's important to pay attention to the way she responds. Her hips will hint at how well your rhythm is working (or if it *isn't*), and if she grasps your head and holds it in place, *don't you dare move*. Now's the time to locate her clitoris, the small, button-y thing near the junction of her inner lips, above the urethra. Tease it with your tongue, but don't *hammer* it—the clit is incredibly sensitive, and a portion of it actually withdraws into her body during arousal to prevent an overload. Moving your tongue in a Figure 8 motion around the clitoris changes up the pace and helps bring her to orgasm. What should you be doing with your hands? Well, you can work touch into your technique, use your hands to grab her breasts, or place a hand on her stomach; that way you'll be able to sense the muscle contractions that precede an orgasm. And always remember that the vagina is a wonderfully complex thing; if you're not getting the results you desire, ask her for guidance. She'll tell you what she likes, and there's no shame in admitting you've been vexed by the mystery of the vagina. You certainly wouldn't be the *first guy*.

4. Situational Awareness

OK, so it's time to have sex. Do you have a condom? Cool, put it on. Now, take stock of the situation—is this a hot-and-heavy, clearing-shit-off-a-countertop encounter, or a soft-and-sensual, all-night-long affair? Because each requires a different approach. There's nothing wrong with slamming away if the situation demands it (hey, you've got school in the morning), but as a general rule of thumb, it's never a bad idea to switch up speed and stroke. Regardless, *ease* your way into things, don't just stuff it in and start pumping away. There's a good chance you'll know the right way to proceed, and we're not about to tell you there's one *correct* way to have sex. That goes for positions, too. You don't need to get acrobatic, though sometimes it's fun, and you shouldn't always be in control of the situation. Let your partner take the reins every now and again, there's a good chance they'll actually teach you something.

5. Stick Around

The deed is done, but hopefully, you're not. Again, situational awareness plays a key role in everything that happens *after* sex—if it's clear you've got to go, by all means beat a hasty retreat; if it's not, ask them if you can stay awhile. Afterglow is a very real thing, and there's nothing better than basking in your accomplishments with your partner. It will make you two feel even closer, and provides an opportunity to work on those communication skills (which, not surprisingly, leads to better sex). It's probably not the best policy to offer frank performance critiques, but there's no harm in telling your partner what you liked (or didn't). And vice-versa. It's OK to laugh if something silly happened, too. After all, sex is pretty ridiculous if you think about it. But it's also a deeply personal thing, so no matter how it went, it shouldn't just end with a firm handshake or a thinly veiled promise of a repeat encounter. Remember: you liked yourself going into this, it's important to like yourself now that it's over, too.

5

Simple Ways *to* Not Suck *at* Gay Sex

So, you want to have gay sex. That's awesome. Like heterosexual sex, it's an oft-fulfilling, occasionally thrilling way to kill some time and/or fill the chasm inside you. And like heterosexual sex, the more you do it, the better you'll get at it. Here are five commonsense ways to make the learning curve just a little less steep.

1. Stop Cock-Blocking Yourself.

If you're reading this, you deserve good dick. Presumably, you're already putting in the effort to find it, but you can save yourself a whole lot of time if you know what you're looking for.

So be honest with yourself. Sure, that might mean having less sex in the short-term, but it will definitely lead to having *better* sex overall. And it's all about quality, not quantity. If apps

aren't working out for you, there are gay gyms, gay-owned bars, gay book clubs, gay sports teams, LGBT centers and Los Angeles. If it's safe for you, expand your parameters beyond hookup apps. There's something unique in being out and about, then locking eyes with another man you don't know yet. It's foreplay.

2. Take Your Time

Here's the truth: size *is* a factor, but that shouldn't be a hindrance. Even well-endowed dudes can be straight-up lousy at intercourse. That's because sex is between two (or more) people, not just their body parts. So focus on what you can change, not what you can't.

Some things you can change:

> Your confidence
> How comfortable you are in your body
> Your rotation of sex positions
> Foreplay
> Your thrusts
> Your attitude
> Who you're having sex with

Some things you can't change:

> Your penis size
> *His* penis size

If you can make it feel good for you, it'll likely feel good for him.

3. Get Him to Relax.

Here's what you need to know about the ass. It's a muscle that has been trained to be clenched tight our entire lives. Nothing is going in there smoothly, especially if it's not relaxed. So take the time to pleasure his bottom so he can...open up.

If you don't know where to start—*use your tongue.*

Start at the side of the neck. Down the chest. Pin his arms back while you circle your tongue around his nipples. Look for cues on what he responds well to—or you can lightly whisper in his ear, "What do you like?" And work your way down. Even lower.

Next, lick it. Our assholes have a lot of nerves. So when a wet tongue slides across it, there can be a lot of pleasure involved. Pull his cheeks apart and lightly tap his hole with your tongue. Let your breath fall on it, and occasionally mix in some light blows, too. Watch him shudder. Lick in patterns he can concentrate on. Occasionally use your spit and get his hole wet. The point is for him to associate butt play with pleasure.

Give him your digits. Start slowly. Make sure you cut/file down your fingernails beforehand. And finally, play around. Consider using toys like butt plugs to loosen things up before sex. Or you can incorporate them into foreplay. It'll build the anticipation.

4. Find Your Speed.

The right pace and rhythm for sex is completely dependent on the bodies involved. You'll never find either if you don't aim for variety. So alternate your thrusts—go between gentle and slow to rough and fast—and your positions. Don't be afraid to communicate.

It'll take some time, though eventually inhibitions disappear from the room and what's left is two people pursuing what makes them feel good. When he starts grabbing your hips or backing up into you, that's a good sign.

5. Assess the Sex.

Sex is kind of a funny thing. Many people talk *during* it. Not a lot of guys talk after it. And that's kind of a shame, because gay sex isn't talked about nearly as much. It's excluded from so many classrooms and is considered a taboo topic in so many families. For a lot of us, the best way to learn is from each other.

Take the time to express with each other how the sex felt for you. Ask each other how it felt. What'd you like? What can you do differently? Passing on your knowledge will only make sex better for the both of you, even if your next time isn't with each other.

69 Lies *You'll* Hear About Sex

1. Everybody has an orgasm every time...

2. And it happens at the same time.

3. Losing your virginity = having vaginal intercourse.

4. Being good at sex comes naturally.

5. You'll have sex all the time when you're an adult.

6. Sex is better when you're young.

7. It's just like porn.

8. All ladies are bare down there.

9. Only hot people are good in bed.

10. Only sex between a man and a woman is legitimate.

11. It's not really sex if nobody comes.

12. Sex is not messy.

13. Sex shouldn't be funny.

14. Vaginas get "loose" if a girl's had a lot of sex.

1 *Every* movie sex scene makes it seem like everybody always reaches the finish line. That's usually the goal, but in real life, stuff happens—not everybody climaxes every time. **2** Even if everyone gets off, it's pretty unlikely that it will happen simultaneously. The big lesson here? Just because you're done, it doesn't mean your partner is. Keep going until everybody has gotten what they wanted. **3** You lose your V card when you have sex. What constitutes sex is totally up to you—vagina stuff, butt stuff, oral stuff. And really, your virginity is nobody's business but your own. **4** Sadly, no. Your first time is probably going to be pretty weird. Thankfully, sex is pretty fun even when you're bad at it, so keep practicing, ask questions, figure out what you like and soon you'll be a pro. **5** Everybody has a dry spell—days, weeks, maybe even years. Even people in relationships can forget to get it on. Adulting can get in the way of everything fun. Don't be ashamed if you go awhile without getting any. **6** You might have more energy and vigor, but like anything, practice makes perfect. With time, you get to know what you like, and what other people seem to like, too. **7** Porn is to real sex what a county fair caricature is to your actual face. It's hyper-exaggerated, only slightly representational of the real deal and if you stare at it too long, it seems kinda creepy. Don't expect your partner to behave like the people you see in porn, and don't assume they want you to either. **8** Fun fact: women are not naturally hairless creatures, despite what porn would have you believe. Women have pubic hair. Some shave it, some wax it, some trim it and some let it grow. Deal with it. **9** Being a 10 does not automatically make someone good in bed. People of all shapes and sizes can be great in the sack. One study recently found that the higher a man's body mass index, the longer he'll last in bed. **10** Hopefully you know this one is bullshit. Have safe, consensual sex with whomever you'd like, however you'd like. **11** Climax or not, it's sex if you say it is. **12** Sometimes things get sweaty—and sticky. That's part of the fun. **13** Stuff happens. Things slip out. People fart. Someone says something goofy. Sex doesn't have to be something you take super-seriously. Just have fun and relax. **14** The vagina can expand enough to bring a human into the world and, with some time, can return to its normal state. Your member, no matter how impressive, is not going to

15. Squirting.

16. Pulling out is an effective method of birth control.

17. Birth control always works.

18. Two condoms are better than one.

19. Expiration dates on condoms don't matter.

20. Condoms make it more difficult to have an orgasm.

21. She can't get pregnant if she is on top.

22. You can use soda as emergency birth control.

23. Blow jobs involving blowing.

24. You need a big rig to be good in bed.

25. Sex is good exercise.

26. Your foot size is correlated with your penis size.

27. Sex positions are a big deal.

28. All boners look like this:

29. All women have vaginas. All men have penises.

cause any lasting changes. The tightness (or looseness) of a woman's vaginal canal is a product of the strength and tone of the muscles in a her pelvis. **⑮** The science is still out on squirting. Is it a real thing? Is it just pee? Nobody knows. Regardless, maybe it will happen, maybe it won't, but it's definitely WAY less common than anyone that's watched a few hours of porn will think. **⑯** According to Planned Parenthood, out of every 100 women whose partners used the pull-out method, 27 will become pregnant. If you've got your timing right, that number decreases to 4. But that's still not zero...so use a condom. **⑰** While we're on the subject, we should probably break it to you: No form of birth control is 100% effective. If you want to be extra safe, use a secondary form of contraceptive (condoms + birth control). Or be abstinent. **⑱** A secondary form of protection DOES NOT mean you should double-bag it. When you wear two condoms, they rub up against one another, and the resulting friction is more likely to make them BOTH break. **⑲** As latex condoms age, they begin to break down, making them much more likely to rip or tear during sex. An expired condom is still better than no condom, but it's best to keep a fresh supply. **⑳** Studies show that wearing a condom really doesn't affect how long it takes for a man to reach orgasm. You're not going to get a substantial stamina boost from wearing one, either. BTW, you shouldn't use this as an excuse *not* to wear one. **㉑** Gravity isn't that strong. Wear a condom. **㉒** Spraying soda into a woman's vagina is a terrible idea and it WILL NOT keep her from getting pregnant. For the love of God, don't do this. **㉓** Nope. "Blow Job" is definitely a misnomer. During oral sex, penises are treated more like Popsicles and less like balloon animals that need inflating. **㉔** Being good in bed is all about skill, not size. Practice. Ask your partners what they like and don't like. Don't worry so much about what you're packing. **㉕** Sex IS exercise. On average you only burn between 50–100 calories per bone sesh. That's about the same as a 15–30 minute walk. Don't expect to get swole just because you're getting regular action. **㉖** Nope. Studies show there is no consistent relationship between the size of a man's foot and the size of his penis. Stop bragging about your size 14s. **㉗** Anyone who's ever looked at a magazine cover probably thinks sex positions are a really big deal. Being able to do the "reverse upside down scorpion" doesn't make you good at sex. Talk to your partner, try new things and find what works for you. You'll find a few things that work for you and that's OK. You don't need to memorize the *Kama Sutra*. **㉘** Boners come in all shapes and sizes. Just like people. Learn to love what you've got.

30. Masturbating will make you go blind.

31. Women don't masturbate.

32. It's OK to fake an orgasm.

33. Only women fake orgasms.

34. You can tell if a girl is a virgin.

35. You can see if someone has an STI.

36. Girls can't get pregnant when they're on their period.

37. Yes means yes forever.

38. Being drunk or high makes sex better.

39. "Your number" matters.

40. If a girl is wearing _____ or doing _____ she is looking to get laid.

41. You can't get an STI from oral sex.

42. Your parents only had sex one time.

43. Your grandparents don't have sex.

44. The dentist can tell if you've given oral/semen gives you cavities.

45. You always have sex on the third date.

46. Big boobs are less sensitive.

29 Gender and sexuality are fluid and personal. You are whatever gender you identify with, despite whatever genitals you were born with. Be who you want, and love who you want. **30** No it won't. Wank at will. **31** LOL. Studies have found that as much as 75% of women don't have orgasms during sex. If you're not getting them off, who do you think is? (Hint: it's probably her hand or vibrator.) **32** Sex is so much better when everyone is honest and communicates openly. If what your partner is doing isn't working for you, let them know. They're trying to please you and will have more fun if they know how. **33** 35% of men said they've done it too. **34** Nope—nothing breaks, pops or changes. The hymen, which some people cite as proof of a girl's virginity, is actually just a membrane inside the vaginal opening, and most have an opening in them. **35** If someone has a herpes outbreak, or genital warts, you MIGHT be able to tell. But most STI's aren't visible, especially to the untrained eye. Get tested if you're worried, and wear protection even when someone "looks clean." **36** It's a little *less* likely that a girl will get pregnant during her period, but it's far from impossible. Sperm can live up to 5 days in a vagina—plenty of time to linger around and find an egg to fertilize. Just wear a condom. **37** Just because someone agreed to have sex with you once (or even many times) doesn't mean you have *carte blanche* to bone. You have to get consent every time. It's easy, here's what you say: "Do you want to have sex?" **38** Actually, both can make things more complicated. Drinking dehydrates you and makes it hard to get hard and daily pot smokers are 3x more likely to experience erectile dysfunction. We're not saying you need to be stone sober every time you get busy, just don't expect weed or booze to make you into a tantric sex god. **39** The number of people you sleep with doesn't matter at all. Have sex with as few—or as many—people as you want. And the next time someone asks you about your number, tell them to mind their own business. Or lie. Either works. **40** No version of this sentence will ever be true. The only clear sign a girl wants to have sex with you is when she says, "Hey, I want to have sex with you." **41** Herpes, gonorrhea and syphilis can all be transmitted through oral sex. Just to name a few. Be smart, get tested, ask questions. **42** Just for fun, ask *them* if this one is true. **43** In a recent survey, 85% of people in their 70s reported having sex in the last year. In all likelihood, your grandparents are still boning. **44** They can't and it doesn't. Just brush your teeth. **45** First date, seventh date, never—you choose. Have sex when you both want to. Don't assume someone is going to put out on date three. **46** Big boobs can feel

47. She actually wants to go all night.

48. You should be completely naked.

49. Your dick can get stuck in braces during oral sex.

50. You can make your jizz taste better by eating fruit.

51. Circumcised guys have less fun.

52. A wet dream is a ghost jerking you off.

53. Only dudes have wet dreams.

54. Women don't watch porn.

55. You shouldn't have sex during a girl's period.

56. Penis size can be altered.

57. Length is more important than girth.

58. Fetishes and kinks are weird.

59. The first time is painful.

60. Aphrodisiacs will make you super horny.

61. Guys think about sex every 7 seconds.

62. You should jerk off before a date to make you less horny.

63. The G-Spot doesn't exist.

64. Sex before sports leads to bad performance.

just as much as small boobs. Treat boobs of all varieties with care. **47** A recent study found that the ideal duration of actual sex (not foreplay) is 7–13 minutes. Sessions that went 10–30 minutes long were considered "too long." So it's not a sprint, but it's not a marathon, either. Don't dilly dally. **48** Science says that if you leave your socks on you're 30% more likely to have an orgasm. Just saying. **49** If someone with braces decides to put your penis in their mouth, relax (and be grateful). You're not going to get trapped in there. **50** What you eat has little to no effect on the taste of your semen. You can make giving you oral sex more enjoyable by keeping your junk clean, though. Forget the pineapple juice, but not the soap. **51** Nope—being circumcised doesn't decrease pleasure during sex. Researchers poked and prodded, but sensitivity and pleasure nerves reacted the same way. No reason to be ashamed either way! In fact, some studies show that being circumcised can actually reduce your risk of getting STIs. **52** Ghosts aren't real. Your sleeping brain just decided to have an orgasm. **53** 40% of women say they've had one. **54** They definitely do. **55** It's a little messy, but do what you want. There is nothing wrong with having sex when a girl is on her period. **56** Don't click that ad. It's a scam and it will probably give your computer a virus. There is no known drug or treatment to significantly change the size of your piece. Learn to work with what you've got. **57** The average vagina depth is shorter than the average penis length. So having much more than the average 6 inches is kind of a waste. **58** In a recent poll, 30% of people had engaged in some type of "kinky" sex, and over 50% were interested in it, even if they'd never tried it. As long as everyone who is participating is on board, do whatever gets you going. It's not weird. **59** Maybe sometimes, but not always. It depends on what kind of sex you're having, how aroused you are and any number of other factors. Your best bet is to just do what feels good, listen to your body and talk to your partner. **60** In order to fully understand aphrodisiacs, doctors took a look at 50 studies that investigated supposed sexual enhancers. They found that supplements like horny goat weed and chocolate actually didn't directly help in the bedroom. **61** The average 18–25-year-old man thinks about sex 19 times a day, so about once every hour and fifteen minutes. **62** Masturbating before a date hasn't been shown to actually make you less likely to think about sex. It can help calm the nerves though, so stave off the jitters with a little jerking. **63** While it's true that there isn't some hidden button or defined anatomical structure that you can find in a vagina, for most women, the front wall of the vagina

65. Sex on the beach is fun.

66. Sex on a plane is fun/possible.

67. Sex in a car is fun.

68. Nobody but your partner will see your sext.

69. Reading lists about sex facts makes you better at sex.

is known to be extra sensitive, and stimulating it can elicit an orgasm.
64 Although multiple studies have attempted to answer the question, there is no conclusive evidence that sex negatively (or positively) affects your athletic performance. **65** Sand will get in every orifice. Every. Single. One. **66** It's barely possible to wipe in those tiny bathrooms, let alone bone. The Mile High Club isn't worth it. **67** Sex in a car isn't as fun as the movies make it seem, but it's more fun than not having sex. If you don't have any other good options, go for it, but be careful. In 1999, two separate couples died of carbon monoxide poisoning while doing it in a garage with the car running. **68** One study found that for every nude you send, the recipient shows it to 3 other people. Plus, 15% of people say they've mistakenly sent a dick pic to a family member. So double-check before you accidentally dick pic your dad. **69** Sorry.

Don't Listen *to* These People

Any advice is a product of the person giving it. If someone offering you sex advice intends to be on the receiving end of said sex—listen carefully. Otherwise be wary.

Because the truth about sex, like most things in life, is that those with knowledge worth sharing tend to do so with discretion. If a guy spends a lot of time talking about sex (whether real or imagined), he's probably doing it to mask his insecurities and inexperience.

It's important to remember that the loudest often know the least—*especially* when it comes to sex. Here's a field guide to the guys you should ignore at all costs.

THE OVERSHARER

IDENTIFYING CHARACTERISTICS: Camera roll full of genitalia (95% sent / 5% received). Inexhaustible supply of purposely vague anecdotes. Innate ability to steer all casual conversations toward sexual innuendo. Has named his penis.

SHARING BEHAVIOR: Too much detail when none is warranted. Derives self-worth from lewd and graphic stories of sexual promiscuity. The scourge of group texts everywhere. Often prefaces outbursts with "Bro" or "Mate."

HABITAT: Leaning over your shoulder with his phone while you are trying to eat.

THE COCK JOCK

IDENTIFYING CHARACTERISTICS: Attractive and overly promiscuous. Distinctive tribal-band tattoos. Unnatural tan. Athleisure obsession. Peaked in college. Pursues sex as a hobby. Probable sociopath.

SHARING BEHAVIOR: Purveyor of super-secret moves gleaned from a lifetime of conquests. Collector of trophy underwear and STIs. Transgressor of generally accepted social norms.

HABITAT: College dorms. Weddings. Las Vegas Day Parties. Tinder.

MR. DOING IT

IDENTIFYING CHARACTERISTICS: Raised eyebrows and audible increase in volume whenever conversation even remotely drifts toward sex. Looks over both shoulders before sharing insights about "doing it." Refers to vaguely defined sexual partners as "them." Unlikely to have actually had sex yet.

SHARING BEHAVIOR: Keen to solicit responses from others. A curator of other people's sexual experiences which he will both covet and traffic.

HABITAT: Pornhub. eSports events. The White House.

THE INNUENDO KING

IDENTIFYING CHARACTERISTICS: Prone to manufacturing sexual innuendo where none exists. Low self-esteem. Three-quarter-length trousers. Dedicated Stern listener. Probably vapes.

SHARING BEHAVIOR: Shares inappropriate jokes and videos of other people having sex. Likes to point. Unnecessarily loud. Refers to himself in the third person.

HABITAT: Bar stools. Amateur sports teams (second-worst player). Divorce courts.

CAPTAIN ATTRITION

IDENTIFYING CHARACTERISTICS: Penis-first decision-maker. Views sex as a numbers game; always probing to see where he might get lucky. Sad/dead inside. Owns a well-thumbed copy of *The Game*. Questionable headwear. "Creative" facial hair. Definitely vapes.

SHARING BEHAVIOR: Dubious understanding of consent. Morally bereft. Believes in "Negging," "Peacocking" and the concept of magic as a courting tool.

HABITAT: The couch at a stranger's house party. Nightclub food emporiums. Boxercise classes.

The
Beginner's
Guide *to*
Anal Sex

You've probably read plenty about the vagina—but what about the butt?

Historically speaking, anal sex has gotten the short end of the stick, but not because dudes' dicks were smaller in the 1800s. Instead, it's long been considered taboo—though, thanks to mainstream media, inclusive sex-ed and Nicki Minaj, attitudes have begun to shift. Still, there's a sizeable stigma associated with anal, which means your most pressing questions probably haven't been answered. Until now.

Q: Is everybody having anal without me?

Not yet. Though they're probably at least talking about it.

A 2016 survey of over 3,000 sexually active millennials revealed 35% of women and 15% of men are engaging in anal sex at least some of the time, while Pornhub data shows that search volume for anal sex videos increased by 120% between 2009 and 2015.

It's really more common than you think. Queer men have been doing it for years, it was commemorated in ancient Greece, and before that, anal apparently inspired a lot of Peruvian pottery; when archaeologists excavated 10,000 pots from the Moche culture between 100 and 800 AD, there were *so many* depictions of anal sex.

Q: Is it safe?

Yes. But it does require extra precaution. The anus does not self-lubricate and is a lot more prone to tearing. Therefore, there is a higher risk for contracting STIs when partaking in anal sex. It's important to use condoms and a lot of lube.

There's also perfectly healthy bacteria that live in the anus, though they can cause some serious infection in other areas. It's always a good idea to change condoms, especially if you're switching to vaginal sex. (See, it's not just for gay guys!)

Q: Why do people do it?

Why do lactose-intolerant people still eat ice cream? It feels good. For men, anal sex allows access to their prostate, which fills with fluid during arousal. Directly massaging the prostate feels great and helps induce an orgasm. While women don't have a prostate, it can still feel good because anal sex stimulates the many nerves of the anus.

Q: Will I encounter poop?

Probably. And that's OK.

If you do come across poop, let your partner know and decide together what to do next. Most bottoms will want to stop and clean up before continuing. Though if you don't care about a little mess, let your bottom know.

Q: Do I have to watch what I eat?

It's your body and you can do what you want. With that said, if you know certain foods make your stomach upset, it's probably best to avoid eating them before receiving anal sex.

If you anticipate having consistent anal sex, it may be a good idea to consider changing aspects of your diet. Red meat, for example, takes a lot of energy for the body to completely digest. A good tip is to increase your overall intake of fiber, through supplements and foods like vegetables, leafy greens, yogurt, fruits and whole grains, as they help the digestive system.

Q: How can I prepare?

Let's talk douching. Douching is the process of squirting water up your butt and then shooting it out, theoretically cleaning out the inside of your butt. You repeat the process until the water runs clear. There are a few ways to do so and the most common way is through an enema.

To douche or not to douche is completely up to you. That said, you want to minimize the timing of the overall process because you don't want to keep water sitting up your butt for a long period of time. Good bacteria does exist in your rectum, so health professionals have advised against overdoing it when it comes to douching because excessive douching can harm your rectal lining.

One to two rounds of cleaning should be plenty. And you can lay down a towel wherever the sex is occurring.

Q: What should I <u>not</u> do?

Don't add unnecessary pressure and tell your bottom to "clean out." It's already a given and telling them to do so will only make them more nervous.

If you're the bottom, don't feel pressured to do it. If you know your body is not ready for anal penetration or you're just not in the mood, don't do it. One reason is that you know your body best. The other reason is that if you or your bottom feel tense, then the sex will be a lot less enjoyable.

Q: How do I talk to my partner about it?

Over frozen yogurt.

NAVIGATING THE MORNING

AFTER

So you had sex last night. Congrats—now comes the hard part. Regardless of the quality of the encounter, the next hour of your waking life will shape how you (and whoever is lying beside you) feel about the whole thing. And as such, whether you're looking to escape or to extend the experience, your goal should be the same: to make your partner feel good about their decision...and themselves.

See, we told you this was going to be difficult. Good thing we've compiled this Morning After Cheat Sheet to help see you through.

Location

Your Place.
Make them feel welcome and appreciated by providing clothing, food and bathroom access (when applicable). If one of your shirts doesn't come back, who cares? Also, breakfast makes everything better. If they want to leave, provide them with a lift home, or offer to walk them back to their place. That's classy.

Their Place.
Say nice things about their home (mentioning décor is always a good move) and be sensitive to the fact that they might not want you in it much longer. Give them an opportunity to say this to you. Buy/make breakfast if that feels like a good idea.

A Hotel Room.
Order room service for two. Don't be cheap.

A Dorm Room.
Like dancing in a nightclub, conviction is everything. If you encounter roommates, greet them with a smile, but refrain from high-fiving them.

Their Parents' House.
Don't skulk out the door. Be respectful and say hello and goodbye to any family member you meet. These could be your in-laws.

Time

You Wake at 6 AM.
Go back to sleep. Escaping in the early hours is rude (unless requested), and wreaks havoc on your constitution.

You Are in a Hurry.
Focus on the time you *do* have with them. If you aren't able to/don't want to rearrange your schedule, make sure you take a moment to make them feel appreciated.

You Have Nowhere to Be.
Know how to read the situation. Give them continual outs by asking what they have planned for the day. Don't get creepy. Also maybe get a job or something.

Scenario

You Don't Remember Their Name.
Man, how drunk *were* you? Instead of guessing or searching the room for clues, ask them for their Facebook ID, or have them enter their contact info on your phone. Also, reevaluate your life.

They Are in a Relationship.
If you knew this ahead of time, ask how they are feeling and behave accordingly. Perhaps formulate a plan. If this is new information, get out of there; but do so with *class*.

This Was a Long Time Coming.
Make it clear that you are happy but don't get creepy.

This Was a One-Night Stand.
Celebrate it. Lean in to the ridiculousness and laugh at yourself. Say kind things before leaving, secure in the knowledge you are an adult capable of no-strings-attached sex.

There Are More Than Two of You in Bed.
Savor it. This won't happen often.

The Aftermath

- Take a shower as soon as possible—you smell worse than you think.

- If you have no toothbrush, coat finger with toothpaste and do your best. At the very least, drink lots of water to combat morning breath.

- Hold in any flatulence until they leave the room. Always remember to air out the sheets afterward.

Conversation

- Try to remember what got you here in the first place. If you were kind and funny last night, stay the course—though take the inherent awkwardness of the morning after into consideration, and turn things down a notch or two.

- Ask them questions—and listen to the answers.

- Show that you are not a scumbag by remembering things you were told last night. If last night is a blur, fake it 'til you make it.

- Avoid pithy one-liners or movie quotes.

- Remember that your behavior here is an advertisement of you. Your responsibility is to be your best you.

The Goodbye

- Offer your number and take theirs.

- Offer a kiss goodbye if this feels right, a hug if not. *Do not* shake hands.

- Say that you had a great time—even if you didn't.

- Leave them somewhere safe.

- Don't make firm follow-up plans if you have no intention of keeping them.

- Remember that this might be the last morning after you have together, so be your best self.

The Follow-Up

- Send them a text the following day to make sure that they got home OK. Tell them that you had a great time and ask if they'd like to do it again. If yes, make firm plans. If no, move on.

- Do not send more than two unanswered texts in a row. Ever.

The Recap

- Gentlemen never tell.

Reasons *You're* Not Having Sex

You are too drunk.

Alcohol decreases your brain's ability to sense stimulation and interferes with parts of your nervous system essential for arousal, orgasm and circulation. Studies show sober men were able to get erections much faster—and maintain them for much longer—than drunk dudes. Also, if you're that wasted, *how* are you reading this right now?

You are in the Friend Zone.

Most friends don't exchange Christmas presents, let alone bodily fluids, so extricating one's self from Palcatraz is a tough task. But it's not *impossible*—one survey found 40% of all couples started out as platonic friends. The key? Knowing if escape is even an option. That requires an honest, open assessment of the situation: Is there *really* the potential for something more? You may think so, but what happens to the relationship if your friend doesn't? Is a "Friends with Benefits" scenario a possibility, or a pipe dream? (Hint: It's probably the latter.) If you're still willing to risk it all, it's imperative to tell your friend *exactly* how you feel about them—be direct, and be willing to live with the results, even if that means moving on. Your friendship doesn't have to end, but your desire to see your friend naked *does*.

You are a gamer.

According to *The Journal of Sexual Medicine* (we have a subscription), if you're playing video games for longer than an hour every day, you may have less sex. On the bright side: Gamers have a lower risk of premature ejaculation. But you'll never know until you put the controller down.

You are eating meat.

A University of Cal-Berkeley study found men who ate a vegetarian diet for two weeks had a "more attractive" body odor than those who ate red meat. So if you needed a reason to switch to soy—and who doesn't?—this is it.

You are dressing wrong.

There are actual studies that suggest wearing red will make you more attractive to the opposite sex, but really, only Kanye and Santa can pull that look off. And while we're the last ones to criticize your wardrobe choices, science has shown that polyester fabrics actually *decrease* sex drive...in lab rats. But do you really want to risk it? On a related note: If you're still wearing polyester in 2018, maintaining your sex drive probably isn't your biggest problem.

You are gross.

We're not here to talk about your physical appearance, body odor or table manners (though would it kill you to chew with your mouth closed?). But we would like to have a brief chat about your behavior toward others—because there's a good chance the biggest hindrance to you having sex is, well, *you*. Do you frequently offer unsolicited commentaries, critiques or compliments? Did you read that question and wonder "Does catcalling count?" Have you ever used derogatory language to describe or insult someone? Are you rude to waiters? Would you describe yourself as a "Men's Rights Advocate"? Do you feel like the government should decide what a woman can do with her body? Do you often feel superior to others? Do you often let them know it? Have you ever used a position of authority as a tool of coercion? Are you quick to fire off a dick pic? If you answered "Yes" to literally any of those questions, congrats: You're gross—and, unless you change, doomed to die alone.

You are dirty.

You know that algae-covered stack of dishes in your sink? Wash them. The tumbleweeds of pubic hair blowing around your bathroom? Grab a broom. The mound of dirty clothes barricading your closet? Do a load of laundry. It's not difficult to go from being a total slob to a (slightly) functioning adult, but it does take a modicum of effort—and some elbow grease. Seem insurmountable? Start by making your bed, since we assume it's not getting a lot of use at the moment—nobody wants to do it with a dirty dude, after all.

You are trying <u>way</u> too hard.

You might not believe it, but sex isn't everything. Almost every single person on the planet has had it—or will have it at some point in the future. So if you're hyper-focused on making it happen, it's probably a good idea to chill. Instead of constantly being on the prowl, consider having actual conversations. Learn to read a room—and a situation. Understand that not every scenario will end in sex...in fact, most won't. If that depresses you, well, you probably shouldn't be allowed to have sex in the first place. Go easy on the scented body sprays. Don't touch unless touched first. If your advances aren't being reciprocated, know when to call it quits. You might have to stop chatting up girls at the gym, or start wearing sleeves, but it's for the best.

You aren't trying hard enough.

That's not to say you should go full-on Fassbender in *Shame*...but would it kill you to put in a little effort? Even the slightest bit of exercise increases blood flow and stimulates the production of feel-good hormones like

oxytocin. Remember, you're trying to convince a stranger to allow you to enter them—the least you can do is put on a clean shirt.

You are too confident.

You might think you're incredibly interesting (or handsome), but that doesn't mean your date does...and even if they do, that doesn't mean sex is a foregone conclusion. So if you find yourself focusing the conversation on *your* accomplishments, preening in the mirror or repeatedly forcing the issue of sex, you're probably too confident. And said confidence is probably not warranted.

You aren't confident enough.

According to just about every sex survey in the universe, confidence leads to coitus. But there's a fine line between assertive and asshole—the key to remaining on the right side of that divide is *perspective*. Tom Hardy carries himself with confidence because, well, he's Tom Hardy. You probably aren't, but confidence comes in many forms. Focus on the things you genuinely like about yourself...if it's a physical trait, great. If it's the gift of gab, a sense of humor or a genuine compassion for your fellow man, even better: They'll be around long after your abs have disappeared. If your source of inspiration is true, your confidence can only come across as genuine—and people will respond in kind.

You are a bad kisser.

The truth hurts. Aside from being a total asshole (or a magician), not knowing how to kiss may be the single greatest sexual deterrent on the planet. So make sure to check your breath beforehand. Use your tongue efficiently, and to great effect—don't jam it down their throat, but don't abandon it entirely, either. Vary your kissing speed and pressure. An occasional touch of the face is always good, but avoid forceful grabs (come to think of it, that's a pretty good rule for life in general). And for God's sake, don't kiss with your eyes open. That's just creepy.

You are being unrealistic.

This isn't your fault. You are a product of your environment, and there's a pretty good chance that environment is crammed with misleading and misguided messages about sex. It's how companies get you to buy crap you don't need, after all. So even though it's tough to do, it's important to block out most of that ephemera—or at least run it through a filter. Remember, sex is a deeply personal thing, and no director, copywriter or Instagram model knows what's best for you.

You are giving off bad body language.

A UCLA study found that 55% of communication comes from body language. And that's bad news if you avoid eye contact, have bad posture, often cross your arms or can't sit still, because you're sending out bad vibes—and probably repelling any potential mates. And according to experts, "bad body language" also includes an inability to respect personal space, making too many hand gestures or even raising your eyebrows. So maybe it's best to just stay inside and never interact with another human ever again.

A Series of Sexy Venn Diagrams

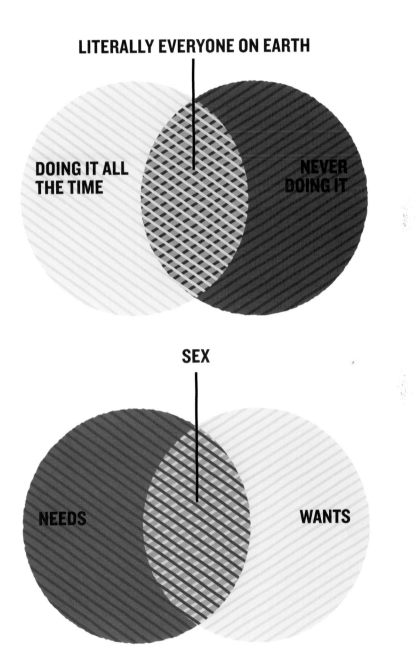

LITERALLY EVERYONE ON EARTH

DOING IT ALL THE TIME

NEVER DOING IT

SEX

NEEDS

WANTS

SUPER DONG

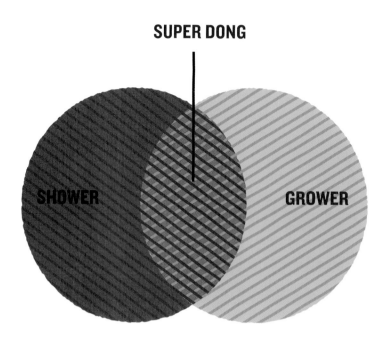

SHOWER

GROWER

GOOD SEX

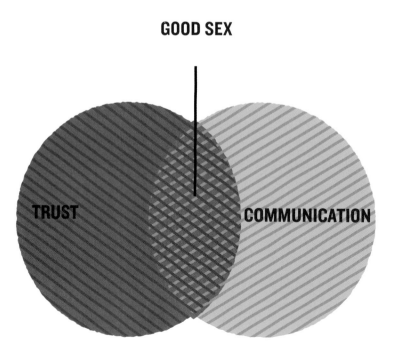

TRUST

COMMUNICATION

"FUCK"

THINGS YOU SAY DURING SEX

THINGS YOU SAY EVERY DAY

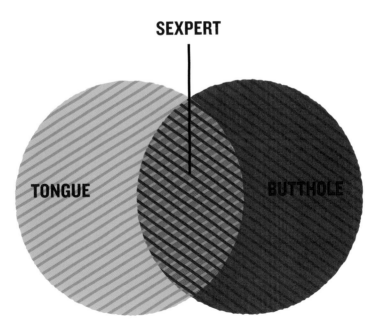

SEXPERT

TONGUE

BUTTHOLE

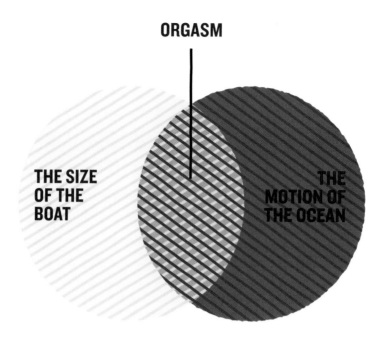

ORGASM

THE SIZE OF THE BOAT

THE MOTION OF THE OCEAN

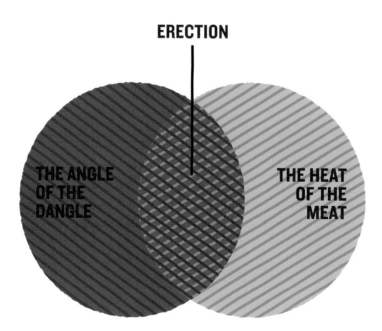

ERECTION

THE ANGLE OF THE DANGLE

THE HEAT OF THE MEAT

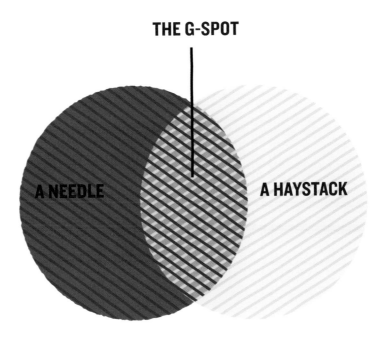

THE G-SPOT

A NEEDLE · A HAYSTACK

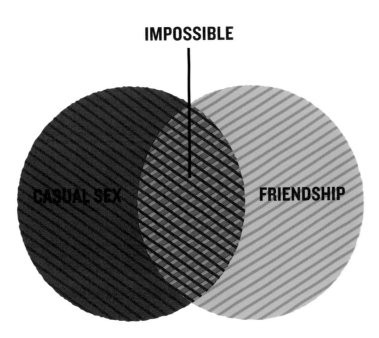

IMPOSSIBLE

CASUAL SEX · FRIENDSHIP

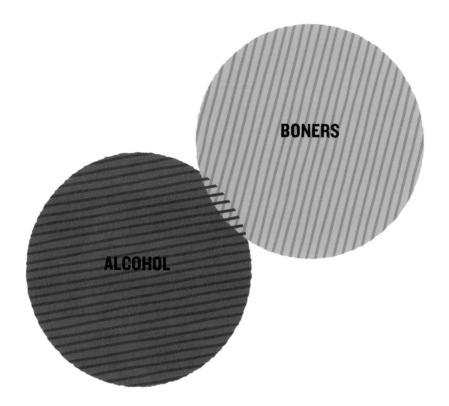

BONERS

ALCOHOL

PENILE
FRACTURE

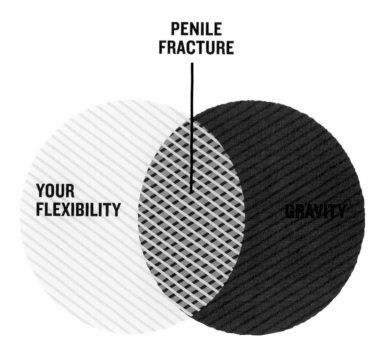

YOUR
FLEXIBILITY

GRAVITY

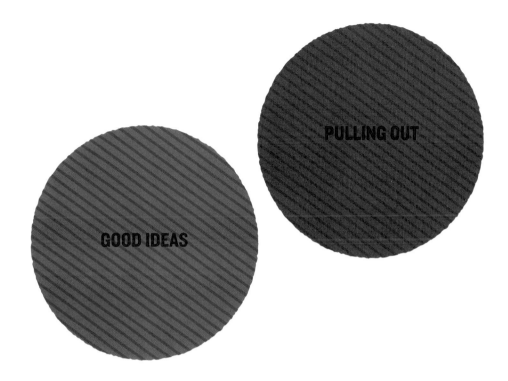

GOOD IDEAS

PULLING OUT

SHOWER SEX

DEATH WISH

BODILY HARM

JEREMIH
BIRTHDAY
SEX

GENDER IDENTITY
SEXUAL ORIENTATION
BIOLOGICAL SEX

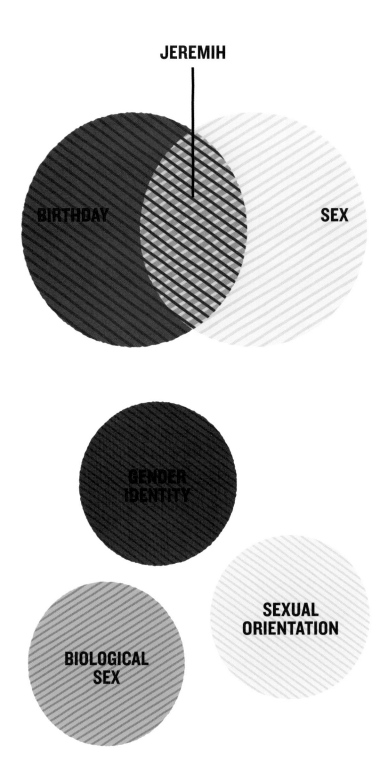

PORN

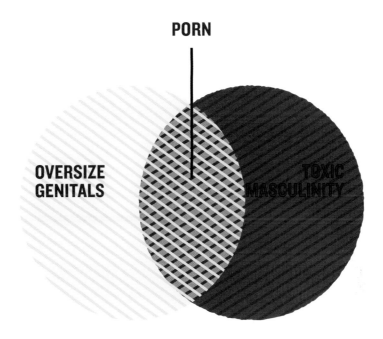

OVERSIZE
GENITALS

TOXIC
MASCULINITY

NORMAL SEX

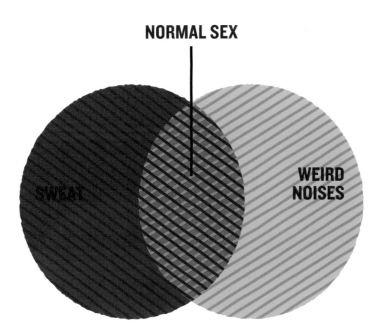

SWEAT

WEIRD
NOISES

YOUR PARENTS

PEOPLE THAT HAVE SEX

JK, ACTUALLY

PEOPLE THAT HAVE SEX

YOUR PARENTS

SEX IN MOVIES

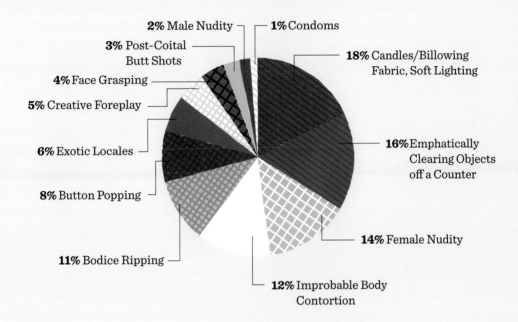

2% Male Nudity
3% Post-Coital Butt Shots
4% Face Grasping
5% Creative Foreplay
6% Exotic Locales
8% Button Popping
11% Bodice Ripping
12% Improbable Body Contortion
1% Condoms
18% Candles/Billowing Fabric, Soft Lighting
16% Emphatically Clearing Objects off a Counter
14% Female Nudity

SEX IRL

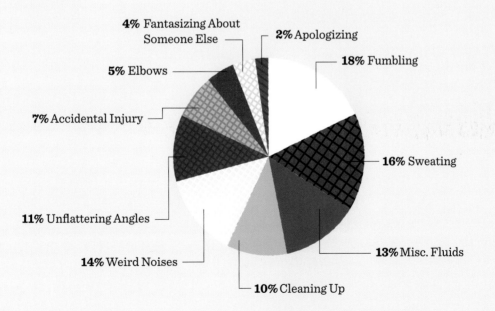

4% Fantasizing About Someone Else
5% Elbows
7% Accidental Injury
11% Unflattering Angles
14% Weird Noises
10% Cleaning Up
2% Apologizing
18% Fumbling
16% Sweating
13% Misc. Fluids

Sex After *the* Apocalypse

If you're reading this, that means you survived the global mass extinction. Congrats, now you can do whatever you want—except have sex. Then again, that's probably not all that different from your life *now*. Except that everyone is dead, obvs.

Anyway, here are some helpful strategies to deal with those lustful urges.

1. When **masturbating**, try not to think about how **everyone you've ever known and loved is dead**. It's a real boner-killer.

2. Also, avoid **remembering the warm, intimate embrace of a woman**. Especially since you'll never experience **physical love** again.

3. Since **pornography will be scarce**, look to nature for boner inspiration. One day you may notice **the subtle beauty of the midday sun playing on the obsidian fields**—and *voila!*

4. Ever **seen clouds like *that* before?** Woah, who let in all of these sexy clouds?? And *voila!*

5. You start to understand why **Georgia O'Keeffe paintings** are so powerful. And... *voila!*

6. Or even try **creating your own tasteful erotic art** - hey, those cavemen were on to something.

7. **The Stranger**. Trust us.

8. If **self-love isn't doing the trick**, try flexing your arts and crafts muscles to create a **handmade chastity device**.

9. Gather **scrap metal from a nearby blast crater** and turn it into a **crude pleasure receptacle**.

10. The radiation has probably **mutated some plants into living Fleshlights**, so have at it.

11. Think about **that chick with three boobs in *Total Recall***.

12. Or, self-flagellate (the medieval kind, you pervert).

13. Don't have **sex with animals**.

14. Don't have **sex with dead bodies**.

15. Don't have **sex with dead animal bodies**.

16. You can always **fuck pumice**.

An *Unsexy* Discussion About Pornography

In ancient times—like way back in the 1990s—pornography wasn't just a click away. We didn't even have things to click. Instead, it had to be *obtained*, clandestinely removed from your dad's sock drawer or mined beneath your older brother's bed. You would lead expeditions to locate stashes of old *Playboy*s in the woods, like Francisco Vazquez de Coronado searching for a lost City of Gold, or head down to a seedy video store, fake I.D. in hand, to purchase previously viewed tapes from the discount bin.

It was a lot of work. But we didn't care.

Because that expended effort, coupled with overall scarcity, meant porn was a highly prized commodity, like Beryllium or Rhodium, and nearly as valuable. On the open market, porn commanded a princely sum: at least a black-bagged copy of *The Death of Superman*, or maybe even a lesser Super Nintendo game like *Killer Instinct*.

It was a simpler time, to be certain. You could even call it "innocent," if you ignore the fact we weren't just using porn to get free video games. But the fact that porn is no longer a valuable bartering tool *does* prove a larger point: There's way too much of it today.

Porn now pervades every aspect of our lives; it is instantly available on your phone, any time, anywhere, and there's a 100% chance you've looked at some within the past 24 hours. In a vacuum, that's not necessarily a bad thing (vacuum porn, on the other hand, *is*). Pornography allows us to explore aspects of ourselves—and our sexuality—without fear of judgment. Masturbation is a normal, healthy thing. Sometimes school is *super* boring.

But increased availability—and, to a degree, acceptance—has brought with it increased expectations and lowered decorum. Whether you view porn as a How-To Guide is entirely up to you, though if you're furiously scribbling down notes (with your other hand), you should know that what you're watching isn't a realistic depiction of sex. At best, porn is fantasy. At worst, it's beyond problematic—according to the California Women's Health Survey, 37% of women in porn are forced victims of childhood sex. There's also the very real chance that the participants might not have even given consent: The Data & Society Research Institute says about 1 in every 25 Americans have either been threatened with, or are victims of, "nonconsensual image sharing"... aka revenge porn.

The problem with porn's prevalence is that you probably *didn't* know that. Why would you? It has become a disposable product, on par with football scores or videos of dogs doing dumb things or anything else you swipe through while sitting on the toilet.

Yet unlike those distractions, porn can fundamentally impact your life. There's a good chance you've grown up with a full supply of it in your arsenal, ready to be deployed at a moment's notice, and an even better chance that you've viewed it as a teaching tool. What else are you supposed to do, read a book? That's led to toxic, downright deplorable standards and behaviors—assumptions about gender roles and consent, unreasonable expectations about sex itself, a lack of empathy—and a generation of guys who shoot first (usually on the face) and ask questions later. In many ways, sex has become as unrealistic as porn. And nearly as problematic.

This is not meant to bum you out, or to come across as a bit of "Back in my day" nostalgia (though, to be honest, it kind of does *both*). There's no question that porn was, is and always will be problematic on some level, which is why barriers to entry are important. Not every kid—and we mean *kid*—with a phone should be looking at it, because they don't possess the critical-thinking skills necessary to discern fact from fantasy. But *you* do. So it's time to start viewing porn in a different way. Realize that these are people getting paid (hopefully) to fuck on camera, and judge their actions accordingly. Stop using porn as a measuring stick, a guide, or an excuse. Or try V.R. We hear that shit is *incredible*.

Are *You* Masturbating Too Much?

Probably.

How Much Sex *Is* <u>Too</u> Much?

TOO MUCH

Your penis is bleeding.

You hear someone say, "Come here" and take it as a challenge.

You own a sex swing.

You ejaculate dust.

You charge admission.

Your sex tapes have special effects.

You've finally filled the gaping chasm inside you.

You use the phrase *mise-en-scène* when discussing dick pics.

You're sponsored by Durex.

Your pubic hair is occasionally singed.

You have the luxury of turning sex down.

You have free time to do other things, like watch porn.

JUST RIGHT

You understand the concept of "not enough sex" is merely an ideological construct of the patriarchy.

You don't complain about not having enough sex.

You are able to view the paintings of Georgia O'Keeffe without discomfort.

You don't feel the need to buy Magnum condoms just for show.

Your Bumble profile features a mention of your spotless driving record.

You sleep well at night.

You are fine with masturbating sometimes, to be honest.

You are in year two of a relationship.

NOT ENOUGH

You have at least entertained the idea of paying for it.

You find yourself staring longingly at raw oysters.

You find yourself fucking raw oysters.

Your Tinder profile comes with a "Buy One, Get One Free" coupon.

Your penis has entered the witness protection program.

You've watched all the porn.

You've forgotten how sex works.

You're anxiously awaiting the day when sex with robots is no longer frowned upon.

You own a Fleshlight.

You are brought to the brink of orgasm by a stiff breeze.

You are the author of the Brother book.

A HANDY GLOSSARY OF TERMS

69—A sexual position in which both partners give and receive oral sex simultaneously. Usually involves lying side-to-side or on top of each other, head-to-toe, so your bodies look like the number 69. Also usually involves a willingness to stare directly into your partner's butthole.

Abstinence—Not engaging in sexual behaviors. As a personal ethos, it's totally fine. As a sexual-education method, it leaves *a lot* to be desired.

Anal Sex—Totally cool if the other person is into it.

Analingus—Stimulation achieved by contact between mouth and anus. Seemingly verboten, it's actually totally normal—and criminally underrated.

Androgynous—Someone or something that is gender neutral or non-gendered.

Areola—The area of skin around the nipples that is darker than the rest of the breast. Both guys and girls have them, and both enjoy when you work them into foreplay.

Ass to Mouth—Withdrawal of the penis from the anus, followed by immediate insertion into the mouth. Seems like gross porn stuff, but if your partner's into it, hey… who are we to judge?

Balls—You know, your testicles.

Banging—Aggressive sex, in the parlance of our times. Avoid use, if possible.

Beaver—Slang term for the vagina that hasn't been popular since the 1970s.

Blue Balls—The uncomfortable sensation in your testicles that occurs when ejaculation *doesn't*. Fun fact: Girls can also get Blue Balls.

Bi-Curious—Someone who is primarily attracted to people of a different sex, but also has feelings for, or attractions to, people of the same sex.

Bisexual—Someone who is attracted to people of different genders.

Birth Control—Any method used to prevent pregnancy. Pulling out isn't one of them.

Blow Job—Slang term for performing oral sex on a man. Does not involve any actual blowing.

Boner—A slang term for erection. Best used among friends, not anyone you'd ever actually have sex with.

Boobs—A slang term for breasts. Boobs rule.

Condom—A sheath-shaped barrier used during sex to prevent pregnancy and the spread of sexually transmitted infections. All different shapes, sizes and flavors are available, and they are made of different materials to accommodate certain allergies. Female condoms are also widely available. You should always use one.

Consent—Agreeing to an action or behavior. In order to consent, a person must not be mentally disabled, under the influence of drugs or alcohol or under the age of consent. Literally the most important thing involving sex.

Cowgirl—A sexual position in which one person rides atop the other.

Cisgender—A person whose gender identity matches their biological sex. Probably includes you.

Clitoris—Highly sensitive organ located above the opening of the vagina. Its only function is sexual pleasure, so find it and make it your friend.

Contraceptive—A barrier, hormonal or surgical method used to prevent pregnancy. Most contraceptives—condoms notwithstanding—do not offer protection against HIV or other sexually transmitted infections.

Cowper's Glands—They make your pre-cum.

Cunnilingus—The act of performing oral sex on a female. Don't let the weird name stop you from doing it.

Cunt—Derogatory term for a vagina and, by extension, the woman attached to it. There is no excuse for actually using this word.

Cyber Sex—Something your parents probably did in a chatroom. Ask them about it (and then ask what a chatroom was).

Dick—You know, your penis.

Doggie Style—A sexual position where one partner gets on their hands and knees, and the other enters them from behind. Not to be confused with the Snoop Dogg album *Doggystyle*.

Double-Bagging—Using two condoms at once, presumably to prevent pregnancy or worse. Actually a really dumb idea,

as it increases the risk of the condoms breaking or tearing. Oh, and also because it doesn't offer extra protection.

Dry Sex—Having sex without actually *having* sex. It involves rubbing genitalia together while fully or partially clothed. If you're into it, go for it.

Ejaculation—The release of semen from the tip of the penis during orgasm. Women can also ejaculate.

Ejac—A term for semen itself. It's more socially acceptable than "cum" anyway.

Endometrium—The lining of a woman's uterus that grows, then sheds, during her menstrual cycle. Also where a fertilized egg implants itself at the beginning of pregnancy.

Epididymis—The coiled tube in the testes where sperm is stored pre-ejaculation. Fun to say.

Fingering—The act of using one (or several) fingers to touch a woman's genitalia. Can escalate to full-blown finger-blasting if the situation demands it.

Flaccid—The resting state of your penis when it is not erect. That includes right now, presumably.

Foreplay—All activities that occur before sex, with the goal of arousal.

Foreskin—Retractable hood-like skin that covers and protects the head of the penis. You might have this, or you might not. Either way is cool with us.

G-Spot—An area roughly two inches inside the vagina that can produce intense sexual pleasure when stimulated. Short for the Grafenberg Spot. Definitely not a myth.

Gender—Societal and cultural norms related to what it means to be masculine or feminine. Usually bullshit. Differs from gender identity, which is how a person feels and understands themselves, and sex, which is biological and usually refers to genitalia.

Group Sex—When more than two people are having sex simultaneously. If you find someone who's into this, keep them in your life *forever*.

Hand Job—The manual manipulation of another person's genitals. Sometimes you're in a hurry and a handy works just fine.

Heterosexual—Being sexually and romantically attracted to someone of a different sex.

Hooking Up—Basically beyond definition, as it means different things to different people. Generally speaking, it refers to when two people are sexual with each other, but whether that means kissing, touching or boning is sort of up to those people.

Homosexual—Being sexually and romantically attracted to someone of the same sex. Kind of dated, to be honest, and can definitely be used in the pejorative sense. Go with gay, lesbian or queer instead.

Intersex—A person born with a combination of genitals and/or chromosomes that differ from an XY male or an XX female. Formerly known as "hermaphrodite," which is a derogatory term.

Labia—The pairs of lips surrounding the vaginal opening. The outer lips are called the labia *majora*, while the inner lips are the labia *minora*.

Lubricant—A substance that decreases friction and increases sexual satisfaction. Water-based lubes are safe to use with condoms, petroleum-based lubes aren't.

Masturbation—The manual manipulation of one's genitals for sexual satisfaction. Ninety percent of all hands you shake are used for masturbation.

Menage-a-Trois—A French term that refers to three people having sex simultaneously. We have never witnessed this term

successfully deployed in the wild.

Menstruation—When the uterus sheds its tissue lining and it is expelled from the vagina. Usually occurs once every month. Also known as a period. It's still OK to have sex during a period, if she's into it.

Misogyny—A hatred of women. Fucking gross and dumb. It's 2019, dude.

Missonary Position—A sexual position that involves one partner lying on top of the other. Don't listen to the haters; missionary is surprisingly effective.

Mono—The so-called "kissing virus" your parents probably warned you about. It's a real thing though, with symptoms that include sore throat, swollen glands and low-grade fever.

Nipples—The tips of the breasts that are sensitive to touch and temperature (so focus on them during foreplay).

Nookie—A slang term Fred Durst uses to describe the act of sex.

Oral Sex—Genital stimulation that involves the mouth and tongue. A prerequisite if you are a decent human being.

Ovary—An organ in women than produces, stores and

releases eggs. Women are usually born with two of them. Ovaries also produce hormones like progesterone and estrogen.

Penis—Your entire *raison d'être.*

Perineum—The area between the vagina (or scrotum) and the anus. Colloquially known as "the taint."

Phone Sex—Something your parents did back when people actually used phones for talking.

Pornography—Difficult to define, though in general, it relates to movies, magazines or videos about sexually related topics that are designed to arouse or titillate. To paraphrase Supreme Court Justice Potter Stewart, you know it when you see it.

Pregnancy—Can be the end result of sex. It's the process by which an implanted, fertilized egg develops into a fetus. If this happens to you, you'd better have a plan, man.

Premature Ejaculation—When you ejaculate shortly after becoming erect with little or no sexual stimulation. It happens to the best of us.

Premenstrual Syndrome—Also known as PMS, it's the set of symptoms many women experience during their periods. It's not a catch-all way to dismiss any emotions, BTW.

Pubes—Coarse hair around the genitals that begins growing during puberty. Everyone has it, so just deal with it, dude.

Pussy—A derogatory (yet widely accepted) term for female genitalia, or for your friend who won't do the rope swing.

Reverse-Cowgirl—A sexual position in which one person rides the other while facing away from them. Yee-haw!

Rim Job—Contact between the mouth and the anus. Basically just analingus.

Scrotum—It holds your balls, bro.

Sex—A person's chromosomes and/or genitalia that designates them as male or female (independent of how *they* themselves choose to identify). Also the engaging of sexual behaviors including oral, anal or vaginal intercourse.

Slut—A shitty term that you should never use.

Sexually Transmitted Infection—Spread though sexual behavior or contact, including skin-to-skin or through bodily fluids. Most (but not all) are treatable, so get tested. Also known as a Sexually Transmitted Disease.

Transgender—A term to describe a person whose gender identity doesn't match their biological sex. Don't refer to them as "transgendered," as that makes it sound like they have an affliction.

Urethra—The tube in men and women that carries urine. It's *not* the clitoris...trust us.

Vagina—A woman's magical cave of wonders. Also the passageway from the uterus to the outside of the body.

Virginity—The societal definition of someone who has never had sexual intercourse. What constitutes sexual intercourse, however, is up to the individual.

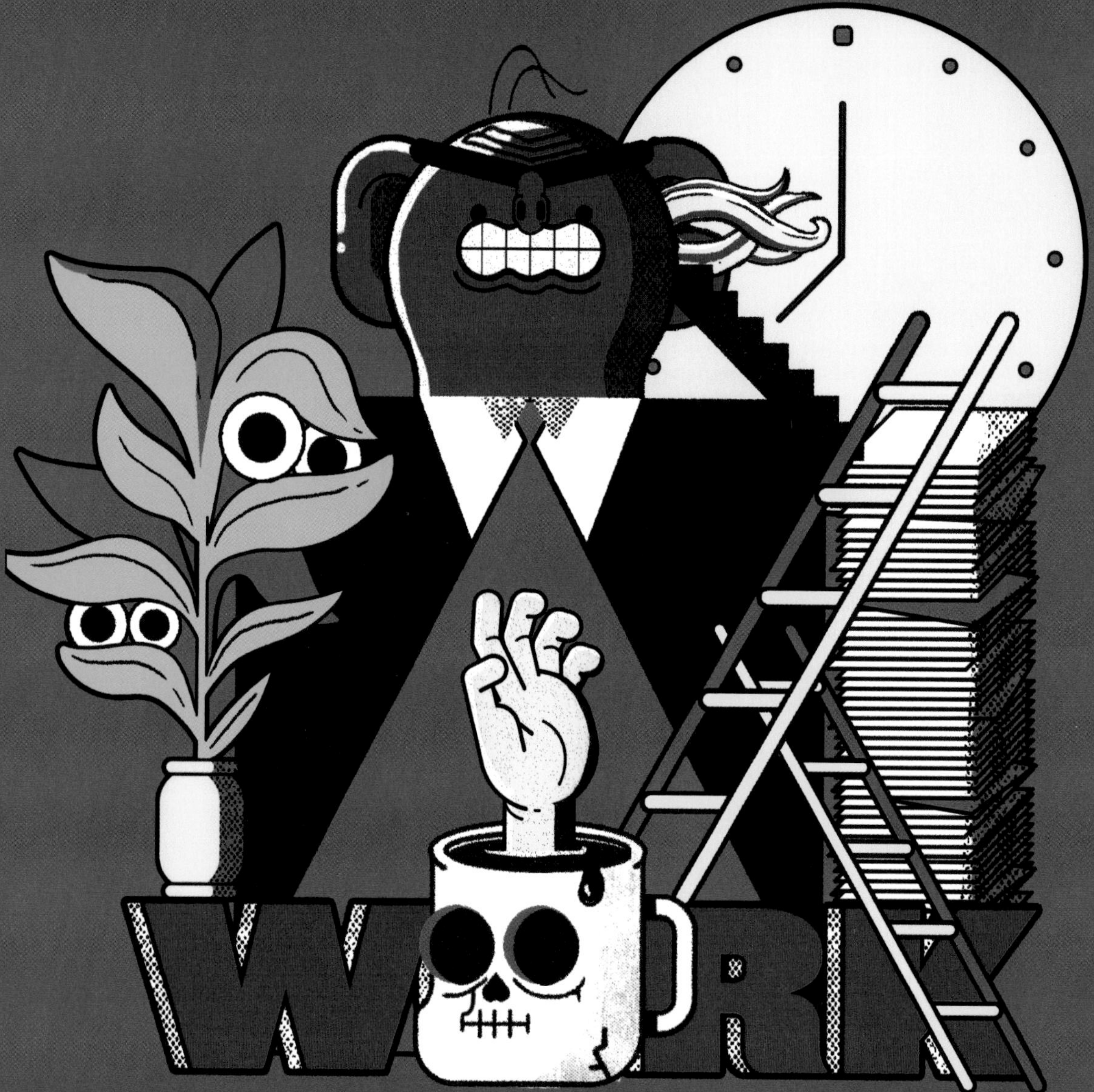

Work stinks. It is an annoyance, an inconvenience, a rather cruel sociological experiment that often involves name tags. They literally have to pay you to do it (unless you're an intern), because you'd never subject yourself to its myriad indignities *for free*.

You will be forced to work in close proximity to people you cannot stand, submit to the rule of a frustrated (at best) or vindictive (at worst) boss, grapple with your own mortality and your feelings on mankind in general. You must show up when you are told, and can't leave until someone says so. On a daily basis, you will interact with sycophants, hypochondriacs, alpha males, amnesiacs, illiterates, martyrs, sociopaths, pessimists, optimists, burnouts and social climbers—with only periodic breaks for lunch and perhaps the odd vacation day thrown in if you're lucky (and chances are, you are not lucky). Sometimes there are also PowerPoint presentations.

Worst of all, you'll basically be working until you die, a level of commitment rivaled perhaps only by marriage or ISIS. And both of those are pretty shitty institutions.

Undoubtedly, someone will try to tell you none of that is true, that work offers not only a creative outlet, but the opportunity for deep personal fulfilment. This person is either: A) lying, B) delusional or C) both. Work is not supposed to make you happy, it is the very definition of a means to an end—you do it to acquire money, which, in turn, you use to acquire things like food, shelter, clothing and iPhones. There is no deeper purpose, and the sooner you realize that, the better.

So why bother? Well, for starters, you pretty much have to. But there's another reason to keep punching the clock: With its litany of petty annoyances, menial tasks and forced acquaintances, work is essentially a microcosm of life itself...and if you can deal with it (or at least make it through the day without strangling someone), there is *nothing* you can't handle. Honestly.

Whether it was intended to or not, work teaches you how to coexist with your fellow man, how to foster a sense of camaraderie with—and develop empathy for—a collection of people you have absolutely nothing in common with, outside of an overwhelming desire to simply make it through the day. Conveniently enough, those are all requirements for functioning in society, too. You will earn the gift of *perspective*, learn that sometimes life isn't fair and that often, obligation is the only course of action. You will be overburdened and underappreciated, find yourself in situations that you are wildly unprepared for and frequently be let down by those closest to you. You will learn to bullshit, how to bide your time and when to exact revenge. You will develop a healthy mistrust of authority, and an innate ability to read people and understand their inner machinations. You might also get to have sex sometimes.

Point is, there *are* benefits of work that go beyond learning how to sweep floors or change printer cartridges—real, genuine life skills that will benefit you much more than a paycheck. **Hey, if you have to do it, you might as well make the best of it.**

MASLOW'S HIERARCHY OF WORK NEEDS

Everything necessary to ascend, find fulfillment and become the person you were meant to be.

SELF-ACTUALIZATION

ESTEEM NEEDS

BELONGINGNESS AND LOVE

SAFETY NEEDS

PHYSIOLOGICAL NEEDS

 SELF-ACTUALIZATION—Becoming the boss, not becoming a dick.

ESTEEM—Salary, promotion, benefits.

BELONGINGNESS AND LOVE—After-work drinks, office fantasy league, mutual dislike of office printer, mutual distrust for management.

 SAFETY—High-walled cubicle, computer monitor positioned away from coworkers' prying eyes, lax attendance policy, health insurance (LOL, yeah right).

 PHYSIOLOGICAL—Coffee, lunch, computer, attractive coworkers, decent boss, *laissez-faire* dress code.

Appropriate Responses *to* Lies *Your* Dad Will Tell *You* About Work

"A job's a job."

Getting paid to clean toilets is not the same as getting paid to eat ice cream.

"Learn a trade—you'll never regret it."

You will regret it when you are replaced by a robot.

"Work builds character."

So does diarrhea.

"There's no such thing as a free lunch."

We have free lunch every Wednesday. It's usually Subway, but it still counts.

"These will be the best years of your life."

As a wage slave these best years will be stolen from you.

"You make your own opportunities."

Opportunities only lead to more work.

"Nothing will be handed to you."

Unless you are related to the boss.

"There is no substitute for hard work."

I wish I could find a substitute to work for me.

"Hard work is its own reward."

Are you sure you know what a "reward" is?

"Don't dip your pen in the company inkwell."

Hooking up with coworkers is basically the only reason to have a job.

"Be first in and last out and they'll notice you."

Be first in and last out and they will own you.

"Dress for the job you want."

Just getting dressed for the job I have should be enough.

"Shine your shoes—people notice your shoes at work."

Converse are more comfortable than dress shoes.

"The suit and tie make the man."

The suit and tie make the mortgage broker.

"Your first paycheck will be the proudest moment of your life."

Your first paycheck will be insulting.

"Always carry a newspaper to show you are ahead of the game."

Nobody reads newspapers anymore.

"Keep your head down, work hard, and good things will happen to you."

Good things only happen to bad people. Especially at work.

"The right job is a job for life."

There are no longer any jobs for life.

"Look after your company and your company will look after you."

Your company will replace you with a robot.

"It isn't what you know, it's who you know."

OK, this one is actually true.

What *You* Should Know Before Taking Any Job

HOW MUCH PRAISE WILL YOU RECEIVE?

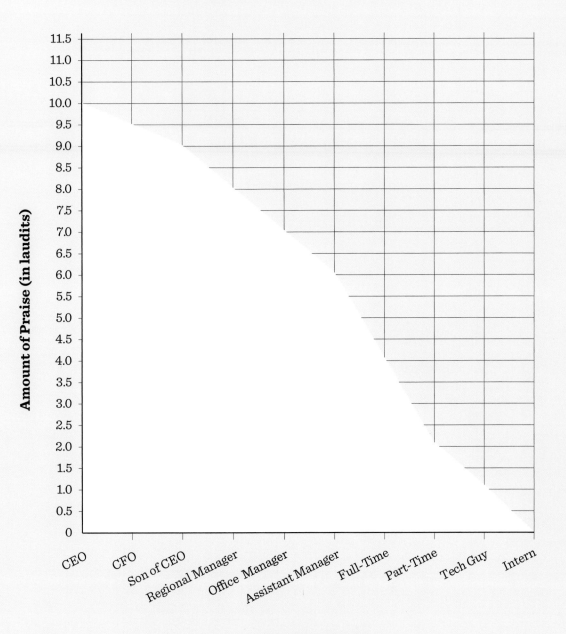

HOW MUCH SHIT WILL YOU EAT?

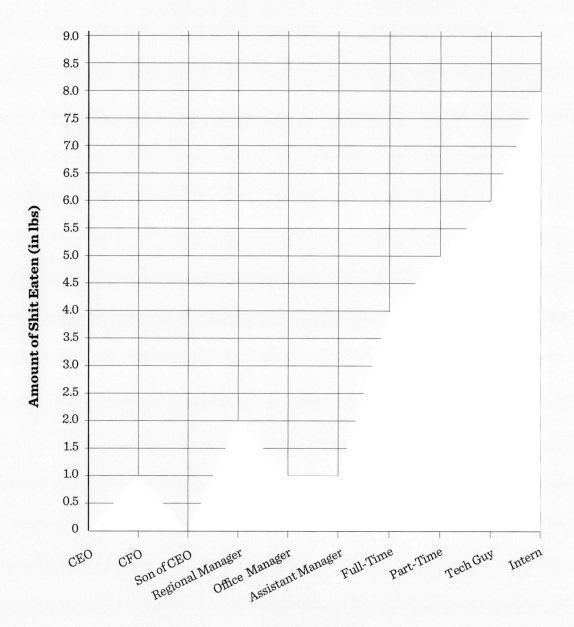

Amount of Shit Eaten (in lbs)

9.0
8.5
8.0
7.5
7.0
6.5
6.0
5.5
5.0
4.5
4.0
3.5
3.0
2.5
2.0
1.5
1.0
0.5
0

CEO · CFO · Son of CEO · Regional Manager · Office Manager · Assistant Manager · Full-Time · Part-Time · Tech Guy · Intern

Employee Level

HOW MUCH BLAME WILL YOU RECEIVE?

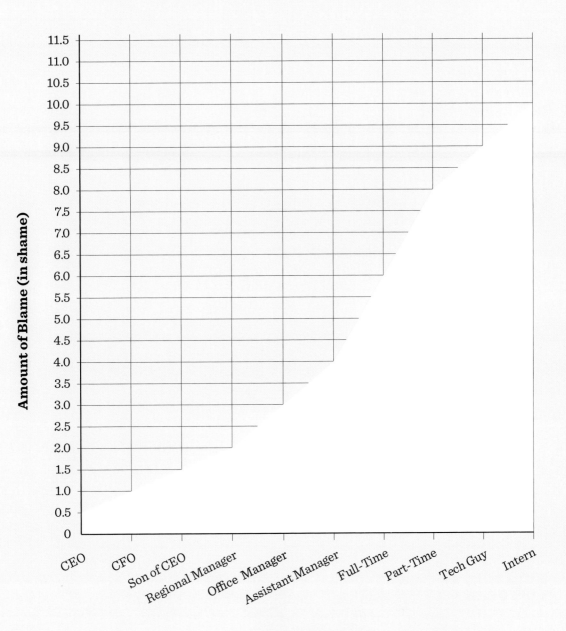

Amount of Blame (in shame)

Employee Level: CEO, CFO, Son of CEO, Regional Manager, Office Manager, Assistant Manager, Full-Time, Part-Time, Tech Guy, Intern

HOW MUCH WORK WILL YOU DO?

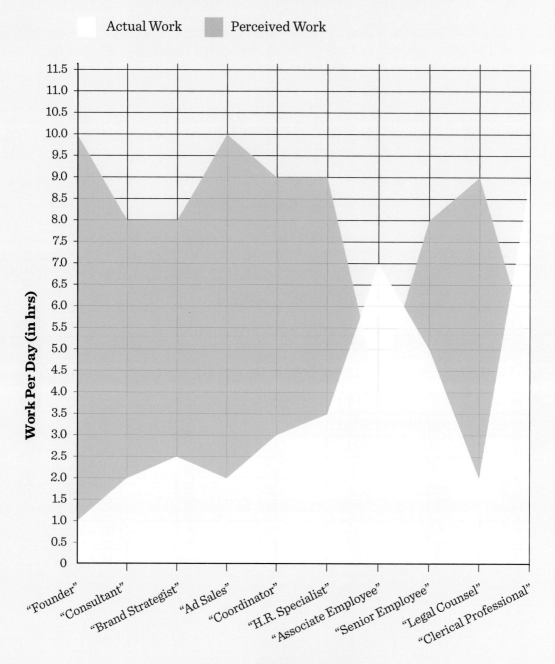

Actual Work   Perceived Work

Work Per Day (in hrs)

11.5
11.0
10.5
10.0
9.5
9.0
8.5
8.0
7.5
7.0
6.5
6.0
5.5
5.0
4.5
4.0
3.5
3.0
2.5
2.0
1.5
1.0
0.5
0

"Founder" "Consultant" "Brand Strategist" "Ad Sales" "Coordinator" "H.R. Specialist" "Associate Employee" "Senior Employee" "Legal Counsel" "Clerical Professional"

Employee Level

WHAT WILL YOU ENDURE?

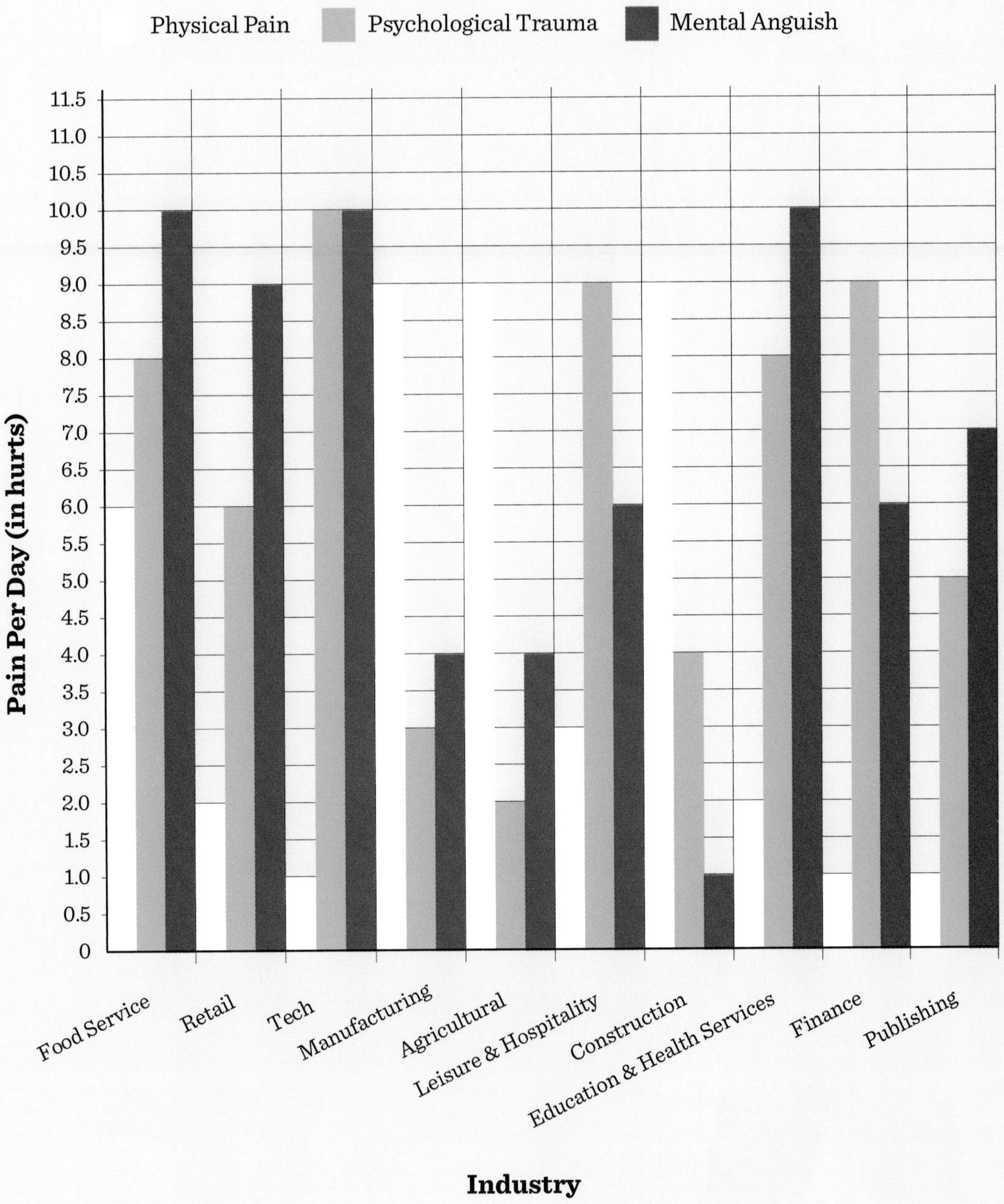
Physical Pain
Psychological Trauma
Mental Anguish
Pain Per Day (in hurts)
11.5
11.0
10.5
10.0
9.5
9.0
8.5
8.0
7.5
7.0
6.5
6.0
5.5
5.0
4.5
4.0
3.5
3.0
2.5
2.0
1.5
1.0
0.5
0
Food Service
Retail
Tech
Manufacturing
Agricultural
Leisure & Hospitality
Construction
Education & Health Services
Finance
Publishing
Industry

The
30 Types *of* People You Will Work With

The Alcoholic

The dude (and it's always a dude) who gets waaaay too drunk—and probably too emotional—at the holiday party. Is always 45 minutes late (at minimum), and frequently calls in sick on Mondays, which means you have to cover for him. Cannot be depended on in any circumstance. Has an inner rage burning inside him. Is the reason you can't have beer in the office.

The Alpha

Must dominate any conversation, and must be proven right no matter the cost. Views every single interaction as a competition. Has always done something better or faster than you have. Is weirdly aggressive in ways that go far beyond normal workplace decorum. Has a handshake like a vice grip. Master of the double Windsor knot. Probably serves as the commissioner of the office's Fantasy Football League, and probably takes that responsibility more seriously than their actual job. Doesn't even have to be a guy.

The Alpinist

The dude (again, it's always a dude) who is hell-bent on climbing the corporate ladder, especially if it means knocking you down a few rungs in the process. Proudly flaunts his perceived symbiosis with the powers that be, often anointing himself the unofficial mascot of upper management. When something goes right, he's the first to take credit, and when something doesn't, he's the last to accept any responsibility. Considers himself to be a "team player," despite all evidence to the contrary. Definitely won't help organize any extracurricular activities, but you can be damn sure he'll be in attendance—and attached to his boss' hip. Often overdresses for the office.

The Anarchist

Always fighting The Man, even if that means creating more work for everyone else in the process. Considers any request from management to be a slap in the face, and is always trying to recruit coworkers to join the resistance (even if he considers them to be sheeple). Frequently taking stands. Probably shouldn't be allowed around other people. Definitely vapes. Just wants to watch the world burn.

The Athlete

Worked out this morning, and makes sure you know it. Often rides a bike to the office. Frequently changing in the bathroom. Finds a way of working marathon times into every conversation. Packs the fridge with specially prepared meals—which cannot be moved without grave consequences—and is usually drinking some sort of shake. Is an asshole.

The Babe

The resident "incredibly attractive person" who somehow works here. Like The Highlander, there can be only one, and it is never a good idea to take a run at them...especially not at the holiday party.

The Boss

Comes in two varieties: Stoic figurehead and good-time guy, both of which are terrible. The former doesn't interact with you, most likely because they don't know who you are (and aren't interested in changing that). The latter considers themselves to be your contemporary, which is hilarious when you consider they make roughly seven times what you do and are directly responsible for keeping it that way.

The Chimer

Always willing to weigh in, whether it's during a conversation or (more probably) on an office-wide email. Never actually contributes anything of substance, but still lets their voice be heard—if only to cover themselves in the event something doesn't go according to plan.

The Community Activist

Consumed by the concept of "corporate culture," they organize innumerable groups dedicated to tackling the most minute of problems, most of which involve kitchen etiquette. Sender of many passive-aggressive emails with the subject line "Hey Guys." Wildly ineffective.

The Conspiracy Theorist

A close cousin of The Anarchist. Is unable to take even the simplest request at face value, content instead to try and piece together a larger scheme, especially if that takes 10 times longer than completing said request would. Cites their lack of advancement as evidence of a massive plot against them. Trusts no one.

The Creative

Self-centered visionary. Purveyor of many big ideas, most of which require you to do the work. Adverse to deadlines and feedback of any kind. Considers even the most concise of critiques to be an affront to their artistry. Doesn't let an actual lack of talent stand in the way of achieving their dreams. Will one day do a TED Talk.

The Creep

Always a guy, and always touching his female coworkers. Doesn't understand the concept of personal space. Has had several meetings with Human Resources. Is at his worst during after-work functions. Never open an email from him.

The Dad

Too old to be involved in anything, yet still finds a way to work himself into everything. Buoyed by years of "experience," he's the first to dismiss your ideas, in the most condescending way possible. Oblivious to the fact that if he were actually any good at his job, he wouldn't be dealing with you in the first place.

The Family Guy

Has reproduced, and works that fact into every interaction. Has at least one photo of his children on his desk. Fills you in on every minute detail of fatherhood. Claims to love his family, yet his unwillingness to go home hints at something darker. Will use his offspring as a convenient way of getting out of any extra work.

The Good Cop

Able to see the positive in any situation, even if it's to their detriment. Unwilling to entertain the notion that the boss is a dick and everyone in this office is a goddamn savage. Becomes visibly uncomfortable the second the conversation turns negative. Under no circumstances will they talk shit about anyone, which is like 90% of the reason you even come to work in the first place.

The Gossip

Dispenser of information that makes you uncomfortable. Will gleefully reveal everyone's salaries. Wants to know the dirt on everyone. Lives vicariously through intra-office romances. Despite knowledge being power, does not actually wield any authority. Cannot be trusted, and more than willing to take you down with them.

The Hoarder

Clutters their cubicle with all manner of ephemera, probably creating a fire hazard in the process. Saves every handout from every meeting. Will one day be buried beneath an avalanche of coffee cups. Has at least three action figures on their desk.

The Martyr

The resident Joan—or John—of Arc. Willing to sacrifice their well-being for the benefit of their coworkers, even if no one asked them to. Is always the first to volunteer for any project, and the first to complain about being "too busy." Carries a deep-seated contempt for everyone else in the workplace. Fueled by the belief that one day, they will get the recognition they deserve. Zero fun.

The Mom

The female version of Dad. Takes things to the next level by dispensing advice with an undercurrent of maternal disgust. Wearer of elaborate shawls.

The Narc

Will always throw you under the bus as a means to an end. Will never do this to your face. Has an uncomfortably close relationship with management. Always assessing the situation. Unaware of the concept of snitches getting stitches.

The Ninja

The resident silent assassin. Can bring this entire place down with a single email, and has used that fact as leverage to attain a modicum of success. Will inevitably walk around the corner just as you are talking shit about them.

The Obstructionist

Has a moral objection to seemingly every action, no matter how small. Resistant to change in any form, and willing to go to the mat to prove it. Literally no mole hill they cannot turn into a mountain. Always willing to tell you why something won't work, yet unable to provide an alternative. In love with the sound of their own voice, oblivious to the fact that no one else is.

The Octopus

Has their hands in eight different projects at once, and is fucking up seven of them simultaneously.

The Office Manager

Possessor of keys. Orderer of snacks and supplies. Master of the printer. They are frequently weighed down by the burden of responsibility, and probably take their job way too seriously. They definitely don't have time for your shit.

The Oversharer

Always unfiltered and unable to gauge interest levels, they're always willing to give you an unwanted glance into their life. Whether that means regaling you with stories of their sexual conquests, weekend activities and medical history, or keeping all their social media accounts public, you will undoubtedly know more about them than you ever wanted to.

The Patient Zero

Is eternally sick, or on the verge of being sick. Has a space heater in their cubicle. Always taking medication. First in line for flu shots. Freaks out if you sneeze in their general vicinity. Is probably the social media manager.

The Tech Guy

Cursed with knowledge (and the smug satisfaction that comes along with it), he is destined to die alone. Does not let his complete lack of social skills stop him from interjecting himself into every conversation within earshot. Delusional enough to believe he is irreplaceable, and carries himself as such. Will definitely treat your every tech request with disdain. Probably has a Bluetooth earpiece and keeps his phone in a belt holster.

The Trainwreck

Distant relative of The Alcoholic, is always on the verge of veering wildly off the tracks. Usually disheveled and distant. Creator of convenient excuses designed to cover up their double life. Has probably injured themselves in the workplace. Essentially insulated from being fired because Human Resources is terrified of the repercussions. When they don't show up for work, everyone worries.

The Two-Face

In public, they go above and beyond to demonstrate their enthusiasm for—and/or loyalty to—the company. In private, they let it be known that they hate every last one of you motherfuckers. Can be counted on to ask rhetorical questions during meetings, then bitch about the answers afterward. Like The Gossip, they should not be trusted under any circumstance.

The Wanderer

An old soul who is eternally searching for a deeper purpose, he is apparently not old enough to realize that work is just some bullshit you have to do for 9 hours a day.

A Beginner's Guide *to* Workplace Communication

You don't have to like your coworkers. In fact, you shouldn't. They're assholes. But you do need to coexist with them—after all, you're around them for a minimum of 40 hours a week.

A lot of that can be accomplished by listening. Not to what they say (because most of that is total bullshit) but to what they mean. That's a lot easier said than done, because unlike any other language, most workspeak defies traditional translation. So we've prepared a helpful cheat sheet to help you read between the lines, and figure out just who's trying to fuck you over. Listen up.

"I'll get it to you by Friday."

TRANSLATION
TRANSLATION
I'll get it to you Monday afternoon.

"There's no such thing as a bad idea."

TRANSLATION
That was a really bad idea.

"How was your weekend?"

TRANSLATION
Have you done the work you owe me yet?

"We're a team."

TRANSLATION
Someone fucked up, but it wasn't me.

"Do you want to sign Mary's birthday card?"

TRANSLATION
Sign Mary's goddamn birthday card.

"That's so funny!"

TRANSLATION
Get back to work.

"Thank you."

TRANSLATION
Fuck you.

"Nice tie!"

TRANSLATION
I am dead inside.

"Nice to e-meet you!"

TRANSLATION
I am a terrible person.

"I understand."

TRANSLATION
You will have to explain this to me again
in the not-too-distant future.

"I read it."

TRANSLATION
I didn't read it.

"Any feedback appreciated."

TRANSLATION
I don't give a fuck about your opinion.

"Have you seen my thing?"

TRANSLATION
I know you took my thing.

"Just going to grab lunch."

TRANSLATION
You will see me again in 4-6 hours.

"Running a few minutes
late this morning."

TRANSLATION
I am slightly hung over.

133

"I'll be working from home today."

TRANSLATION
I am moderately hungover.

"I'm sick."

TRANSLATION
I am incredibly hungover.

"I have a doctor's appointment."

TRANSLATION
I am interviewing for another job.

"There are cookies in the break room.
Help yourself!"

TRANSLATION
Please love me.

"This shouldn't be a problem."

TRANSLATION
This will inevitably become a problem.

"Any volunteers?"

TRANSLATION
Volunteer or else.

"It isn't mandatory."

TRANSLATION
I will doubt your level of commitment
if you don't show up.

"Happy to help!"

TRANSLATION
I am not happy to help.

"Sounds like fun!"

TRANSLATION
That sounds terrible.

"It's a collaborative effort."

TRANSLATION
Get ready to do all the work.

"It will only take 5 minutes."

TRANSLATION
Clear your calendar.

"I'm really swamped at the moment."

TRANSLATION
I don't want to be bothered with this.

"Got a minute?"

TRANSLATION
You're fucked.

"I'm going to set up a meeting."

TRANSLATION
I want to hear myself talk.

"Let's table this discussion for now."

TRANSLATION
This will never be dealt with.

"What do you think?"

TRANSLATION
Tell me I am right.

"I'm not sure that kind of language is appropriate."

TRANSLATION
You are nearly fired.

"Did you do this?"

TRANSLATION
You are definitely fired.

[Silence during conference call]

TRANSLATION
I have my phone on mute and am pantomiming masturbation.

Work, in Actuality

AN OFFICE JOB, ACCORDING TO ADULTS:

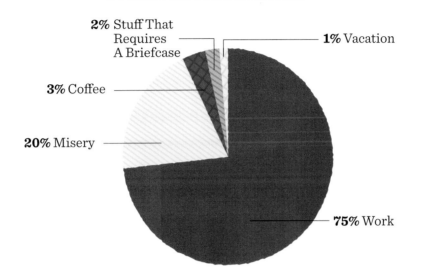

2% Stuff That Requires A Briefcase

1% Vacation

3% Coffee

20% Misery

75% Work

AN OFFICE JOB, IN ACTUALITY:

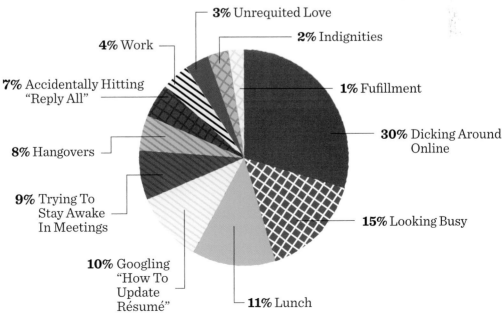

3% Unrequited Love

2% Indignities

4% Work

1% Fufillment

7% Accidentally Hitting "Reply All"

8% Hangovers

30% Dicking Around Online

9% Trying To Stay Awake In Meetings

15% Looking Busy

10% Googling "How To Update Résumé"

11% Lunch

139

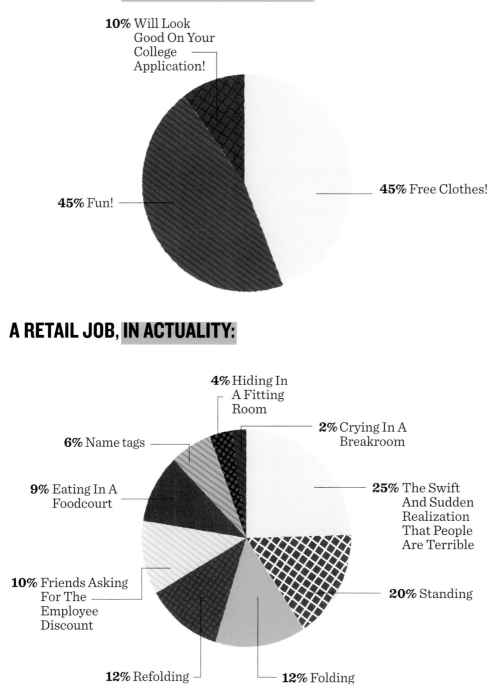

A RETAIL JOB, ACCORDING TO ADULTS:

10% Will Look Good On Your College Application!

45% Free Clothes!

45% Fun!

A RETAIL JOB, IN ACTUALITY:

4% Hiding In A Fitting Room

2% Crying In A Breakroom

6% Name tags

9% Eating In A Foodcourt

25% The Swift And Sudden Realization That People Are Terrible

10% Friends Asking For The Employee Discount

20% Standing

12% Refolding

12% Folding

A FAST FOOD JOB, ACCORDING TO ADULTS:

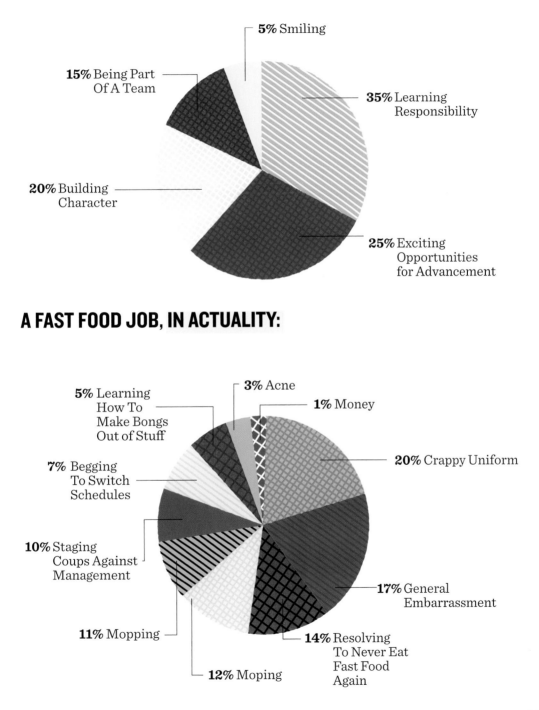

5% Smiling

15% Being Part Of A Team

35% Learning Responsibility

20% Building Character

25% Exciting Opportunities for Advancement

A FAST FOOD JOB, IN ACTUALITY:

5% Learning How To Make Bongs Out of Stuff

3% Acne

1% Money

7% Begging To Switch Schedules

20% Crappy Uniform

10% Staging Coups Against Management

17% General Embarrassment

11% Mopping

14% Resolving To Never Eat Fast Food Again

12% Moping

The
Coworker
Code

Employee of the Month

It doesn't matter how many "team-building" exercises your boss subjects you to, there's really only one tie that binds us working stiffs—the unyielding desire to get through this shit and go home.

In that regard, work is a lot like prison: We're all counting down the hours until we're free (though, to be fair, you're a lot less likely to get shivved in the office). Both are also governed by an unspoken set of rules—in jail, it's known as The Convict Code— designed to keep the peace, foster unity and mete out punishment when appropriate. If you feel like your coworkers are slipping, it's probably because they're unaware of those rules...they *are* unspoken, after all.

So here they are. All of them. Feel free to tear out these pages and post 'em in the breakroom—it's a lot easier than sharpening a toothbrush and stabbing someone in the mess hall.

Don't snitch.

Don't get too close to management.

Don't talk about how busy you are.

Don't go out of your way to be the Employee of the Month.

Don't take anything personally.

Don't disappear for hours.

Don't pass the buck.

Don't expect a raise just because you've been here a year.

Don't Reply All.

Don't CC fellow employees without warning.

Don't schedule a meeting for 5 p.m. on Friday.

Don't schedule a meeting for 9 a.m. on Monday.

Don't ask rhetorical questions.

Don't come into the office if you're on the verge of death.

Don't play up a potential sick day with dramatic coughs.

Don't call in sick on a Monday. Everyone knows you're hung over.

Don't take the last cup of coffee without making more.

Don't touch anyone's food.

Don't leave a passive-aggressive note if someone does touch your food.

Don't stack dirty dishes in the sink.

Don't reheat fish in the microwave.

Don't burn the goddamn popcorn.

Don't sprint for free food. Have some pride.

Don't be upset if you're too slow and miss out on the free food.

Don't post photos on social media during work hours.

Don't let your desk become a disaster area.

Don't light a scented candle.

Don't run a space heater in your cubicle.

Don't put your feet up on your desk.

Don't decorate for the holidays.

Don't blast music.

Don't carry around a Thermos.

Don't wear open-toed sandals.

Don't wear shorts.

Don't go too heavy on the cologne.

Don't talk politics.

Don't guilt coworkers into sponsoring your charity run.

Don't mention your GoFundMe project.

Don't schedule "after-work drinks" that start 90 minutes after work.

Don't be mad if people don't come to your stupid "after-work drinks."

Don't think biking to work makes you better.

5 Ways to Get the Job You Deserve

Don't wear a suit if you don't have to.

Don't use one of those standing desks.

Don't bring your dog to the office.

Don't bring your kids to the office, either.

Don't hoard office supplies.

Don't interject yourself into conversations.

Don't ask personal questions.

Don't crow about personal accomplishments.

Don't watch porn.

Don't find out what anyone else makes.

Don't be a creep.

Don't touch.

Don't cry.

Don't interrupt female coworkers.

Don't get *too* drunk at work functions.

Don't abuse the interns.

Don't talk down to younger coworkers.

Don't ignore the IT guy.

Don't be condescending if you *are* the IT guy.

Don't act like you're any better than anyone in the mail room.

Don't be the "office prankster." Everyone hates that guy.

Don't try to figure out the printer on your own.

Don't use the last roll of toilet paper.

Don't treat the bathroom like an abattoir.

Don't forget to flush.

1. Don't Chase Salary

Are you getting paid what you deserve? Is anyone? Rather than getting angry, get even. Use your current shitty job to figure out what you're good at—then get better at it. Hopefully, it's something that will hold your interest; ideally, it's something that people will actually pay you for.

Sure, you might never become a billionaire, but if you're making money doing something you enjoy, you definitely won't mind.

2. Stop Climbing

Scaling the corporate structure sucks and is a waste of time. Ladders only go two ways—you're forced to either keep climbing or give up and go back down. That's how your job tricks you into doing things today that you won't be compensated for until

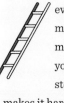

tomorrow (if ever). So jump between companies and jobs, even if that means making a lateral move, and create your own unique story. That only makes it harder for people to put a value on what you do.

3. Realize Everyone Is Faking It

This applies to just about every aspect of life, but nowhere is it quite as apparent as the office. There's a very good chance you could run your company better than your boss does; he's just sat behind a desk longer than you have. Everybody would rather be somewhere else. A tie is just a stupid strip of fabric you knot around your neck. Work is essentially one long exercise in disbelief; the quicker you realize that, the more fun you will have.

4. When You Don't Know Something, Say "I Don't Know"

To know you are fallible—and to share that knowledge—is to be confident in who you are. If you know what you don't know, and are willing to admit it, it will carry more weight when you share what you do know.

5. Don't Try to Compete with Workload

Outworking people is never fun, even if you can sustain it. And, to be honest, most bosses disdain a brownnoser and are looking for people willing to do things differently. Don't read the industry press and spend your life on work; if your office is full of people pouring over *The Wall Street Journal,* read comic books instead. Finding inspiration elsewhere will give you an edge and help create a distinct point of view that stands out from the pack.

Are You Workplace Appropriate?

1) You have an idea to increase productivity. What's the first thing you do?

Ⓐ Call a meeting to get my fellow employees' feedback.

Ⓑ Scrawl the idea on a piece of paper and stick it to the wall with a knife.

Ⓒ Just go ahead with it. Fuck 'em.

2) Your office has implemented a "Casual Friday" policy. How do you respond?

Ⓐ With a *short-sleeve* button-up. Maybe.

Ⓑ By wearing my leather daddy costume to the office.

Ⓒ With shorts. Fuck 'em.

3) Your boss is doing a bike ride for cancer and has hung a sponsorship form in the break room. How do you react?

Ⓐ By begrudgingly pledging $50.

Ⓑ By donating $5 more than a person you hate in the office.

Ⓒ Ignore the form and continue microwaving your Swanson Hungry-Man Dinner.

4) You have a disagreement with a coworker. How do you resolve things?

Ⓐ Ask your Human Resources rep to act as a mediator.

Ⓑ By exacting revenge.

Ⓒ A duel in the parking lot.

5) A female coworker has just made a valid point in a meeting. How do you respond?

Ⓐ You say, "That's an excellent point."

Ⓑ Wait 2–3 minutes, then repeat exactly what she said.

Ⓒ Provide her with a nuanced *male* perspective that invalidates everything she just suggested.

6) You see a female coworker eating lunch. What's your course of action?

Ⓐ Say "Hi." Join her if she offers. You know, the same way you'd interact with any *employee*.

Ⓑ Pull up a chair. Comment on the nutritional value of her lunch.

Ⓒ Tell her she looks pretty.

7) Your dirtbag friend sends you an email full of attachments. What do you do?

(A) Open it at home.

(B) Look at it on your phone.

(C) FWD it to your boss.

8) You have hooked up with someone in the office? What happens next?

(A) You notify your Human Resources rep about your indiscretions.

(B) Depends…is it your boss? If so, can you finagle a raise out of it?

(C) Tell everybody about it.

9) Whoops, you accidentally hit Reply All on an email. Now everyone knows how you feel about Tom in accounting. How do you rectify the situation?

(A) Frantically try to recall the message.

(B) If it's too late, apologize to Tom in person. Blame stress or something.

(C) Double down with a Reply All. Apologize for nothing.

10) It's someone's birthday. How do you celebrate?

(A) Get a cake and lead a "Happy Birthday" sing-along with your sensuous baritone.

(B) Gather at their desk, and silently mouth the words to "Happy Birthday."

(C) Get your coworker in an affectionate headlock.

11) How would you best describe your cubicle décor?

(A) Professional: Maybe a motivational poster mixed in with the odd photo of a loved one.

(B) Cluttered: Old coffee cups and papers, perhaps the odd rodent living in the detritus.

(C) Dad's Garage: Promotional posters featuring bikini-clad women, the odd beer can (or six).

12) The company needs to downsize. You have been let go. Now what?

(A) Thank the team for their time and support. You have learned a lot and you hope better times are ahead for the company. Offer to keep coming to work anyway.

(B) Tell HR that you have seen your coworkers do inappropriate things in the workplace environment. See if this moves the needle.

(C) Turn on your online stationery store, selling the stock you have taken from the office over the previous 12 months.

HOW DID YOU DO?

Mostly A—You're workplace appropriate! Enjoy the next five decades of your life!

Mostly B—With proper guidance, you will probably be OK.

Mostly C—You should probably be in jail.

HOW TO
ASK YOUR BOSS FOR A RAISE, ACCORDING TO THE ACTUAL BOSS OF

BROTHER

So you want more money? Great idea—it's that kind of innovative thinking that makes you deserve a raise. Hell, you deserve two raises.

But who, when and how do you ask and how much more money should you be asking for? We've got you.

The Day Before the Ask

In theory, you have been setting up for this raise all year—you know, with hard work and a good attitude and all that. But that probably sounds too much like work, so let's focus on the day *before* your ask.

Come into the office with donuts for the team. Ask everyone if they need any help (there is no need to actually follow through on this offer) and spend lots of time pretending to be on the phone with people who are really impressed by you. When engaging with colleagues, say things like "Don't worry—I'll fix this for you...*again*." Make sure your boss hears this. At the end of the day, send an email asking your boss if you can if grab five minutes with him at some point tomorrow. Make this communication as vague as possible so he doesn't know what you have in store. Ideally, he will fear you are going to quit and your asking for a raise will come as a relief—meaning you will catch him off guard.

Finally, show your dedication by working late, even if you have nothing to do, and loudly say "Good night!" to anyone who leaves before you. Before you leave the office, set up lots of meetings the following day—all scheduled between morning and your meeting with your boss. It doesn't matter what they are about...it's always better to *appear* busy.

Raise Day

Dress like a winner. If you work in an office, wear a tie. If you work in a store, wear pants. If you work in a hospital, wear both. Make sure you are in bright and early, leading some to ponder whether you ever *actually* went home last night. Thursday is the ideal day to ask for a raise, since the end of the week is in sight and your boss has only marginally begun to formulate his weekend plans. Never ask for a raise on a Monday (everyone hates Mondays) or a Friday (you will be ignored and pushed to next week).

Spend the morning looking busy. Attend all of the meetings you scheduled the night before—ideally you have them set up in and around your boss' workspace and he can see from his desk how important and occupied you are. Carry pieces of paper back and forth and make sure you take lots of notes, then spend the remainder of the day forming "action items." Bosses love "action items."

Shaping the Ask

In order to decide how much money you deserve, ask yourself these questions:

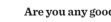

1. **Are you any good at your job?**
It doesn't actually matter either way, but if you are good at your job, you can enter the conversation with even more confidence.

2. **Does your boss know you are good at your job?**
If so, make a realistic ask in line with your level of competence.

3. **How much money do you currently earn?**
If you are being paid less than you deserve, ask for a 25% raise—and expect to get 5%. If you are being paid more than you deserve, ask for 30%. Your boss obviously doesn't know what he's doing.

4. **How much effort and cost would it take to replace you?**
If it is low effort and low cost, decrease your demand by 5%. If it would be painful or expensive to replace you, raise your demand by 5%.

Making the Ask

You have laid the groundwork, set your meeting and figured out your target number. Now it's time to close the deal. The following script should help you do it.

Boss: Good afternoon, come on in.

You: Is it?

Boss: I'm sorry?

You: Are you?

Boss: Uh... you wanted to discuss something—what's on your mind?

You: Money. M. O. N. E. Y. (spell this really slowly while looking in to their eyes for dramatic effect)

Boss: I don't understand. There's a money issue?

You: Indeed. Indeed there is. I'm going to need more of it. A lot more.

Boss: You're talking about a raise?

You: *We're* talking about a raise.

Boss: We tend to cover raises at the end of each work year—you're obviously doing great work here, but you've only been with us for three days.

You: 25%

Boss: What's 25%?

You: A fair offer is 25%. If you can give me a 25% bump, I'm happy to keep doing what I'm doing here. It's exhausting but I'll do it... because I care about what we're building here. And I care about you.

Now wait for your boss to respond. Revel in the awkward silence—he will be hoping you speak first, while he tries to figure out a counteroffer in his head. Hold firm and the raise is yours. Shake hands and leave. Congratulations...you deserve it.

Should You Launch a Start-Up?

1) Have you dreamed up/stolen an idea that will "disrupt the marketplace"?

(A) Yes, digital pottery is the future.

(B) Not yet, but I *do* enjoy using phrases like "disrupt the marketplace."

(C) Depends...how much money can I make?

2) What would you call your start-up?

(A) PTTRY. Vowels are a vestige of *old* media.

(B) Whatever looks best in a cutesy font.

(C) Probably something like "Cash Grab."

3) Do you enjoy prostrating yourself before Venture Capitalists?

(A) I am willing to do whatever it takes to turn my dream into a reality.

(B) Definitely. Venture Capitalists are the engines that drive ingenuity.

(C) Depends...is there bottle service?

4) What is your monetization strategy?

(A) A soft launch, followed by the gradual introduction of "freemium" content.

(B) In-app purchases, baby!

(C) Sponsor some sick parties.

5) Do you enjoy making decisions?

(A) Yes I do. And I stand by all of them.

(B) Sure, but I make a whole lot of mistakes along the way.

(C) Let me get back to you on this one...

6) How would you describe your managerial style?

(A) Brute charm—and if that doesn't work, brute force.

(B) I place my employees in positions to succeed, and provide them with the necessary resources to do so.

(C) Once a year, I will interact with my underlings at the holiday party. The rest of the time, I'll be on my yacht.

7) Women in the workplace are:

(A) Vital, and I will take every opportunity to say as much before making my frat brother the CFO.

(B) A necessary annoyance, so long as they don't complain about the patriarchy too much.

(C) The only reason to come to work, *right fellas?!?!*

8) Do you like working really long hours?

(A) Hard work is who I am.

(B) I am driven, but I try to work smart and get things done as quickly as possible.

(C) No. That's what the developers are for.

9) What do you wear in the office?

(A) A hoodie, just like Zuck!

(B) A suit. I'm the boss, after all.

(C) Whatever my stylist has decided will make me look "approachable" to my underlings.

10) What is a founder?

(A) The guy who gets the glory.

(B) The guy who has to make it all work.

(C) The guy who gets the girls.

11) Are you willing/able to consign your lofty dreams of changing the world to the permanent void of naked capitalism?

(A) If necessary, yes. I can always change the world later.

(B) Duh. My philanthropy doesn't come until Stage 2.

(C) Fuck yeah!

12) When your start-up fails, what will you do?

(A) It won't fail—I never lose.

(B) Apply what I have learned to my next venture.

(C) Go live with my parents. They're rich.

HOW DID YOU DO?

Mostly A—You have watched *The Social Network* one too many times. Don't do it.

Mostly B—You are idealistic to a fault. Your start-up will probably survive a year.

Mostly C—You are driven by a craven desire for wealth. Launch your start-up *ASAP*.

Post-Apocalyptic Career Aptitude Guide

Just because the world has ended doesn't mean you can't start a successful career—if anything, there will be a lot less applicants, making it easier for you to rise to the top. Like Jon Taffer says, embrace solutions, not excuses!

But since your liberal arts degree has even less relevance now that the world has ended, let's use this moment to reassess your relative strengths and weaknesses, and find the right job for you. It's not Doomsday, it's a New Day!

BOUNTY HUNTER / MERCENARY

WHAT YOU DO: Hunt people down for money, possibly murder them.

RELEVANT SKILLS: Tracking, trapping, firearms, hand-to-hand combat, looking cool in mirrored sunglasses.

PROS: You can finally live out your fantasies of being Boba Fett.

CONS: You'll probably get killed by other bounty hunters as you're easy to spot in that Boba Fett costume, nerd.

WARLORD

WHAT YOU DO: Recruit and lead an army of survivors, burn and pillage, wear spiked shoulder pads.

RELEVANT SKILLS: Verbal communication, hand-to-hand combat, outsized ego, a lack of remorse.

PROS: All that you survey can be yours.

CONS: An endless stream of challengers to your throne, a lack of indoor plumbing.

PROSTITUTE

WHAT YOU DO: You have sex with people for money.

RELEVANT SKILLS: Seduction, looking attractive in a radiation suit.

PROS: You have sex with people for money.

CONS: You have sex with people for money.

JUNK SHIP CAPTAIN

WHAT YOU DO: Pilot a sand skiff over irradiated dunes, harvest the charred remnants of our once-great society.

RELEVANT SKILLS: Boating or pilot's license, wearing many layers of robes and rags, a thousand-yard stare.

PROS: All the sweet scrap metal!

CONS: Radiation poisoning, constantly pursued by marauding hordes of mutants.

FOOD SAFETY TESTER

WHAT YOU DO: Sample foods before other people eat them to detect poison or malicious tampering.

RELEVANT SKILLS: A deft palate, a strong constitution, a hearty appetite.

PROS: All you can eat, baby!

CONS: You will probably die of dysentery.

TEACHER

WHAT YOU DO: Pass along the teachings of our once-great society before they are lost to the ever-encroaching sands of time.

RELEVANT SKILLS: Teaching degree from an accredited university, an optimism that knows no bounds, an inquisitive mind.

PROS: Summers off, baby!

CONS: You realize that without the Internet, you're pretty much a certifiable idiot.

ARTIST

WHAT YOU DO: Part historian, part documentarian, you are responsible for carrying on human culture and civilization in the new world.

RELEVANT SKILLS: Painting, drawing, sculpting, the ability to stretch animal hides into crude canvases.

PROS: You can be an eccentric asshole because you're "creative."

CONS: You're kind of insufferable to hang out with.

SERF

WHAT YOU DO: Till the soil for your feudal lord.

RELEVANT SKILLS: Agriculture and irrigation, a green thumb that wasn't caused by exposure to gamma rays.

PROS: Your new blue-collar gig will make you finally appreciate those Springsteen records your dad played.

CONS: You're an indentured servant.

ARTISANAL JENKEM VINTNER

WHAT YOU DO: Create inhalable hallucinogenic gas from fermented human waste.

RELEVANT SKILLS: Basic chemistry, brewing and bottling, a strong stomach.

PROS: Demand for inhalable hallucinogens will be high after most of society has crumbled.

CONS: You have to shit into glass bottles.

GRAVEDIGGER

WHAT YOU DO: Dig the holes to bury the bodies.

RELEVANT SKILLS: Basic shovel operation, a strong back, lack of a sense of smell.

PROS: Always in demand, flexible schedule.

CONS: Fending off any potential graverobbers, packs of wild animals and/or zombies that are fixing to undo your work.

A HANDY GLOSSARY OF TERMS

110%—Amount of effort expected of you by your employer at all times; the fact that it's an imaginary percentage doesn't matter.

401(k)—Tax-qualified, defined-contribution pension plan offered by some employers. Sounds like a cool idea until you realize you can't touch it until you're 59 1/2 years old, unless you want to pay an excise tax.

5 Minutes—Term used to preface any time-consuming request; is essentially arbitrary, since said request will inevitably take much longer than 5 minutes.

Action Plan—A course of action your boss asks you to formulate whenever he/she is too busy...which is always.

All Hands—A meeting that all employees are required to attend. Usually a harbinger of bad shit on the horizon.

ASAP—Timeframe in which a top-priority request is expected to be addressed. Tough shit if you're doing something else.

Bandwidth—Your daily capacity to do work. Often used before a coworker bails on a project.

Benefits—Non-wage compensation (including health insurance) offered to employees who make more than you.

Bonus—Additional compensation paid out to employees, whether they deserve it or not.

Boss—The bane of your existence.

Brainstorm—A banal exercise in groupthink, often deployed when a supervisor or team leader can't come up with any ideas of their own.

Busy Work—Work designed to keep you busy. Often has little to no actual value.

Cal Invite—Short for Calendar Invite. Used by assholes.

Circle Back—Officespeak for "revisit at a later date," or more accurately, "forget about completely."

Closing—The worst shift at any retail or food-service job. Involves sweeping, mopping, restocking, refilling, rethinking your life.

Creative—The visual aspects of any project, or the team tasked with developing said visual aspects. Neither will be understood by superiors.

Deck—Any part of a visual presentation (like PowerPoint). Often used because "busy work" would be too demeaning.

Deep Dive—To take a closer look at something. Used by assholes.

Delegate—Only used as a verb in the context of an office, where it means "dump this crap on someone who makes less than me."

Download—To inform your boss about the details of a project, the overwhelming majority of which he or she will forget immediately.

Dress Code—What you are expected to wear to work. Oppressive.

EOD—Short for "End of Day," usually means "Middle of next week."

Full Disclosure—Term used when an employee is about to weigh in with useless information, or drop an excuse pertaining to why he/she can't do a given task.

Human Resources—Overworked, underpaid team of employees tasked with resolving the most minute of workplace disputes.

In the Weeds—Term used when an employee is excessively busy, or excessively incompetent. Usually the latter.

LinkedIn—Useless pseudo social-networking platform masquerading as an employment service. A great way to be contacted by people you went to college with and never wanted to speak to again.

Lunch—Fleeting period of freedom used to break up the monotony of the workday. Sometimes involves crying in your car.

Offline—Verb that means "discuss outside of a meeting." Used by assholes.

OOO—Short for "Out of Office," also short for "You won't hear from me until Monday."

Optional—Applied to any work-related event in which attendance is actually mandatory.

Organic—Something created naturally, without the aid of a third party. So almost nothing.

Per Our Discussion—Phrase that prefaces bad news.

Performance Review—Meeting with your superior in which he/she assesses your strengths and weaknesses, undermines any real shot you have at getting a raise.

Ping—To alert when something is ready. Used by assholes.

PowerPoint—Soul-wrenching presentation program, often used by Human Resources.

Raise—Something you will never get.

Résumé—A list of accomplishments that your dad still updates.

Salary—What you are paid for the job. Is never enough.

Self-Assessment—A project in which you are tasked with honestly evaluating your performance. An exercise in futility.

Spit-Balling—Phrase that inevitably follows any terrible idea that falls upon deaf ears.

Swing By—A brief visit requested by your boss. Never a good thing.

Synergy—Officespeak for the interaction of various coworkers meant to produce great results, even if said interaction never really does.

Table—Verb that means "to put on hold for the time being." Anything tabled will forever be lost to the sands of time.

Time to Lean—In the retail and food-service industries, it's a preamble to your manager telling you to do work—used in conjunction with "...Time to clean."

Town Hall—Mandatory meeting in which your company's founder/CEO is theoretically supposed to answer questions from employees, but instead spends the entire time gesturing wildly while wearing a headset microphone.

Tribal Council—Potentially problematic officespeak for a meeting involving select team members, who discuss issues that have no real bearing on the office.

Work from Home—Phrase used when an employee doesn't want to come into the office, but doesn't want to burn his/her sick days. Should probably be called "Occasionally Check Email from Home."

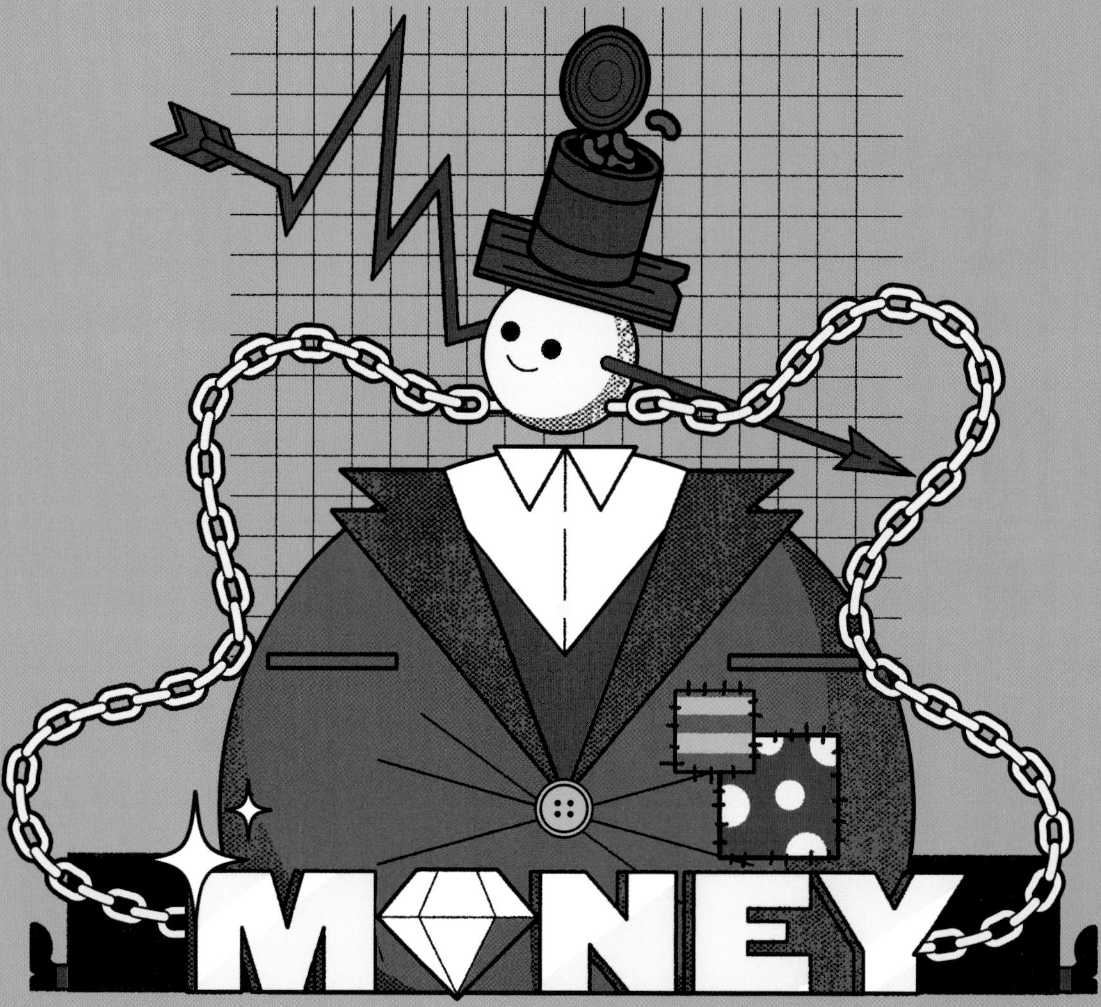
MONEY

M oney isn't important. That's something rich people like to say, usually in-between sips of 25-year-old scotch. They're not lying, either; money *isn't* important when you don't have to worry about it.

But for everyone else, money is *very* important. And not just because it gets you food, clothing and shelter, three things that are pretty essential to life. Money buys access, power and status. It affords you opportunities and allows you to take risks. It provides a compelling reason to keep showing up to work every day. You also need it to pay your phone bill and buy whatever ugly sneakers Kanye just designed. Money is a necessity—or, more specifically, a necessary evil.

Should you pursue it with every waking minute? Probably not. Should you forsake it entirely? Not unless you're also willing to forsake all comfort and security (like bathrooms or locks). Perhaps it's more realistic to split the difference and view money for what it actually is: a means to an end. Work for your money, but also let your money work for you.

That's not supposed to sound like a pitch for a high-yield savings account. Instead, it's supposed to force you to figure out what *you* want to do with your money. Perhaps you want to buy a house, or go on vacation, or get a jacket. Maybe you actually want to open a high-yield savings account. There are no wrong answers— again, it's *your* money—though there are a few wrong approaches, most of which involve making the accumulation of wealth your sole purpose in life.

Because, really, that's no life at all. You'd be better served learning to live with money, to understand that it will come and go, that you will probably never have as much of it as you want. The balance in your bank account does not define you, or make you a better (or worse) person. What you decide to do with that balance does.

Maybe money will buy you a wealth of experiences. Or maybe it will just make you wealthy. Regardless, you earned it, and you use it to do the things *you* want to do. Either way, you're rich—which means you can start telling people money isn't important. **And that's really the point, right?**

MASLOW'S HIERARCHY OF MONEY NEEDS

Everything necessary to ascend, find fulfillment and become the person you were meant to be.

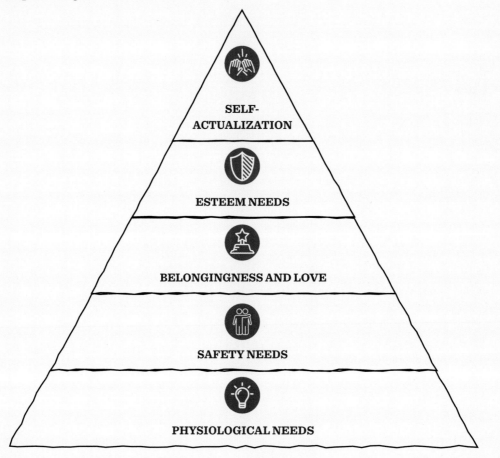

SELF-ACTUALIZATION

ESTEEM NEEDS

BELONGINGNESS AND LOVE

SAFETY NEEDS

PHYSIOLOGICAL NEEDS

 SELF-ACTUALIZATION—Having so much money you no longer have to worry.

ESTEEM—A bit of savings, a 401(k) or pension plan, being able to buy the things you want.

BELONGINGNESS AND LOVE—Bonding with coworkers over mutual dislike of boss, buying a round of drinks for friends, someone to buy dinner for.

SAFETY—No-slip work shoes, one of those back braces, sturdy gloves, helmet, employer-provided health insurance.

PHYSIOLOGICAL—A brain, a strong back, an even stronger work ethic, the stamina to survive endless meetings, the willpower to avoid not choking your coworkers.

How to
Live Like a Millionaire
(Without Actually Being One)

Are you a millionaire? Feel free to skip this section—and feel free to cut us a check. If you're like everyone else on the planet, read on. Chances are, you're probably dreading work right now, and perhaps even wondering how much longer you'll be forced to punch the clock. The bad news? It's forever. The good news? It doesn't have to feel that way.

Turns out, you can actually live like the rich and famous; you just need to forget about the "rich and famous" part. Wealth is a state of mind, and finding inner peace is a lot easier than you might think. All it takes is doing these four things.

Find Something You Love Doing. Get Good at It.

Good enough for someone to pay you to do it. This covers everything from playing a sport to scooping ice cream—though more of the latter than the former. It's a lot tougher than it sounds, and will probably require more work than merely submitting a résumé, but it's worth it. If your passion is also your profession, it won't really *matter* how much you're getting paid (and if you're the world's greatest ice cream scooper, you probably won't get paid all that much). You'll actually enjoy going to work...and you can't put a monetary value on that.

Have Perspective. There's nothing wrong with taking a job just for the paycheck...but you forfeit the right to complain about it if you do. The same goes with a job you love; chances are, you won't be making the big bucks, but that's not why you did it, remember? Always look at the big picture and keep the finish line in sight—it will make the daily slog just slightly more bearable, and you'll have the peace of mind that *usually* only comes with having millions in the bank.

Define Success. Want a big house and a nice car? There's a job for that. Want to live in a yurt and raise yaks? There might not be...but that doesn't make it any less valid. It's up to you to determine what success means—be it financial security, complete independence or literally anything in between. The beauty of making up your own definition is that you can never, ever be wrong. Unless you want to be a lawyer; we have way too many of them already.

Treat Yourself (Occasionally). Despite your best efforts, you will probably have to get a job at some point. So you should reward yourself for showing up every day. Don't go crazy and blow through your entire paycheck, but find one big-ticket item and gradually save up for it. It'll remind you why you put up with all the bullshit, and will inspire you to keep going back for more. Of course, if you want to buy something like a private island, you'll be going back for more *forever*.

How to
Live on a Budget
(Without Living Like a Crazy Person)

It's important to save money—but what's the point if it means living like a coupon-clipping granny? Based on just about every "budgeting basics" article we've read, the only ways to spend less involve buying in bulk, gifting friends repurposed garbage from your house and sitting in total darkness, wrapped in a shawl (gotta keep those heating and electric bills down). In other words, crazy cat lady stuff.

Keeping a few extra bucks in your bank account shouldn't mean becoming a shut-in. In fact, with just a few sacrifices—and a tiny bit of suffering— you can save money and still have a social life. Don't worry, you still get to drink.

Make Stuff at Home. You spend *way* too much eating at restaurants; if you're the average American, it's about $1,500 a year (plus another $1,200 on coffee). So buy some goddamn groceries. Start with dried goods; pasta, beans and rice are cheap, won't go bad and can be the basis for lots of meals. Buy fruits and vegetables that will keep for weeks—like onions, apples, potatoes, carrots and beets—and a bit of protein, since it tends to be more expensive (though almost all meat, fish and poultry can be frozen).

That's enough to make most of your meals for a week, and save yourself as much as $100 per month. Want to up that amount? Buy good Tupperware to keep leftovers longer, and brew your coffee at home and take it with you. If the thought of meal prep seems daunting, start small, and keep everything in perspective: Every meal you *don't* eat at a restaurant is literally money in your pocket.

Delete Your Apps. They make your life easier; they also make it more expensive. If you don't have delivery apps installed, you definitely won't be spending money on them (though you definitely *will* miss the midnight pizza). Get rid of shopping apps, too—you spend more than $12 per purchase, on average—and anything with in-app purchases (which

is pretty much everything); they cost you another $10 per month. It's not shocking—by removing the ability to make spur-of-the-moment purchases, you will actually *make* less spur-of-the-moment purchases.

But Not <u>All</u> Your Apps. You're still going to be social, so you're going to need to score some deals. Luckily, there are apps like Groupon and FourSquare (and dozens more) that exist solely to provide you with access to said deals. Of course, if it sounds too good to be true, you should probably check out a few Yelp reviews before booking. Technology is a wonderful thing.

Buy Cheap Booze. To put it simply, plastic bottles are your friends. We're not saying you should get the stuff that tastes like paint thinner, but there's a surprising amount of decent booze that comes in bottles that won't break (Smirnoff and Wild Turkey are time-tested

favorites). Your friends won't tell the difference unless they're assholes—and if they are, buy a couple decanters from IKEA (they're like $4) and pour the booze in there. *Voila*, instant class!

Go to Museums. But whatever you do, don't *pay* to go to museums. This is actually way easier than it sounds—some museums have a pay-what-you-can option, and just about every one offers free admission at least *once* a month—and there are apps that will help you locate them (hopefully you didn't delete those ones). A trip to the museum makes a great date, and let's face it, you could use a little more culture.

How to
Make More Money
(Without Working All That Hard)

I t's the dream. But it can also be your reality. If you've got a relatively open schedule, a sense of adventure and a willingness to be studied by the occasional guy in a lab coat, you can make a pretty decent living. Or at least enough for a pretty decent weekend. Don't worry, you won't even have to break a sweat.

Get Paid to Poop. You do it every morning (hopefully), so why not get paid for it? Believe it or not, there are stool banks out there that will pay you $40 per pop. The only downside is that someone else will see your poop.

Sell Your Hair. Do you have long, lustrous hair? Is it red? Great, you can sell it for as much as $80 per inch online, through one of the (what we assume to be) fairly reputable human hair marketplaces. Oh, and if you're not a ginger, you can still get paid. Blonde hair goes for about $60 per inch, and brown can fetch as much as $30.

Get Naked. Nude models for figure-painting classes make about $30 per session. Not a huge sum, but probably the only time in your life someone will pay you to get naked.

Give Plasma. A classic. So long as you don't mind hanging with the blood bank crowd, donating plasma can earn you $50. Plus, you will save lives (and get a juice box!).

Give Your Opinion. Want to earn money while shitting on various products? Join an in-person focus group, where you will make anywhere from $75-150 per hour to give your largely uninformed opinion to a group of people holding clipboards! There literally *are* no wrong answers. A quick Google search will turn up plenty of opportunities for quick cash in your area.

Have a Sale. Or do some shopping. Some stats: There are an average of 165,000 garage sales each week in the U.S., generating $4.2 million in revenue. Items *bought* at garage sales can be resold on eBay for a profit margin of 462%. You undoubtedly have a ton of junk lying around—or live in a neighborhood populated by old people who don't realize they're sitting on a ton of treasures. So get on the garage sale circuit, either as a buyer or a seller. Preferably both.

Donate Sperm. Finally, getting paid to do what you love. Some sperm banks will pay as much as $200 per donation, but they're looking for a few good men—between the ages of 19 and 38, currently attending (or having graduated from) college, in good health, standing 5'9" or taller. If you meet those requirements, start jacking. Once you're at the sperm bank, obviously.

Get Tested. There are literally hundreds of thousands of clinical trials happening all around the world, and almost all of them are looking for guinea pigs. That's where you come in. If approved, you can make up to $300 per session, and hey, there's at least a 50/50 good chance whatever medication they're giving you is a placebo.

Get the Biggest Bang for Your Buck!

NET WORTH	WHAT TO BUY
<$100	Pop Rocks.
$100	100 packets of Pop Rocks.
$500	A beat-up car that still runs.
$1,000	A pinball machine
$10,000	An Airsteam trailer.
$100,000	A water jetpack.
$1,000,000	A private island off the coast of Belize.
$10,000,000	A minor league baseball team.
$100,000,000	16 Six-Million Dollar Men.
$1,000,000,000	A Major League Baseball team.
All the money	The U.S. Presidency.

How to
Get Rich

Chances are, you would like to have more money. It's too bad, then, that the ultra-rich control half of the world's wealth, because sharing isn't exactly their strong suit.

So if you want to get your hands on the other half, your best bet is to try and emulate their success. But that's easier said than done—no one said amassing wealth was going to be easy. In general, rich people get rich in one of four ways, each with its own unique set of pros and cons. Pick your poison.

#1 | WORK FOR IT

Believe it or not, some millionaires actually *are* self-made. But committing to earning your future wealth will require a trade-off—you'll have to hand over control of your waking hours in exchange for financial compensation. The more fun the job, the less likely it will pay well. Do you want to have a blast as an aspiring DJ (and live in a tent) or sell your soul to high finance and retire with a heart condition at 40? The choice is grim, but it is yours to make.

PROS: You get to wear a suit and eventually boss around your subordinates.

CONS: Initial humiliation that eventually gives way to a gradual disintegration of your soul.

#2 | DISRUPT IT

This is a relatively new approach, one born in Silicon Valley on the backs of millions of startups, each powered by a "big idea" designed to "disrupt" an existing marketplace. Are you guaranteed to be successful? Definitely not—but with high risk comes high reward. Plus, you'll probably get to work in an open-plan office space with a foosball table.

PROS: You probably won't get your hands dirty, you definitely will get your own TED Talk, all that foosball.

CONS: You have to spend all your time with Silicon Valley types and use the phrase "disrupt."

#3 | INHERIT IT

DADDY
(1919-2019)

A classic. Did you know a full 40% of the *Forbes* 400 inherited a sizeable chunk of their wealth from a family member or spouse? Of course you didn't—that would ruin the illusion of hard work! It's easy for the offspring of the very rich to "earn" their own fortune—often they simply collect excess money their parents accidentally drop around the house. If you aren't close to a wealthy person, you'd better start ingratiating yourself to one soon.

PROS: Low effort and hard to fuck up.

CONS: Equally hard to go through this experience and not be a dick.

#4 | STEAL IT

Perhaps even easier than inheriting it. Sure, crime carries obvious risks, but most of them don't apply to the very wealthy. At worse, you spend a couple years in a minimum-security prison, which is basically a resort (only with bars). Even better, "stealing" is a relative term—it's not illegal *per se* to trick a tribe of indigenous people into signing over the rights to their land, or selling a few suckers on the concept of adjustable-rate mortgages. And, hey, it's a lot more enjoyable than actually working.

PROS: Minimal effort, maximum gain.

CONS: Prison showers.

DO YOU HAVE ENOUGH MONEY?

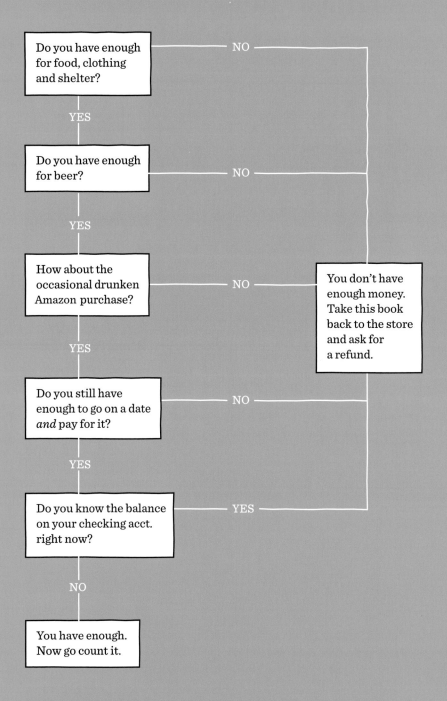

Do you have enough for food, clothing and shelter?

NO →

YES ↓

Do you have enough for beer?

NO →

YES ↓

How about the occasional drunken Amazon purchase?

NO →

YES ↓

Do you still have enough to go on a date *and* pay for it?

NO →

YES ↓

Do you know the balance on your checking acct. right now?

YES →

NO ↓

You have enough. Now go count it.

You don't have enough money. Take this book back to the store and ask for a refund.

Six Truths About Money, According *to* Someone Who Has *a* Lot *of* It

1. Money Is Only Relevant in Extremes.

Having too little money to eat, have a home or feel safe sucks. Having so much money that you don't ever have to think about it is fun. But most people live in between these two extremes, and spend their life talking about it. They will never go hungry, but they won't buy an island, either. So aim for the island or let it go. If you ever catch yourself talking about mortgages you are dead inside.

2. Money Is a Prick.

Money is a fair-weather friend. It is hardest to find when you need it most. When you need it least, everything is free and money comes pouring in. Fuck money (but obviously don't *literally* fuck money—you need it to buy things).

3. Enough Is Enough.

The moment you can afford to buy anything you want from Amazon you have won. Don't let anyone try and distract you with bigger or shinier things. Stuff is just stuff.

4. Giving Is Better Than Receiving.

Share the wealth. That could mean donating to charity, organizing an elaborate, condition-filled giveaway a la *Brewster's Millions*, or merely using it to elevate the lives of those closest to you. Money is best used for adventures—and adventures are best experienced with friends. And ironically, even though you can afford to buy the bar, you will never pay for a drink again.

5. Money Makes You a Dick.

If you do find yourself with a bunch of money, it is usually best to forget about it and carry on like a normal person. Money can turn kind, intelligent, rational people into cruel, greedy, covetous monsters; so don't let it. Instead, hire someone to take all manner of verbal, psychological (and even physical) abuse from you—at least they'll be getting paid.

6. Money Can Set You Free.

An underrated benefit of money is that it affords you the opportunity to make some decisions based on merit—rather than financial need. Harper Lee was given a year's salary as a gift from her friends. She left her job and used the time to write *To Kill a Mockingbird*. Do that.

CAN MONEY BUY YOU THIS?

THINGS MONEY CAN'T BUY	THINGS MONEY CAN BUY
Happiness.	Literally everything else.
Self-respect.	
Dignity.	
Class.	
Taste.	
Friendship.	
Ability.	
Skill.	
Joy.	
Love (the real kind).	
Charm.	
Wit.	
Work ethic.	
Manners.	
Common sense.	
A happy home.	
An honest opinion.	
Talent.	
Inner peace.	
Tranquility.	
Kindness.	
Enlightenment.	
Style.	
Perspective.	
Patience.	
Trust.	
More time.	

Make Your Own Money!

Establishing financial independence is pretty easy when you can *literally* print your own money. Just make some copies of this page, cut out the Brother bucks, then attempt to pass them off in exchange for goods and services!

Is that illegal? Depends; is counterfeiting against the law where you're from? And like they say, fortune favors the bold!

What *to* Do with Your Money After *the* Apocalypse

One of the benefits of surviving the nuclear war is that, by default, you're now one of the richest people on the planet. (Suck it, atomized corpse of Jeff Bezos!) And while most survivors you encounter will likely mention that money has no applicable value anymore, don't listen to them—they're just jealous of your wealth.

If anything, there's *never* been a better time to make your money work for you. Here's how:

Burn It. Not only will it keep you warm during those frigid nuclear winters, but there's a pretty good chance inhaling the fumes from smoldering dollars will also bring you one step closer to the sweet release of death, or at least make you hallucinate. It's a win/win!

Trade It. Sure, *you* know money is worthless now that society has crumbled, but the mutant hordes don't—so take full advantage of their ignorance! Trade your legal tender for goods that will help you survive. Note: You will always get a better exchange rate with coins, since most mutants are fascinated by shiny things.

Eat It. You are probably starving, and you could do *a lot* worse. Remember that time you were forced to subsist on thin slivers of flesh carved from your traveling partner's corpse?

Save It. Eventually, society will recover, and if you're alive to see it happen, you're going to need a nest egg. So save your money. You'd be amazed at the favorable interest rates currently being offered by the Coffer Tenders of Southern Necroshire—we're talking annual percentage yields of 5–7%!

Invest It. Use your money to purchase any and all remaining cryptocurrencies. Now that *every* bank is decentralized, you will essentially control the entire marketplace. Plus, it's fitting that you'll be using a currency with no current fundamental value to purchase something that never had one.

Bury It. And not just for safekeeping. We've all seen the things that sprout from the irradiated Dacite fields of Eurasia, so there's a pretty good chance you might be able to grow an *actual* money tree—not the kind that your in-laws gave you after your wedding. Try not to think about how they're dead now.

Wear It. Why let the Warlords have all the fun? You can match the splendor of their elaborate bone headpieces by simply stitching a few dollars together. In fact, there's nothing stopping you from dressing head-to-toe in dollars and proclaiming yourself to be the Money God. If your costume is convincing enough, you *might* even pick up a few followers!

Fuck It. Like literally have intercourse with it. Again, you could do *a lot* worse…and we both know you have.

LIKE MY MAN PUFF SAY...

Problems
Money

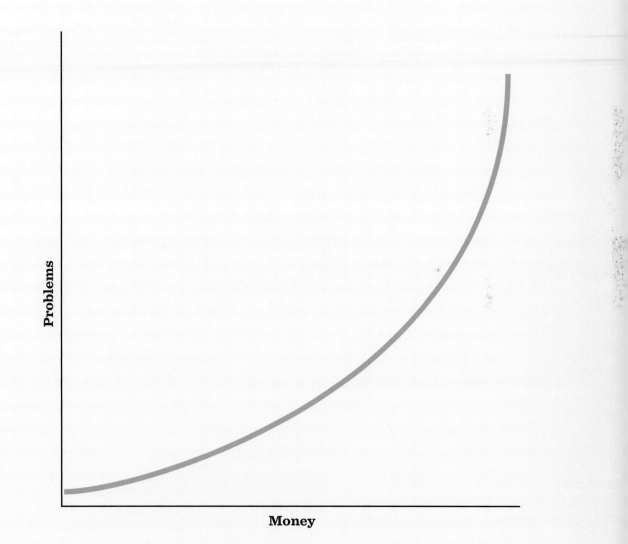

HOW TO
TAKE IT
WITH YOU

Right now, you might not have a lot of money—but by the time you die, that will (hopefully) change. And while prevailing wisdom has long held that you can't take that money with you when you depart this earthly plane, we're here to tell you that you *literally* can. And probably should.

Take a lesson from the pharaohs of ancient Egypt, who were buried with their fortunes to aid them in their journey through the afterlife—and to prevent their descendants from paying inheritance taxes, which were exorbitantly high in 1,000 B.C. Back then, said fortunes consisted mainly of gold, jewels and jars filled with organs, all of which were pretty unwieldy (hence the pyramids...plenty of storage space). But luckily for you, it's *much* easier to take your wealth to the afterlife these days. Here's how to get started:

Over the next few decades, while you wait for death, don't update your will—instead, slowly begin to withdraw all of your cash from the bank and place it in sacks. Somewhat annoyingly, while most financial institutions will provide you with sacks, they are not the kind with a comically large dollar sign printed on them—so you'll have to add that flourish yourself. Accumulate enough wealth to fill a minimum of three sacks.

Take one of the sacks to a funeral home and purchase a casket for yourself. Do not wait until death—because then, your family will most likely choose a casket for you (or, if they're cheap, they'll just have you cremated). You didn't spend all those years avoiding them for nothing! If the funeral director inquires why you're paying for the casket with a bag of cash, say something about how Anubis, the God of the Afterlife, demands it. He or she will probably understand.

Next, create a posting on Craigslist, Taskrabbit or another reputable work-for-hire site. You're looking for an honest stranger who will agree to keep your final resting place a secret in exchange for a sack of money. If you doubt his or her honesty, make passing mention of a curse that will be placed upon your burial site—it worked for the pharaohs and will usually help keep your grave unmolested for millennia, too.

Finally, lie in your newly purchased, premium casket—comfy, right?—and have the stranger pour the contents of the remaining money sacks over you. Your casket is now your deathbed, and you have successfully cut out the money-hungry mortician middlemen, leaving you with even more riches for the afterlife! Just don't forget to place two coins over your eyes for the ferryman Charon, who will ensure you've paid your toll to cross the

River Styx into Hades. The stranger will then shut and lock the casket as you both go to your graves with this secret. You've already got a head start!

While you wait to die, reflect back on all the things you did in your life to distract you from this inevitable moment. Think of all the hilarious content and memes you consumed. Remember that time you mastered *Angry Birds*. Have a laugh about the angry comments you left on Reddit. Ponder the hours you spent working to accumulate all this cash. Was it worth it? You bet. Money took care of you in life and will now provide for you in death. You earned this moment. Breathe in that sweet, sweet money scent. It's all yours, and no one can take it away from you now!

6 Unexpected Benefits of Being Interred with Your Fortune!

 It acts as insulation, keeping your casket at a cozy 72 degrees in the cold, dark dirt.

 It will distract graverobbers who are looking to harvest your precious organs and/or molest your corpse.

 The green ink is a natural worm repellent, preventing them from boring into your skull.

 If your casket is flooded, the dollars will act as a cocoon, keeping you safe from a watery grave.

 As you decompose, you will become one with your money, becoming indistinguishable from the treasures you worked so hard for in life.

 In the event that you are reanimated, you will still have all of your riches with you—meaning you won't be a vagrant zombie, but a wealthy undead person!

A HANDY GLOSSARY OF TERMS

Amortization—The process of paying off debt in regular installments over a fixed period of time. Only used by old-timey bankers with cigars clenched between their teeth.

ARM—Acronym for Adjustable Rate Mortgage, in which the interest you pay on your outstanding balance rises and falls, often significantly. If your family used to live in a newly constructed two-story, four-bedroom, three-bathroom house, but is now skipping from motel to motel under the cover of darkness, your parents probably got tricked into signing up for one of these.

Assets—The entire property of a person, corporation or estate that can be used in the payment of debts. Can also be used to describe the physical attributes of a female coworker, if you're making an inappropriate workplace joke.

Blockchain—Digital database containing information that can be used and shared within a large, decentralized network. The reason dudes have boners over Bitcoin.

Bonds—Debt investments in which you lend money to a government or corporation for a fixed period of time, in exchange for interest payments. When bonds mature, you also receive the loaned amount. When *you* mature, you refrain from making a "Bonds... James Bonds" joke here.

Capital—Assets that add to the long-term net worth of a corporation. Combined with labor, it creates value (we read that on a whiteboard somewhere).

Capital Gain—Profit from the sale of property or an investment. Having to pay taxes on capital gains is the second-leading cause of death amongst rich old white dudes (Viagra overdose is the first).

Compound Interest—Interest earned on savings or investments, *plus* interest accumulated over time, or interest charged on a loan, plus interest added to your balance over time. You'd prefer the former to the latter.

Credit—Provision of money, goods or services with the expectation of future payment. You ability (or inability) to do that directly impacts future provisions, and, essentially, your entire life.

Cryptocurrency—Currency that only exists digitally and has no central issuing or regulating authority. Instead, it relies on a decentralized system to record transaction, and cryptography to prevent fraud. Sound sketchy? It sure does!

Debt—Obligation to pay or repay an entity in return for something received. If you do not meet said obligation, a large gentleman will pay you a visit and break your leg.

Deduction—Anything that can be subtracted from taxable income—i.e. student loan interest, reinvested dividends, charitable contributions, *this* book.

Dependent—Person who is financially dependent on your income, and therefore helps reduce your taxable income. Sadly, you cannot claim your dog as a dependent.

Dividend—Sum of money paid regularly by a corporation to its shareholders out of its profits or reserves. Making finance jokes is hard. Let's move on.

Escrow—Process in which a deed, bond or piece of property is held in a trust by a third party until a financial transaction is completed. Sounds like a cool Spanish crow you'd party with in Ibiza.

FICO—Number used by banks and financial institutions to measure your credit worthiness. Developed by ironically named data analytics firm Fair, Issac and Company, it uses your credit history and mathematical algorithms to thoroughly fuck you over forever.

Happiness—A state of mind. Money cannot buy you it.

Interest—A charge for borrowed money, usually based on a percentage of the amount borrowed, or a profit from money made on invested capital. You're probably more interested in the latter.

Loan—Money lent at interest. Pro tip: Avoid if possible.

Liability—A debt or financial obligation. Or, any loose-cannon officer in a buddy cop movie.

Mortgage—Agreement in which a bank or creditor lends you money at interest in exchange for the title of your property. Once you pay it off, the property becomes yours, though don't worry, you never will.

Net Worth—Your assets minus your liabilities. Essentially, this is what you're worth—but you're so much more to us.

Premium—Payments to an insurance company, in return for protection from financial loss. We know, that's a pretty boring definition for such a classy word.

Principal—The original sum of money borrowed in a loan, or put into an investment. Also the head of a school who definitely hates his/her life.

Simple Interest—Interest earned on savings or investments, calculated on the principal of a loan, not the principal *plus* interest, which is Complex Interest. We're confused too.

Stocks—Shares owned of a publically traded company. Owning them makes you a shareholder, which is definitely something that will impress girls at a bar.

Wealth—The sum of all property that has a monetary value (if you are wealthy), an abundance of spiritual and experiential resources (if you are not wealthy).

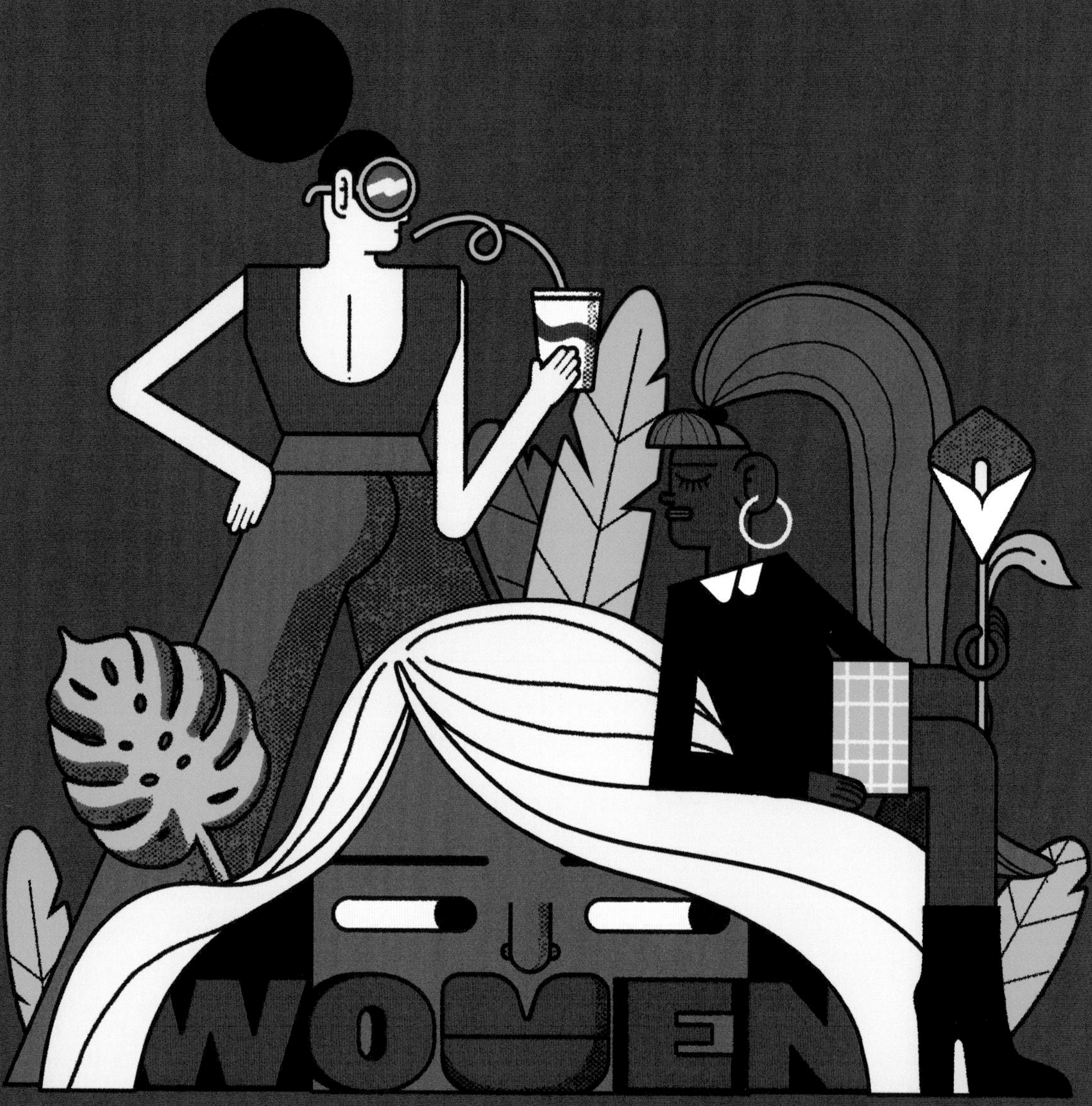
WOMEN

It would be easy to say the truth about women is that they are better, smarter and more compassionate than men; that they display levels of patience, determination and drive that make us look like giant toddlers by comparison; that they survive a daily barrage of judgment, condescension, harassment and general bullshit—while wearing uncomfortable shoes, mind you—because they are tougher and more pragmatic than any man could ever be.

It would be easy to say all of those things because they are all facts.

But you probably don't want to be preached to. So instead, we only ask that you keep those things in mind the next time you interact with a woman. Try to put yourself in her (again, very uncomfortable) shoes. Imagine growing up in a world that subtly—and not so subtly—imposes a series of standards on you, most of which were determined by men, and none of which play to your preternatural strengths. Think about being subjected to an endless stream of messaging designed to make you feel bad about yourself, while *also* being judged solely on your physical appearance. Consider being routinely ignored, intimidated and insulted. And finally, accept that you will be unable to complain about *any* of those things without being considered "emotional" or "unstable," because that's just the way women are.

We know, it's a stretch. After all, you're a man, and as such, have basically been *encouraged* to do what you want, when you want, however you want—without fear of repercussion or judgment. That's just one benefit of growing up in a patriarchal society. So perhaps this analogy will help: Imagine being Superman, and having to wait for FAA clearance every time you want to fly. That's basically what it's like to be a woman.

And to extend that analogy one step further, maybe it's best to treat women like the benevolent superbeings they are. Remember that the girl you just matched with on Tinder comes from a future where man-made implements of war gather dust in museums and everyone eats a macrobiotic diet (there are also elaborate robes involved.) She is capable of creating and nurturing life. Her body runs like clockwork. Your primitive ways probably confuse her—and undoubtedly frustrate her—and it takes every fiber of her *considerable* willpower not to destroy you.

Don't take it personally. You're great. But you could be even *greater* if you realized everything you could learn from her. So consider where she's coming from, what she's been up against, how she's managed to cope with it all. Cut her some slack. Giver her the respect she deserves.

At the very least, don't send her a picture of your dick, you savage.

MASLOW'S HIERARCHY OF WOMEN NEEDS

Everything necessary to ascend, find fulfillment and become the person you were meant to be.

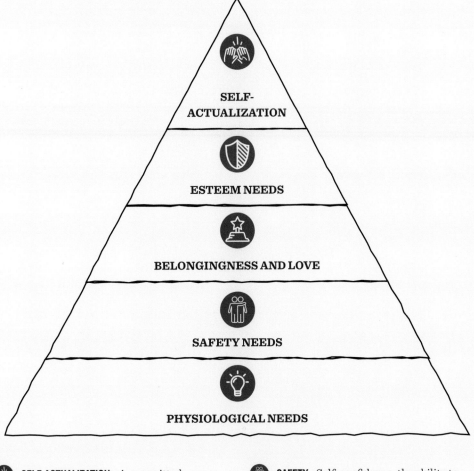

SELF-ACTUALIZATION

ESTEEM NEEDS

BELONGINGNESS AND LOVE

SAFETY NEEDS

PHYSIOLOGICAL NEEDS

 SELF-ACTUALIZATION—A committed relationship.

 ESTEEM—Sex.

 BELONGINGNESS AND LOVE—First dates, unsolicited laughter at your jokes, the occasional handjob.

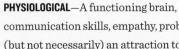 **SAFETY**—Self-confidence, the ability to handle rejection, condoms.

PHYSIOLOGICAL—A functioning brain, communication skills, empathy, probably (but not necessarily) an attraction to women, a relatively clean apartment.

THE GENTLEMAN'S GUIDE TO LADY PARTS

If you giggled your way through health class—or were too busy hiding your boner to actually learn something— don't worry; we've got you covered. We're going to take you through the ins and outs of the female body, because every man should know the basic difference between the vulva and the vagina.

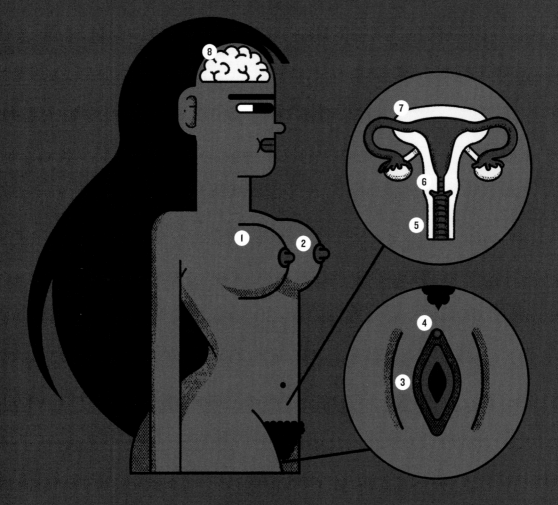

① BOOBS

Human females are the only mammals to have enlarged breasts for all of adulthood, not just when breastfeeding. And human males are the only mammals to be sexually attracted to breasts (they don't even have to be particularly enlarged, either). Scientists can't really explain why—good looking out, evolution!

② NIPPLES

The raised regions of tissue on her breasts. They're primarily used for nursing, *but* when a woman's nipples are stimulated, her brain creates oxytocin—a chemical that makes her (and you) feel happy. Nipple-play also activates the same parts of the brain as touching her genitals does. So stop at second base for a minute or two before you try to slide into home.

③ THAT'S NOT WHAT YOU THINK IT IS

If you're lucky enough to have a naked lady standing in front of you, you probably can't see her vagina. What you can see is the vulva—aka the external female genitalia. The vulva includes the labia—aka lips or folds—and the more delicate features those folds protect, like...

④ THE CLITORIS

The clitoris is a super-sensitive nub nestled above the opening of the vagina. The clit has 8,000 nerve-endings, which is twice as many as the tip of your penis. Unsurprisingly, this little guy plays a big role in sex. Clitoral stimulation not only builds arousal in a woman, but 75% of women actually require it to orgasm.

⑤ THE VAGINA

The vagina is a muscular canal that connects the vulva to a woman's internal sex organs—but you probably know it best as the innie where you can put your outie.

Unaroused, the vagina is typically 2-3 inches deep. During sex, the vagina only extends to between 4-5 inches, with the inch nearest the opening being the most sensitive. So the size of the tool you're working with matters less than how you use it.

The vagina is also pretty magical. It can expand by almost 200 percent to bring a human into the world and, with some time, can return to its normal state. It is self-cleaning, self-lubricating and slightly acidic (it has a pH of about 4, the same as a glass of wine).

6 THE CERVIX

The cervix—or the dead end of the vagina—is the opening to a woman's uterus. Normally, it's open just enough to let a few swimmers through, but can dilate a few inches during childbirth. It's basically a portal to human existence. Also, no, you cannot penetrate a woman's cervix.

7 THE UTERUS AND OVARIES

Just past the cervix, lies the uterus, which is connected to the ovaries, where eggs are created. When an egg is fertilized by sperm, it implants itself into the lining of the uterus and spends nine months there becoming a person. Unfertilized eggs are ejected with the lining of the uterus each month when a woman has her period. If you want to limit how much you need to know about these particular parts of the female body, wear a condom.

8 THE BRAIN

At the center of it all is a woman's brain, which science has shown is more complex and works harder every day than a male brain. So remember, a woman is not just a bundle of fun bits. She is a real person with a brain more impressive than yours and she will use it to decide whether or not to have sex with you.

How *to* **Date** *a* **Woman** (According to an Actual Woman)

It's really not as complicated as it seems. Here's all you need to know:

1. Avoid Confusion—Ask Her Out on a Date.

"Hey, wanna hang?" means nothing. Do you really want to spend three hours on a "maybe-date" wondering what's going on? Nope, neither does she.

2. It's Even Better If You Ask Her Out in Person.

+100 sexy confidence points. Maybe even 200.

3. Make a Plan.

Your "The Future Is Female" T-shirt doesn't excuse letting her arrange all the details of your date. You're not being a feminist; you're being lazy. Putting some thought into your date shows you're genuinely interested. Girls like that.

4. Offer to Meet in Her Neighborhood.

"There is a cool bar right by my apartment," will be understood as, "I don't really care about getting to know you, I just want you to come back to my house to bone."

5. Look Nice, But be Comfortable.

You at the beginning of the date: *puts on tie, hums *James Bond* theme*

You in the middle of the date: *can't stop fucking with annoying tie, looks like a fidgety weirdo*

Also, always remember:

6. Be on Time.

Your phone has at least 12 different apps that can remember where you're supposed to be, and when you're supposed to be there. There's no explanation for being late. Unless you're an apathetic jerk.

7. Don't Get Drunk or High Beforehand.

Buzzed to calm the nerves? Acceptable. Slurring, slobbering and mumbling? Not so much. Not even if you're going to go see a sick-ass IMAX 3-D movie.

8. Don't Have an End Game.

Don't waste your time wondering if you have breath mints, or if your roommate will be home tonight. You'll figure it out. Have fun and pay attention to the person you're with.

9. Be Nice (to Her and to Everyone Else).

There is no clearer sign that you're an asshole than being a dick to the waitstaff. Say "please" and "thank you." Hold doors for people. Don't criticize things she likes.

10. Ask Questions (and Listen to the Answers).

Good

> You: "Do you like to read?"
>
> Her: "Yeah, I read all the time. My favorite books are..."

Bad

> You: "I like to read. Do you?"
>
> Her: "Yeah, I—"
>
> You again: "I love Salinger. Have you read *Catcher in the Rye*? It really speaks to my very unique life experience."
>
> Her: [Attempts to withdraw from society like the actual Salinger.]

11. Make Eye Contact.

Things not to stare at: your shoes, her boobs, the girl at the end of the bar's boobs, the waitress' boobs, the TV above the bar. And on that note...

12. Put Down Your Phone.

Mute it, put it in your pocket, leave it in the car. Hell, throw it in the ocean if you have to. Just don't spend your date texting, looking at Instagram or checking the score of the game (or any of the other 987,923,883 things you do on your phone).

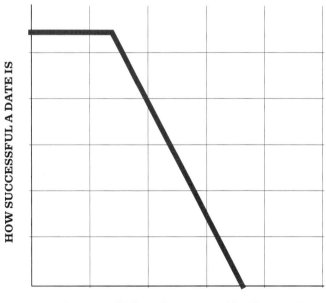

 # OF TIMES SOMEONE MENTIONED AN EX

13. Don't Bring Up Your Exes.

14. Be Honest and Authentic.

Her: "I love *Harry Potter*!"

You: "Wow, so do I!" (lie)

3 months later

Her: "I got us tickets to a 36-hour *Harry Potter* Marathon!"

karma

15. Ignore Your Idiot Friends and "Pick-up Artists."

Girls are not video games, there are no cheat codes that you can learn from nerds on the Internet. *This* advice, however, is in a book, so you know it's good.

16. Accept You're Going to Say or Do Something Stupid, and Get Over It.

The sooner you tell a dumb joke, spill beer on your shirt or accidentally make one of those weird spit bubbles, the sooner you can stop worrying if you're going to mess up. You're a human—you will. And *most* mistakes are endearing, not repulsive.

OVERRATED/UNDERRATED DATES

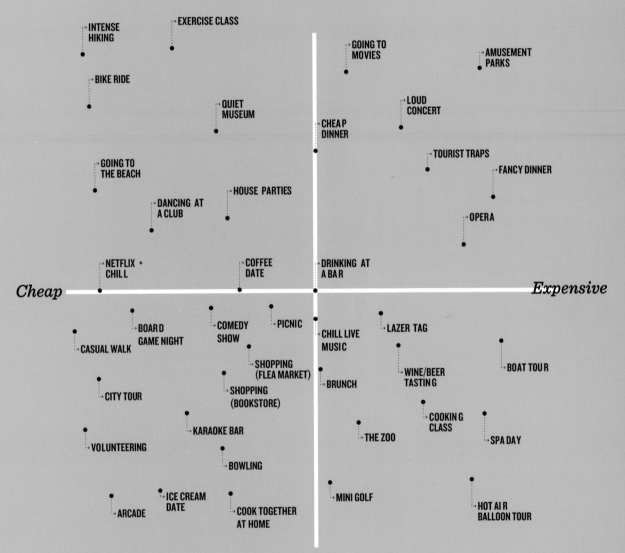

Overrated

INTENSE HIKING

EXERCISE CLASS

GOING TO MOVIES

AMUSEMENT PARKS

BIKE RIDE

LOUD CONCERT

QUIET MUSEUM

CHEAP DINNER

TOURIST TRAPS

GOING TO THE BEACH

FANCY DINNER

HOUSE PARTIES

DANCING AT A CLUB

OPERA

Cheap

NETFLIX + CHILL

COFFEE DATE

DRINKING AT A BAR

Expensive

BOARD GAME NIGHT

COMEDY SHOW

PICNIC

CHILL LIVE MUSIC

LAZER TAG

CASUAL WALK

BOAT TOUR

SHOPPING (FLEA MARKET)

WINE/BEER TASTING

CITY TOUR

SHOPPING (BOOKSTORE)

BRUNCH

KARAOKE BAR

COOKING CLASS

VOLUNTEERING

THE ZOO

SPA DAY

BOWLING

ARCADE

ICE CREAM DATE

COOK TOGETHER AT HOME

MINI GOLF

HOT AIR BALLOON TOUR

Underrated

201

The Truth About Dick Pics

Weren't expecting that, were you? Welcome to being a woman. Here's a follow-up question: Are you aroused? No? Well, that's what it feels like to get a picture of a dick you didn't ask for. It's surprising, maybe a little funny, but to some it's also really offensive and gross.

So don't send unsolicited dick pics. They're not likely to make her want to have sex with you and are very likely to either make her laugh or creep her out. Neither is good for you.

Consensual sexting can be fun if that's what you're both into—but before you hit send, remember:

PEOPLE YOU THINK WILL SEE YOUR DICK

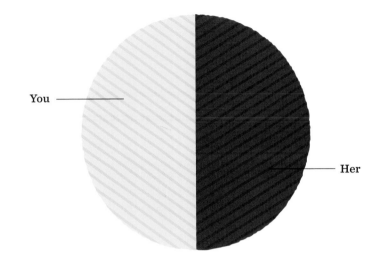

You

Her

PEOPLE WHO WILL ACTUALLY SEE YOUR DICK

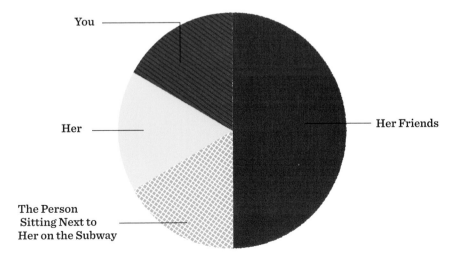

You

Her

Her Friends

The Person Sitting Next to Her on the Subway

Is It Time *to* Move On? Probably.

Wayne Gretzky once said "You miss 100% of the shots you don't take," and while that adage may be true for most things—hockey, business, drinking—it definitely doesn't apply to dating.

To be clear, if you're interested in someone, there's nothing wrong with taking a shot. And if there's a rebound, we suppose it's OK to crash the net, too (it's hockey talk—Wayne understands). But if this someone isn't receptive to your advances, it's time to move on. Even the Great One would probably agree with that.

Because no matter how hard you try, you can't make someone like you. Perseverance—the steadfast determination to press on in the face of overwhelming obstacles—is an admirable trait, one that will serve you well in just about every aspect of life; but rarely does anything good come from persistent pestering. At *best*, you will wear someone down until they finally relent (*hooray!*). At worst, you will end up getting slapped with a restraining order (or just slapped).

And at every other stage, you just look pathetic.

Want to avoid that? Move on. If the object of your affection has made it abundantly clear they aren't into you, nothing you can do will change that. No, it doesn't matter if you two are friends—despite what popular culture wants you to believe, there's no escaping the Friend Zone. No, some over-the-top gesture won't convince them to *finally* give you a shot. If anything, they'll just think it's creepy. And, no, you should *definitely* not get drunk and tell them your true feelings.

Oh, and if you're not sure if you should move on, you should move on. People tend to let you know if they're into you or not.

Rejection hurts, and accepting it requires swallowing your pride, but that's better than any of the alternatives. And even though you might not believe it, you'll be OK.

The feelings you have right now will subside, probably a lot sooner than you think. Someone else will come along. You'll score again. Just think about Wayne Gretzky. He took 4,819 shots during his NHL career—and scored 894 goals—meaning he missed 81.5% of the time. But at least he wasn't a creep about it.

How *to* Give Compliments

(Without Being a Total Creep)

It seems easy—you like something about someone, you tell them you like it and then they appreciate the attention, right? Maybe. But it's not always simple. Women are subjected to lots of unwanted attention from men—especially attention of the unwanted, objectifying variety—and that can be at best uncomfortable, and at worst really scary and intimidating. Here's a handy guide to help you navigate giving compliments without being a creep.

Sexual compliments should be reserved for people you have a sexual relationship with.

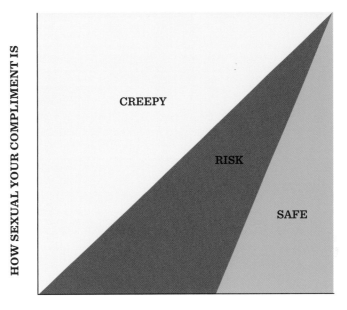

Look for the signs that your compliment is not welcome.

Is she wearing headphones? Is she walking down the street minding her own business? Is she busy with a group of friends? Is she deliberately avoiding eye contact? Is she talking about a serious subject? These are all good clues that your compliment, well-intentioned or not, is probably not welcome.

Consider her personal space.

Saying "I like your hair" while sitting a comfortable distance from a woman at a bar is very different than saying "I like your hair" then leaning over and touching it. Don't enter her space unless it's very clear you're welcomed there.

Catcalling is dumb. Don't do it.

Who actually likes catcalling?

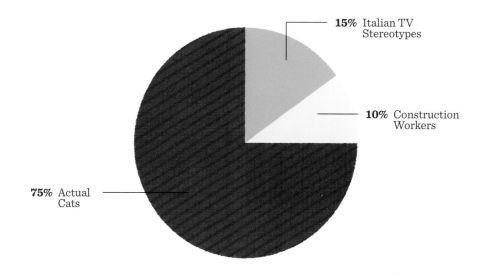

15% Italian TV Stereotypes

10% Construction Workers

75% Actual Cats

Giving someone a compliment doesn't entitle you to anything.

Not even a "thank you." Don't assume that just because you said something nice to a girl, that she will suddenly be smitten with you. And if she doesn't acknowledge or appreciate your compliment, don't lash out or belittle her out of retaliation.

There's so much more to compliment than a woman's appearance.

Things women are often complimented on

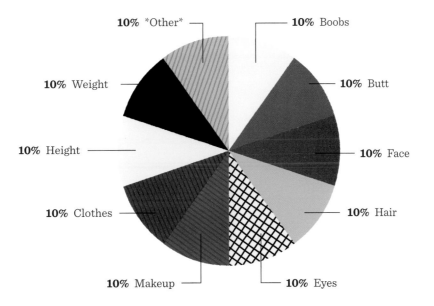

10% *Other*

10% Boobs

10% Weight

10% Butt

10% Height

10% Face

10% Clothes

10% Hair

10% Makeup

10% Eyes

Things women SHOULD BE complimented on

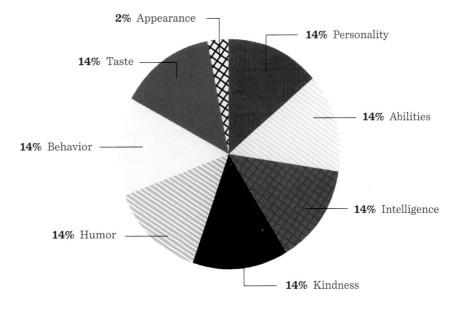

2% Appearance

14% Personality

14% Taste

14% Abilities

14% Behavior

14% Intelligence

14% Humor

14% Kindness

Don't objectify.

Even when you're complimenting a woman's appearance (to her face or to someone else), don't talk about her like she is a thing. Talk about her like she is a person. Focus on what makes her unique and special.

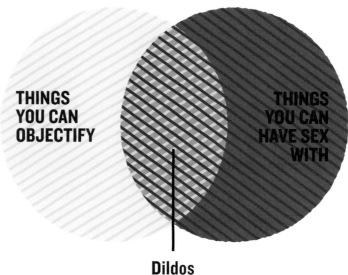

Dildos
& Fleshlights

If someone says they don't like your compliments, listen.

No matter how "nice" you thought you were being, if someone asks you to stop, stop.

How to Compliment Coworkers

Keep the majority of your compliments work-related. Focus on her talent, abilities and skills to show that you value her as a coworker.

Did she get a new haircut or outfit? It's pretty safe to compliment someone on these sorts of things, but you should never give her sexualized compliments about her body.

GOOD: "Those new glasses look great!"

BAD: "Your butt looks great in those jeans!"

How to Compliment Someone You're Interested In

Don't overuse generic compliments—"You're cute"—or cheesy pick-up lines; they're the IRL equivalent of copy-paste Tinder lines. Show her that you are interested in *her* specifically. Pay her compliments that are unique to her personality and appearance—"I love the way your cheek dimples when you smile."

Until she's said she is also interested in you, don't talk about her body or give the sexual compliments. You might ruin your chances by creeping her out. And whatever you do, avoid phrasing anything in a manner that will seem condescending. Telling a girl "You're funny" or "You're smart" makes it seem like she's an incredibly rare specimen, as if all women aren't funny or intelligent.

How to Compliment Your Girlfriend

Don't stop complimenting a woman after she becomes your girlfriend. Too often, guys think that compliments are just a strategy for getting girls. Once they've got one, they stop telling her how much they admire and appreciate her. Then **poof** girlfriend vanishes.

To have a healthy relationship, regularly compliment her on all the things you like about her—her laugh, her kindness, her body. As long as she is into it, it's totally OK to pay her sexual compliments. Just make sure they're not the ONLY aspect of her that you're appreciating.

These Aren't Compliments, Don't Ever Use Them

"You're not like other girls."

What you're really saying: "Other girls are bad. You're OK. I might be a misogynist."

It might be true that the woman you're speaking to is very unique, but focus on what makes her great. Don't disparage other people to raise her up.

"Wow you're really smart/athletic/creative/___." or the more egregious "Wow, you're really smart/athletic/creative/_____ for a girl."

What you're really saying: Again, "I'm surprised by your talents because I underestimated you or your entire gender."

Instead of expressing surprise at a woman's talents or skills, tell her how admiring and impressed you are.

"I love short/Asian/curvy/blonde/___ women."

What you're really saying: "I'm not interested in you. I'm interested in the part of you that matches my fetish."

Fixating on a woman's physical characteristics that fit your "type" minimizes the way in which she is uniquely special and attractive. Plus, it makes the compliment more about you than her.

"That dress is pretty, but I don't think red is your color."

What you're really saying: "I read about negging on a pick-up artist website, and because I'm a lowlife loser I've decided to try it on you!"

Don't be this guy. Negging is a cruel way to make someone feel insecure and vulnerable so you can more easily take advantage of them. Plus, most women will see right through your game.

"Wow, you're so pretty when you wear makeup/wear a dress/do your hair."

What you're really saying: "Typically, you're not that great to look at. I'm surprised by how attractive I find you right now."

Compliments like this are just thinly veiled suggestions about how someone should typically look. It's nice to compliment someone when they've put in extra effort to look nice, but don't use it to imply they usually look like crap. Generally, it's best to avoid any compliment that comes with a caveat.

"You remind me of my mom."

What you're really saying: "I have never read *Oedipus*."

Your mom is probably wonderful, and yes, you'd be lucky to find a woman as great as her. That being said, no woman wants to be compared to her significant other's mom. It's deeply unsexy and can be really confusing and creepy.

Ways *to* Meet Women After *the* Apocalypse

Look, you're gonna have to procreate—it's the only way to ensure the survival of the human species. Here's how to find a willing partner.

1. Play it cool; women like confidence. Just because you may be the last man on Earth doesn't mean she's into you!

2. Learn to play "Despacito" on the acoustic guitar. It will showcase your musical talent and confidence. Also, that song is essentially the musical equivalent of a cockroach, and will unquestionably survive a nuclear holocaust.

3. Most likely the Internet won't exist, so **create a flier of your face along with some of your interests, turn-ons, and turn-offs.** Place these fliers around town with a designated meeting time to see if any survivors are interested in meeting IRL. Be careful not to tip off your location to any radioactive mutants roaming the countryside.

4. Read her body language. If she's turned toward you and making eye contact, she's engaged in the conversation. If she's screaming at the horror of your blistered, irradiated visage, don't take it personally; she's most likely disinterested.

5. Ask her questions about herself—what she loved doing before hellfire rained down upon us all. Show her you're interested!

6. Be both a hunter and a gatherer; it will show her that you are a provider. Wearing trophies of your conquests (garlands of herbs, bones or defeated foes' ears) will get the point across.

7. Demonstrate you're an intellectual by ranking Truffaut's films from best to worst, and mention that Jonathan Franzen was an overrated pontificator.

8. Be prepared to compete in feats of strength or hand-to-hand combat with fellow suitors.

9. In the event that there are no dog parks after the Apocalypse, **feel free to take her on a date** to watch wild packs of wolves roam the black forests, picking over the charred corpses.

10. Volunteer.

11. Draw pictures of grumpy cats on cave walls. **Memes are timeless!**

12. Organize a social sports league for adults, such as kickball or dodgeball. If rubber needs to be conserved for the rebuilding effort, feel free to get creative with discarded skulls for balls.

A HANDY GLOSSARY OF TERMS

Ally—People who support a group who are commonly the subject of discrimination, prejudice or harassment, but who are not members of that group. You should be a feminist ally.

Baby Crazy—A thing that women who think babies are cute are accused of being.

Bitch—A word you should never call a woman.

Cunt—Another word you should never call a woman.

Cosmetics—Products or substances used to enhance or alter appearance. Has become a $445 billion industry worldwide, thanks mostly to preying on women's insecurities.

Dating—A Sisyphean beauty pageant that occasionally leads to deep personal connection. *Very* occasionally.

Douche—Vagina cleaner. Most women don't actually use it because vaginas are pretty much self-cleaning. Also, a fitting term for an obnoxious human being.

Emotional—Word often used to describe women by people who scream at a television while complete strangers throw/kick/hit a ball around. Note: Crying does not count as being "emotional."

Emotional Intelligence—The ability to understand, empathize with and communicate about emotions. Women are pretty good at this. Men usually aren't, though the rare ones with high emotional intelligence are highly prized as BF/husband material.

Feminism—The belief in, and pursuit of, social, political and economic equality between the sexes. If someone says this is a bad thing, they're an asshole.

Feminazi—Term insecure men often use to describe women who are vocal about their feminism.

Harassment—To annoy repeatedly and persistently. Can come in many forms, both overt (catcalling, etc.) and subtle (psychological), none of which are good. If you see a guy doing it, tell him to stop.

Heels—Medieval torture devices that have somehow made it through the Geneva Convention.

"I'm Fine"—A thing women say when they are probably not fine, more than likely because you did something stupid. Routinely followed by 60–90 seconds of crushing silence.

Insecurities—Uncertainties or anxieties about oneself, presumably caused by growing up in a society that sets unrealistic standards of beauty and values aesthetics above all else. If you're a guy, you have no idea what any of that means.

IUD—Short for "Intrauterine device"—aka fancy birth control that goes in a woman's uterus and stays there for a few years.

Mansplaining—When a man, without prompt, explains something to a woman that she already understands or is totally capable of figuring out herself. Watch how often this actually happens; you'll be amazed/horrified.

Mars/Venus—Two planets that neither men nor women come from. Turns out we're all just flawed people from Earth.

"No, Thanks"—A polite way of saying, "I'm not interested." Sadly, some men confuse it with an invitation to pursue or pester a woman more aggressively.

Patriarchy—Very real hierarchical structure that favors and empowers men over women. Believe it or not, it still exists today. Also, a thing one should smash wherever and whenever possible.

Period—Monthly scourge that makes existence uncomfortable and annoying. In addition to the bleeding, common symptoms include acne, bloating, swelling, weariness, irritability and mood changes. Literally imagine if *you* had to go through that shit every four weeks.

Planned Parenthood—Bane of conservatives everywhere, often (incorrectly) cited as providing "government-funded abortions," it's actually a lifeline to women, providing low-cost reproductive health care, birth control, emergency contraception and abortion counseling. Donate to it today.

Pink Tax—Term for the actual practice of putting a higher price on products targeted to women, relative to the same products targeted to men. The Patriarchy is everywhere.

Pubes—A thing that women are totally allowed to have. It's 2019; women shouldn't be obligated to get rid of any of their body hair.

Sephora/Ulta—Cosmetics retail stores where it's remarkably easy to spend a stupid amount of money—a stupid amount of money you should have no snarky comment or opinion on.

79 Cents—How much money the average woman makes for every $1 a man makes. Not fair.

Sex—A thing girls are allowed to like too.

"She's Crazy"—Something shitty guys say about ex-girlfriends who were probably not crazy, just annoyed by their bad relationship.

Slut—Derogatory term for a woman who engages in the exact same sexual practices a man is routinely lauded for.

Spanx—Spandex undergarment designed to keep all her wiggly bits from wiggling. They are not sexy, or comfortable, but they *do* make clothes look better. Don't make fun of them.

Tears—A relatively harmless way of expressing emotion that you shouldn't make a woman feel bad about.

Vagina—Tubular part of the female genital tract that extends from the vulva to the cervix. A magical cave of wonders/self-cleaning oven that is also the portal to life itself. You *wish* you had one.

Waxing—Form of semi-permanent hair removal in which wax is spread over the skin then quickly, painfully yanked off. Why do women do this? Good question.

"Whatever"—A thing women say at the end of an argument. Roughly translates to, "I'm annoyed, but I don't feel like fighting about it. Let it go." Ironically, she will never let it go.

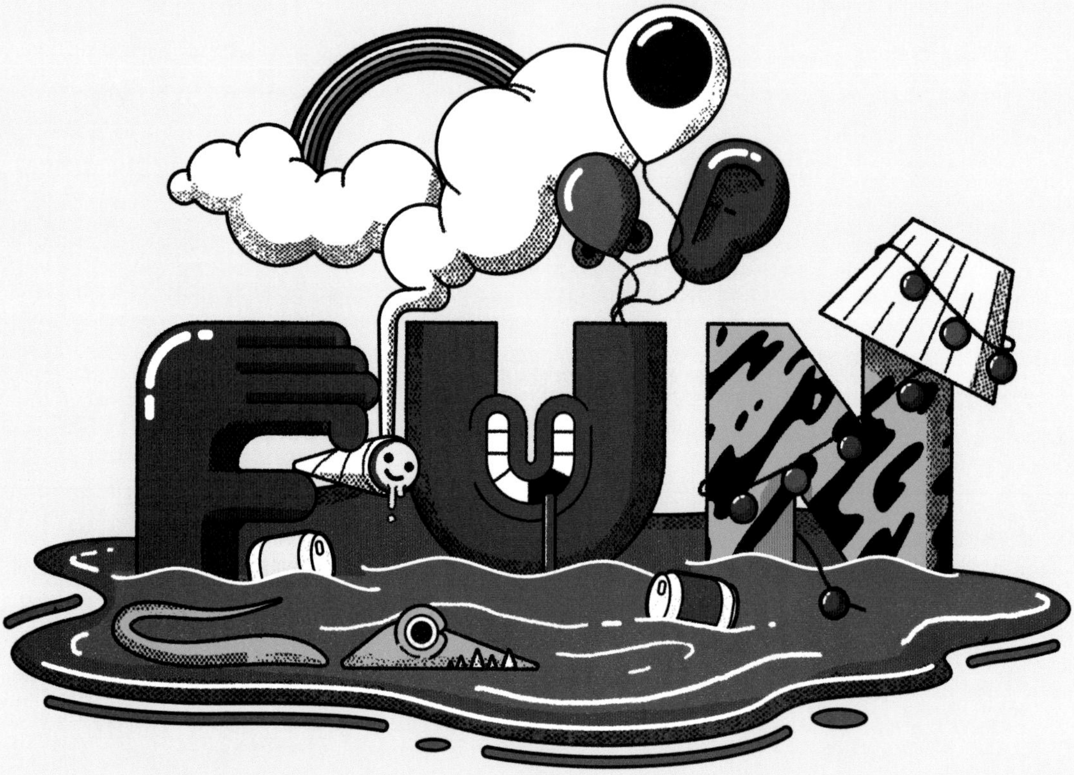
FUN

When was the last time you had fun?

If you are between the ages of 13 and 24, your answer is probably something like "Last night" or "Five minutes ago," because you are young and unbowed, still relatively unburdened by life and the sundry responsibilities that come along with it. You can still do whatever you want, and get away with most of it. You are "burning down the highway skyline on the back of a hurricane," as Brandon Flowers put it, and you don't even know it.

You *won't* know it, either—not until that storm slows and spontaneity gives way to stasis. This is something that happens to everybody, whether they want it to or not, BTW. It's called growing up. It's not much fun.

As you get older, you realize fun is one of those things that go away, like your hair or your ability to understand rappers. So you begin rationing it. You find yourself *making plans* to have fun, and assessing the fun postmortem by proclaiming, "That was fun!" And if you need reassurance that something was fun, it wasn't. You *know* when you're having fun.

But you are young. None of that applies to you. So *have some fucking fun.*

What does that mean? Whatever you want it to. The beauty of fun is that it's subjective. Anything that offers escape, relief or release is fun. Action and inaction are both equally fun. Presumably, work is fun. It's up to you, and you have the methods and resources to make it happen *right now*. Your mortgage payment isn't going to stop you.

But some day, it will. Or if you're still renting, replace "mortgage payment" with literally any other dumb thing your parents have to deal with on a daily basis. Fun doesn't stop in adulthood, the opportunities to *have* fun do. Are you having fun right now? Why not? Quit your job. Ditch that negative person in your life. Go outside. Stave off the advances of adulthood, even for an afternoon. "Rage against the dying of the light," as someone not named Brandon Flowers put it.

Fun is finite. One day you will wish you had more of it. That's the truth.

MASLOW'S HIERARCHY OF FUN NEEDS

Everything necessary to ascend, find fulfillment and become the person you were meant to be.

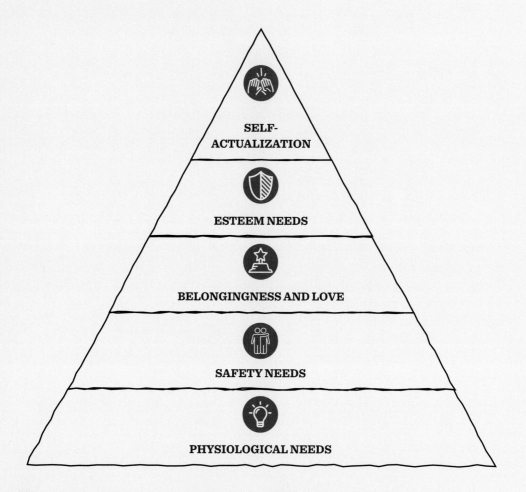

SELF-ACTUALIZATION

ESTEEM NEEDS

BELONGINGNESS AND LOVE

SAFETY NEEDS

PHYSIOLOGICAL NEEDS

SELF-ACTUALIZATION—Winning, having fun.

ESTEEM—Prizes/trophies, the satisfaction that comes with doing your best.

BELONGINGNESS AND LOVE—Friends (real or imaginary), teammates, coworkers.

SAFETY—Protective gear, health insurance, the ability to swim, good reaction time.

PHYSIOLOGICAL—A body, hand-eye coordination, imagination, freedom, a willingness to occasionally look ridiculous, strong thumbs, tolerance (for pain or alcohol).

GENERAL RULES FOR HAVING FUN

General Rules to Observe While Having Fun at a Sporting Event.

Refrain from starting a wave.

Keep all inflatable objects at home.

Avoid using the pronoun "we" when discussing your team. You are not on the roster.

Never discuss the fortunes of your fantasy team—no one cares.

Be drunk...but, like, *fun* drunk.

Don't fight. It's a goddamn game.

Always tip vendors and concession stand workers.

Don't complain about the price of beer—this isn't a bar.

Don't complain about the price of food—this isn't a restaurant.

The floppy flask is your friend.

Don't throw objects onto the field of play.

Put your phone away.

Sing–alongs and chants are only acceptable at football matches.

Only wear apparel pertaining to the teams on the field.

If you choose to wear a jersey or kit, *never tuck it in.*

Retire all relevant jerseys or kits once a player has left your team.

Refrain from burning said jerseys or kits and posting it on social media. You'd leave for more money, too.

Use body paint sparingly. Don't treat every game like Halloween.

If attending a baseball game, don't bring your glove. You are not six years old.

If you catch a foul ball or home run anyway, give it to a child seated nearby.

Always sing "Take Me Out to the Ballgame." Only sing "God Bless America" if you really feel like it.

Ask yourself, "Is what I'm about to yell problematic?" If the answer is even "maybe," keep it to yourself.

Never cheer when a player is injured.

Always applaud when an injured player is taken off the field.

Try not to curse like a sailor around children.

Don't *try* to get on the Jumbotron or TV. If it happens, it happens.

Avoid participating in anything involving a T-shirt cannon.

Wait for a break in the action before leaving your seat.

Only stand during pivotal moments.

Never cry after a loss. Crying after a victory, however, is encouraged.

General Rules to Observe While Having Fun at a Concert.

Refrain from starting a wave.

Keep all inflatable objects at home.

Put your phone away.

Never wear apparel pertaining to the band/artist performing.

Be drunk...but, like, *fun* drunk.

Don't fight. It's a goddamn concert.

Stop talking once the artist starts playing.

Don't throw hard objects onto the stage.

Thinking of lifting your girlfriend up on your shoulders? Don't.

Be considerate of others while in the pit.

Don't push your way to the front of the crowd.

If you are *at* the front of the crowd, you forfeit the right to personal space.

If you can't see, stand up. Or move.

Don't bring a five-course meal, complete with table settings and wine pairings, to an outdoor show.

Leave the oversized blanket at home, too.

Never grope a crowdsurfer.

Don't antagonize the opening acts.

Be courteous when artist is performing songs from the new album.

Please don't shout out requests between songs.

Only clap/sing in unison if the artist specifically requests it.

If you feel the need to play air guitar/drums, keep your range of motion in mind.

The same thing goes for dancing.

Avoid cropdusting or flatulence of any kind.

If you spill someone's drink, offer to replace it.

If you are tall, offer to stand behind shorter concertgoers.

If you are short, don't make everyone else feel bad about it.

Don't be the cool guy. If you're going to stand with your arms crossed for the entire show, do it off to the side.

General Rules to Observe While Having Fun at a Bar.

Refrain from starting a wave.

Keep all inflatable objects at home.

Pace yourself. A proper night out is a marathon, not a sprint.

Tip your bartender. If you are unsure if tipping is customary, ask another patron.

Never shout or gesture wildly to get a bartender's attention.

For the love of God, don't reach *over* the bar.

Read your surroundings, then order appropriately—you should know if this is the kind of place that makes a skinny margarita.

The same logic applies when playing songs on the jukebox.

HAVE YOUR ORDER READY WHEN YOU APPROACH THE BAR.

If someone was at the bar before you, let them order first.

If you are considering buying a drink for a female patron, ask first.

If she accepts, don't assume the drink guarantees you anything more than conversation.

Help yourself to the peanuts—they're free!

Actually, *don't* eat the peanuts, they've got fecal matter on them.

If there's a dance floor, use it. If there isn't, there's probably a reason why.

If it's a karaoke bar, don't sing more than three times over the course of a night.

And don't sing any fucking show tunes. No one cares you were in drama club.

Don't cut in line while waiting for the bathroom.

Don't strike up a conversation with girls waiting to use the bathroom.

Don't use the opposite gender's bathroom, even if it's empty.

Only urinate in appropriate receptacles.

Make sure your fake I.D. is on point.

Don't fight the bouncer.

Know when it's time to make an exit.

Don't step on people's toes—figuratively *or* literally.

Don't be the loudest person in the bar.

Dress appropriately.

If you want to watch a game, *ask* the bartender to change the TV. Don't demand it.

Never move a drink if it has a napkin on top of it.

Avoid any drink served via ice luge.

Pay for a round when it's your turn.

Don't bum a smoke from the same person twice.

General Rules to Observe While Having Fun at a Club.

Refrain from starting a wave.

Keep all inflatable objects at home.

Don't show up with only guys—you won't get in. Aim for a 5:2 guy-to-girl ratio.

Don't chat up the door guy. He hates you.

Don't grind on random girls.

Flirt effectively. Don't strike up a conversation on the dance floor.

If a girl turns you down, LEAVE HER ALONE.

Go easy on the cologne—remember: a splash, not a tumbler.

Mind the dress code.

Don't pay for bottle service. Have your friends pay for it instead.

The VIP section is never worth it.

Do drugs...but, like, *fun* drugs.

Avoid purchasing drugs *inside* the club.

Always knock before entering a bathroom stall. Trust us.

Always tip the bathroom attendant—he's definitely earned it.

Sometimes it's a good idea to drink water.

Never ask the DJ to play a song.

In fact, never congregate around the DJ booth unless invited.

Avoid hitting on the girl selling shots. She hates you.

Don't be a wallflower.

If attending a gentlemen's club: Put your phone away, don't get suckered into visiting the champagne room, tip appropriately and *never* touch the dancers.

Just accept getting kicked out. You probably deserve it.

General Rules to Observe While Having Fun at a Festival.

Feel free to start a wave.

Inflatable objects are OK, so long as they are not sex dolls.

Banners/flags are also acceptable, and double as a homing beacon for your friends.

Plan ahead for inclement weather.

But leave the umbrella at home; ponchos exist for this exact scenario.

Dress appropriately. That probably doesn't mean wearing an Indian headdress.

Always wear shoes.

Pace yourself. A festival is a sprint, not a marathon.

Be drunk...but, like, *fun* drunk.

Do drugs...but, like, *fun* drugs.

Avoid taking drugs given to you by strangers.

Avoid purchasing drugs inside the festival.

If you must vomit, do it in an out-of-the-way location.

The floppy flask is your friend.

Don't complain about the price of beer—this isn't a bar.

Don't complain about the price of food—this isn't a restaurant.

Note set times and plan accordingly.

If you must dash across the field to see a band, be courteous to your fellow festivalgoers.

Accept that everyone has the same shitty view—that's why they put giant screens on either side of the stage.

Thinking of lifting your girlfriend up on your shoulders? Go for it! A festival is about the only scenario in which this is acceptable.

If you have spread a blanket on the ground, don't get mad when someone steps on it.

If you are camping out, make friends and share your stuff.

Know the location of at least one medical tent.

Invest in wet wipes. Trust us.

When using a portable toilet, remember that someone *else* will use it after you. And chances are, that someone will be a girl.

Humor any activists attempting to collect signatures.

Shun anyone else trying to sign you up for something.

If attending Coachella, do not feed the celebrities.

Wear your wristbands as badges of honor.

Admit to yourself that if you sprung for the VIP ticket package, you are not actually attending the festival.

General Rules to Observe While Having Fun Playing Video Games.

Don't be a brand loyalist. Microsoft, Nintendo and Sony don't give a shit about you.

Also, are you playing on a PC? Cool, no one cares.

Don't rage-quit.

Don't troll.

Don't grief.

Don't make memes. We don't need to know you took an arrow to the knee.

Resist the urge to shoot a Let's Play series.

Refrain from cursing at adolescents during online play. We realize this is difficult.

Refrain from being a creep. We realize this is *also* difficult.

Refrain from being a racist. This *shouldn't* be difficult.

Don't use hacks in multiplayer.

Don't join a clan unless you absolutely *need* to.

Only join a raiding party if you are able to carry your weight.

Avoid confusing video-game skills with *actual* skills.

Remember, being an elite gamer is not always something to be proud of.

When choosing a gamertag, avoid Xs, excessive spacing, epithets, unnecessary capitalization or the numbers 420 and 69.

There's no need to be an achievement hoarder.

Or a farmer—play the game the way it was intended to be played.

If you are spending actual money on in-game microtransactions, perhaps it's time to reconsider things.

If playing an FPS, avoid camping in one location to rack up kills.

And *really* avoid camping out next to a spawn point. Spawn killers suck.

DLC is cool, but, like, not *that* cool.

If armed with a sniper rifle, don't quick scope—aim like God intended.

Go outside every once in a while. And not to play on a handheld.

General Rules to Observe While Having Fun at the Beach.

Refrain from starting a wave. The ocean does that for you.

Inflatable objects are OK, so long as they are not sex dolls.

Always remove your shirt—it's weirder if you *don't*.

Always wear sunscreen. In fact, it's probably time to reapply.

Avoid wearing sandals with socks.

Don't smoke cigs on the beach.

Drink responsibly.

Keep the glass bottles at home.

Only toss/kick balls around in open areas.

Leave two-thirds of all beach toys in the car. You won't use them.

Don't flip out if you step on something weird in the ocean. Have some self-respect.

Don't plop your stuff down right next to other people if there is plenty of open space.

But if you set up a massive umbrella, don't get mad if someone encroaches on your space.

Respect the chafing powers of sand.

Refrain from destroying sandcastles when children are present.

Give surfers their space.

Don't read too much into a bikini.

Don't feed the seagulls.

Don't litter.

It's OK to pee in the ocean.

It's *not* OK to poop in the ocean.

If fishing, prepare a witty retort to the question "Catch anything yet?" ahead of time.

Tossing seaweed on an unsuspecting friend is OK, tossing a jellyfish on them *isn't*.

Put your phone away.

But if you *must* take pictures, don't be a creep.

Play music at appropriate levels.

Be mindful of your fellow beachgoers when shaking sand out of your towel.

If exercising on the beach, stop immediately.

General Rules to Observe While Having Fun at Work.

Share your secret with the rest of us, because work sucks.

General Rules to Observe While Having Fun at a BBQ.

Refrain from starting a wave.

Keep all inflatable objects at home.

Never show up empty-handed—when in doubt, bring beer.

Though you should never underestimate the appeal of a well-prepared side dish, either.

Make sure to document any dietary restrictions ahead of time, then thrown the list away. This is a fucking BBQ.

Respect the Grillmaster's authority at all times.

If *you* are the Grillmaster, establish a clear chain of command—Deputy Grillmaster, Toppings Supervisor, etc.—in the event you need to grab a beer or use the bathroom.

Never flip steaks, fish or chops more than once while cooking.

Always let steaks, fish or chops rest for five minutes before serving.

Flip burgers, sausages or chicken as many times as you desire.

There is no marinade too bold.

Drink responsibly if you are grilling. If not, fuck it—get *schwasted*.

If you are vegetarian/vegan, accept the fact your veggie burger will come into contact with meat. The grill is a communal space.

Don't get mad if your burger is over/undercooked—this isn't a restaurant.

Don't get mad if you end up with a turkey burger, even if those things *are* terrible.

Don't get mad if you end up with a cheeseburger, unless you are lactose-intolerant.

Actually, even if you *are* lactose-intolerant, just pick the cheese off.

Remember: Federal law requires all male partygoers spend a minimum of five minutes standing in a loose semicircle around the grill.

Dress appropriately—if you're looking for an opportunity to wear a novelty apron, this is it.

General Rules to Observe While Having Fun at a Wedding.

Refrain from starting a wave *during* the ceremony.

Keep all inflatable objects at home.

Drink responsibly if you are the bride/groom.

Drink semi-responsibly if you are a bridesmaid/groomsman.

Drink irresponsibly if you are a guest. And make sure to give a speech.

If you feel yourself becoming overly emotional, don't be ashamed—but *do* stop drinking immediately.

Refrain from purchasing or using drugs at the wedding.

Avoid taking bets on how long the marriage will last (but three years is a good over/under).

Pay attention during any toasts and/or ceremonial dances.

Remember: There's nothing better than partying in a suit.

When renting a tuxedo, *always* pay extra for the Accidental Damage Waiver. Trust us.

Once the wedding ceremony is complete, it is perfectly acceptable to remove your tie and wear it around your head.

Learn the Electric Slide/Cupid Shuffle/Cha-Cha Slide ahead of time.

Don't shrink from the spotlight—when encircled on the dancefloor, *embrace* it.

If R. Kelly's "Step in the Name of Love (Remix)" is played, you are at a black wedding, and it's going to be amazing.

Always help out during the *Horah*.

If attending an Indian wedding, remember: It's a marathon, not a sprint.

Feel free to complain loudly if there's a cash bar.

If there's an open bar, cut down on long wait times by ordering doubles.

Tip bartenders generously, regardless of bar status. Trust us.

Don't fight. It's a goddamn wedding.

Never show up looking to get laid; you'll be amazed how much this helps you actually *get* laid.

Feel free to use any children in attendance as props, especially if it will help you score points with the bridesmaids.

When singling out a bridesmaid to take a run at, be realistic.

Know when to fold 'em: If you have struck out with 40% of the bridesmaids, it's time to cut your losses.

Always thank the parents of *both* the bride and groom. There's a pretty good chance they paid for all this.

If attending a reception with a prime-rib carving station, congrats: You are at a classy affair.

If attending a reception in a barn, and neither the bride or groom are farmers, congrats: You are at the whitest thing imaginable.

Don't obsess over table selection. You should only be sitting down to eat and/or catch your breath.

The photo booth isn't *just* for taking photos.

Dress appropriately—shorts are only barely acceptable at beach weddings.

General Rules to Observe While Having Fun at Karaoke.

Don't let a lack of talent keep you from singing—that's *literally* the point of karaoke.

If you can sing, limit yourself to one spotlight-grabbing performance. Anything more is excessive—and annoying.

Said spotlight-grabbing performance cannot, under any circumstances, be a show tune.

Ask yourself, "Am I an artist or an entertainer?" Entertainers perform for the crowd—artists perform for *themselves*. Choose songs accordingly.

Never sing more than two songs in a row.

Never start a duet with someone without their permission.

Never get *sexy* during a performance.

Never bail on a performance mid-song.

Never choose a song longer than seven minutes.

For reference, "Don't Stop Believin'" is only 4:11, and "Bohemian Rhapsody" runs 5:55.

Don't just stand there—any lengthy instrumental breakdown or smokin' hot guitar solo should be acted out.

Keep vocal limitations in mind; know your range before grabbing a microphone.

However, if you fail, fail *spectacularly*.

When in doubt, get a private room.

It's always a good idea to sneak in a bit of booze. You'll never regret it.

Be drunk...but, like, *fun* drunk.

Don't stand on the furniture—in most karaoke spots, this is the only rule.

Be attentive and supportive while others are performing.

Avoid using the n-word, no matter *what* the lyrics are.

WHEN DOES THE FUN START?

"You should sleep late, man. It's much easier on your constitution."
—Bill Murray

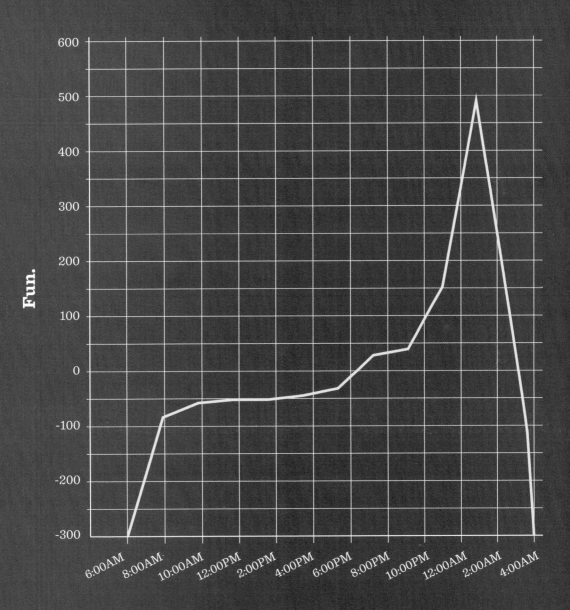

Things That Seem Fun Until *You* Actually *Do* Them

Adulthood.

Binge drinking.

Being single.

Fame.

Sleeping in the top bunk.

Smoking.

Staying up all night.

CrossFit.

Drive-in movies.

Parades.

Being a lifeguard.

Deep-sea fishing.

Ice fishing.

Going to a strip club.

Driving cross-country.

Being in the VIP section.

Methamphetamines.

Mixed Martial Arts.

Attending any All-Star Game.

Sex tapes.

Threesomes.

Sending nudes.

Sex on the beach.

Going to the beach.

Tattoos.

Bottle service.

Hot air balloons.

Marathons.

Marriage.

Crafting.

Virtual reality.

Escape rooms.

Improv classes.

Open-mic nights.

Flying first class.

Owning a trampoline.

Pinball.

Getting your shoes shined.

Theme parks.

Fairs.

Tightrope walking.

Riding in a limousine.

Cruises.

Backpacking.

Sleeping on a futon.

Garage sales.

Scooters.

Surfing.

Boogie Boarding.

Water balloon fights.

Owning a pet.

High dives.

Golf.

Shaving.

Beer festivals.

Owning a pool.

Playing pool.

Waterslides.

Slip 'N Slides.

Foam parties.

Renting a paddleboat.

Being a police officer.

Reading.

Pub quizzes.

Camping.

Eating at a fancy restaurant.

Brunch.

Having children.

Cooking.

Designing video games.

Having a credit card.

Traveling for work.

Binge-watching anything.

New Year's Eve.

Being president.

Playing in a band.

Writing a novel.

Living in a tiny house.

Craft-brewing.

Apple picking.

Pumpkin patches.

Haunted houses.

Hayrides.

Raising chickens.

Writing a clever tweet.

Having a "theater room" in your house.

Owning a popcorn machine.

Russian roulette.

Being Paul Walker.

Yoga.

Writing a list of things that seem fun until you actually do them.

Empathy.

WORTH THE WAIT?

Maximum time you should wait in line (in minutes)

Category	Minutes
Any club	~20
ATM	~10
Bathroom	~10
Booth at Dinner	~5
Coffee	~7
Concert	~45
Concessions	~15
Cupcake You Saw on Instagram	~5
Food Truck	~15
Food Truck (After the Bar)	~30
Hamilton Tickets	~52
Movie	~15
Movie (New *Star Wars*)	~60
New iPhone	Unlimited
New Video Game	~10
Photobooth	~12
Putting in a Song at Karaoke	~17
Pop-Up Shop	~10
Restaurant	~36
Restaurant Serving "Fusion Street Food"	~5
Roller Coaster	~48
Sneakers	~8
Voting	Unlimited

Is This Funny?

There's an old saying—"Comedy is tragedy plus time." But we know you're busy, so rather than waiting around to figure out what's funny, we've done the work for you!

SCENARIO	IS THIS FUNNY?
Your friend has just been kicked in the nuts.	Without a doubt. Laughing at the misfortune of others is a cornerstone of comedy.
Your friend has just suffered a grievous injury.	Depends. Will he recover? If so, yes. If not... maybe?
Your friend has just been dumped.	Publically? No. Privately? Yes—especially if you hated his girlfriend.
You have just witnessed an elaborate slip-and-fall accident.	Yes—as a general rule, the more elaborate, the funnier.
Your coworker has just mistakenly hit "Reply All" on an email.	What did he/she send? If it's something bad about the boss, yes.
Your coworker has just been fired.	No, unless he/she cries.
You have just suffered a grave injury or injustice.	No. Remember, we only laugh at the misfortune of others. Anyone deriving pleasure from your pain is not your friend.
Loud flatulence.	Absolutely.
Loud flatulence in an enclosed space.	No, but laughing will probably keep you from breathing it in.

SCENARIO	IS THIS FUNNY?
Any other overt bodily function.	Yes, unless it's loud breathing. That's just annoying.
Erectile dysfunction.	Only to God, the cruelest comedian of all.
Natural disaster.	Probably not. Give it a decade or so.
Terrorist attack.	See previous answer.
Disaster that doubles as a handy metaphor for man's hubris.	Yes. The sinking of the *Titanic*? Hilarious.
Racism.	No...unless it's at the expense of white men. They have it coming.
Air show mishap.	Were you able to make a pun ("More like the Blew-Up Angels, right?") in the moment? If so, yes. If not, no.
Machinery mishap.	Did the affected lose a funny body part? If yes, then absolutely.
An overweight person has just collapsed a bench.	Publically? No. Privately? Yes. This is Manna from Comedy Heaven.
An overweight person has just collapsed.	Are they dead? Then, no.
You are attending a funeral.	No.
You are attending a clown funeral.	Definitely.
A homophobic, misogynistic, orange-hued reality TV businessman/xenophobe has just been elected President of the United States thanks to an outdated Constitutional mechanism.	Yes. Laughing is the only way to prevent yourself from crying.

Is This Art?

Art can be inspiring, challenging, thought-provoking—and fun to laugh at. But to be in on the joke, you need to be able to tell *actual* art from everyday garbage. Normally, you'd need a fancy degree to do that, but why waste all that time and money when you could just read this?

SCENARIO	IS THIS ART?
A porcelain urinal signed by "R. Mutt."	Yes, it's called "Fountain," created in 1917 by conceptual artist Marcel Duchamp. "R. Mutt" was the pseudonym of a collaborator who sent Duchamp the urinal.
An 18-karat gold toilet.	Yep. It's called "America," created in 2016 by Italian satirical sculptor Maurizio Cattelan and exhibited at the Guggenheim Museum in New York—and, yes, you can actually use it.
A 24-karat gold toilet.	No, but up until a few years ago, it was on display at the Hang Fung Gold Technology showroom in Hong Kong—and, no, you couldn't use it.
A five-foot-long piece of cake made out of foam rubber and cardboard boxes.	Yes, it's called "Floor Cake," created in 1962 by sculptor Claes Oldenburg and inspired by both the burgeoning "Pop Art" movement and Duchamp's "Readymade" works.
A 12,000-pound burrito made out of a single flour tortilla.	No, but according to *Guinness World Records*, it was the world's biggest burrito, created in 2010 by 3,000 volunteers in La Paz, Baja California Sur, Mexico.

SCENARIO	IS THIS ART?
An unmade bed surrounded by trash.	Yes, it's called "My Bed," created in 1998 by English artist Tracey Emin. It was even nominated for the Turner Prize, the award presented annually to a British visual artist.
An empty room.	No. Just kidding—yes. It's called "Concerto in Black and Blue," created in 2002 by American artist David Hammons. Guests were given flashlights and allowed to wander a darkened gallery. There was also Japanese *koto* music.
An empty room in which the lights are periodically turned on and off.	Yes! It's called "Work No. 227: The Lights Going On and Off," created in 2000 by British artist Martin Creed. This one actually *won* the Turner Prize.
A condom filled with raw meat.	No, but it *is* a way to cook meat in water at a low boil, similar to a *sous vide* bag—but way more gross.
A condom filled with potatoes and onions.	It sure was. It was called "Spring Is on Its Way," an installation work created by Belgian multidisciplinary artist Jan Fabre in 2008.
A crumpled-up pack of Newports.	Yes! It's part of photographer Matthew Yake's 2012 series "237 Pieces of Trash Around Bleachers." So while it technically *is* garbage... it's also art.
Plastic bags.	Also yes. Thousands of them were used by Cameroonian artist Pascale Marthine Tayou in 2012 to create a 32-foot-tall beehive called, appropriately enough, "Plastic Bags."
A coffee table littered with empty beer bottles, cigarette butts and nitrous cartridges.	No, this is the remnants of your Saturday night.

SCENARIO	IS THIS ART?
A cabinet filled with $20, $50 and $100 bills.	No. But a handyman in Colorado did discover $1,000 in those bills hidden behind a medicine cabinet while remodeling a client's house in 2015. He didn't keep it, BTW.
A cabinet filled with cigarettes.	Yes. It's called "The Abyss," created by British artist Damien Hirst in 2008. That same year, it was sold at auction for £1.8 million.
Cate Blanchett sleeping inside a box.	No, but Tilda Swinton sleeping inside a box was—the actress took random naps inside glass boxes at New York's MoMA as part of her performance piece "The Maybe."

In short, **not all art is trash—but in the hands of an artist, all trash *can* be art**. The funny thing is, pretty much anyone can be an artist; you don't even need to know the difference between postmodernism and remodernism.

By 21st-century standards, an artist is basically anyone who expresses themselves through a medium...and that medium is entirely up to you. Create a collage of used condoms, symbolically put your phone in a paper shredder, tear up this book and glue it to your face— congrats, you're an artist. You might not make money, but then again, *you might* (Damien Hirst, the dude who put all those cigarettes in a cabinet, has a net worth of £270 million!) though we'd argue that's not really the point. Art isn't supposed to make you rich, it's supposed to make you think, feel, ponder and pose questions.

Then again, if you can convince people to pay millions of dollars for your piles of garbage, we suppose that's art, too. You're not laughing now, are you?

Is Reading Fun?

No.

OVERRATED/UNDERRATED RAP

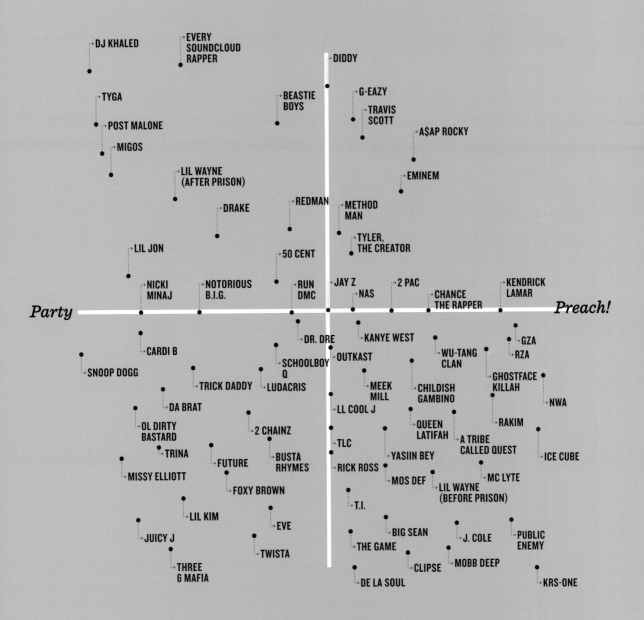

Overrated

DJ KHALED

EVERY SOUNDCLOUD RAPPER

DIDDY

TYGA

BEASTIE BOYS

G-EAZY

TRAVIS SCOTT

A$AP ROCKY

POST MALONE

MIGOS

LIL WAYNE (AFTER PRISON)

EMINEM

DRAKE

REDMAN

METHOD MAN

LIL JON

TYLER, THE CREATOR

50 CENT

Party

NICKI MINAJ

NOTORIOUS B.I.G.

RUN DMC

JAY Z

2 PAC

KENDRICK LAMAR

NAS

CHANCE THE RAPPER

Preach!

DR. DRE

KANYE WEST

GZA

CARDI B

SCHOOLBOY Q

OUTKAST

WU-TANG CLAN

RZA

SNOOP DOGG

GHOSTFACE KILLAH

TRICK DADDY

LUDACRIS

MEEK MILL

CHILDISH GAMBINO

NWA

DA BRAT

LL COOL J

RAKIM

OL DIRTY BASTARD

2 CHAINZ

QUEEN LATIFAH

A TRIBE CALLED QUEST

TRINA

TLC

YASIIN BEY

ICE CUBE

FUTURE

BUSTA RHYMES

RICK ROSS

MOS DEF

MC LYTE

MISSY ELLIOTT

LIL WAYNE (BEFORE PRISON)

FOXY BROWN

T.I.

LIL KIM

EVE

BIG SEAN

J. COLE

PUBLIC ENEMY

JUICY J

TWISTA

THE GAME

MOBB DEEP

THREE 6 MAFIA

CLIPSE

KRS-ONE

DE LA SOUL

Underrated

OVERRATED/UNDERRATED ROCK

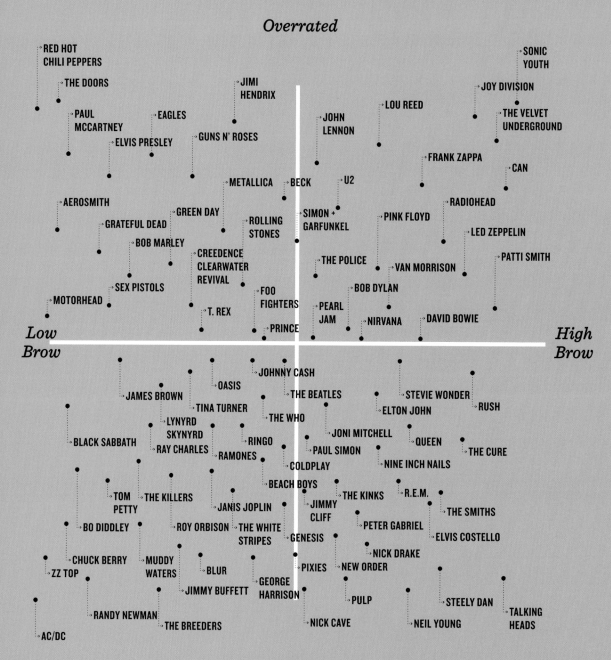

Overrated

RED HOT CHILI PEPPERS

SONIC YOUTH

THE DOORS

JOY DIVISION

JIMI HENDRIX

LOU REED

THE VELVET UNDERGROUND

PAUL MCCARTNEY

EAGLES

JOHN LENNON

ELVIS PRESLEY

GUNS N' ROSES

FRANK ZAPPA

CAN

METALLICA

BECK

U2

AEROSMITH

RADIOHEAD

GREEN DAY

SIMON + GARFUNKEL

PINK FLOYD

GRATEFUL DEAD

ROLLING STONES

LED ZEPPELIN

BOB MARLEY

CREEDENCE CLEARWATER REVIVAL

THE POLICE

VAN MORRISON

PATTI SMITH

SEX PISTOLS

BOB DYLAN

MOTORHEAD

FOO FIGHTERS

Low Brow

T. REX

PEARL JAM

NIRVANA

DAVID BOWIE

High Brow

PRINCE

JOHNNY CASH

OASIS

THE BEATLES

STEVIE WONDER

RUSH

JAMES BROWN

TINA TURNER

ELTON JOHN

THE WHO

LYNYRD SKYNYRD

JONI MITCHELL

QUEEN

THE CURE

BLACK SABBATH

RAY CHARLES

RINGO

PAUL SIMON

RAMONES

NINE INCH NAILS

COLDPLAY

BEACH BOYS

TOM PETTY

THE KILLERS

THE KINKS

R.E.M.

JANIS JOPLIN

JIMMY CLIFF

THE SMITHS

BO DIDDLEY

ROY ORBISON

THE WHITE STRIPES

PETER GABRIEL

ELVIS COSTELLO

GENESIS

CHUCK BERRY

MUDDY WATERS

NICK DRAKE

ZZ TOP

BLUR

PIXIES

NEW ORDER

JIMMY BUFFETT

GEORGE HARRISON

PULP

STEELY DAN

RANDY NEWMAN

TALKING HEADS

AC/DC

THE BREEDERS

NICK CAVE

NEIL YOUNG

Underrated

OVERRATED/UNDERRATED POP

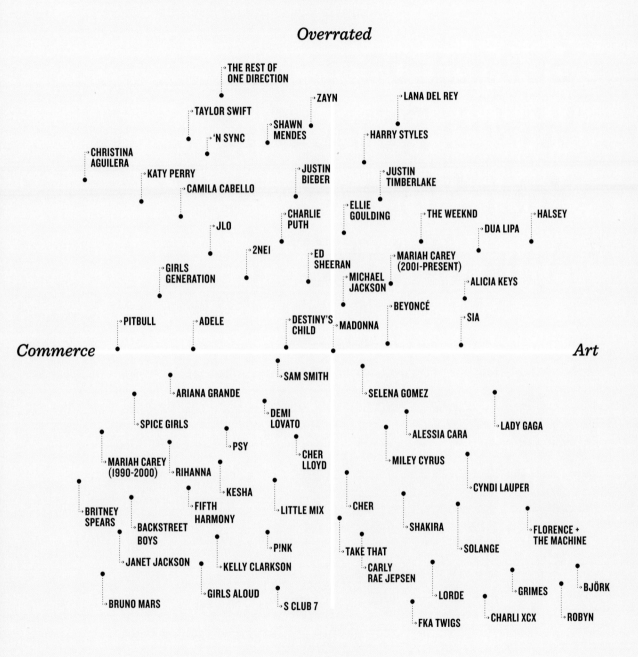

Overrated

THE REST OF ONE DIRECTION

ZAYN

LANA DEL REY

TAYLOR SWIFT

SHAWN MENDES

HARRY STYLES

'N SYNC

CHRISTINA AGUILERA

KATY PERRY

JUSTIN BIEBER

JUSTIN TIMBERLAKE

CAMILA CABELLO

ELLIE GOULDING

THE WEEKND

HALSEY

JLO

CHARLIE PUTH

DUA LIPA

2NE1

ED SHEERAN

MARIAH CAREY (2001-PRESENT)

ALICIA KEYS

GIRLS GENERATION

MICHAEL JACKSON

BEYONCÉ

SIA

Commerce

PITBULL

ADELE

DESTINY'S CHILD

MADONNA

Art

SAM SMITH

ARIANA GRANDE

SELENA GOMEZ

SPICE GIRLS

DEMI LOVATO

LADY GAGA

ALESSIA CARA

PSY

CHER LLOYD

MILEY CYRUS

MARIAH CAREY (1990-2000)

RIHANNA

CYNDI LAUPER

KESHA

FIFTH HARMONY

LITTLE MIX

CHER

BRITNEY SPEARS

SHAKIRA

FLORENCE + THE MACHINE

BACKSTREET BOYS

P!NK

SOLANGE

JANET JACKSON

KELLY CLARKSON

TAKE THAT

CARLY RAE JEPSEN

LORDE

GRIMES

BJÖRK

BRUNO MARS

GIRLS ALOUD

S CLUB 7

FKA TWIGS

CHARLI XCX

ROBYN

Underrated

Scenarios *in* Which Removing Your Shirt *Is* Appropriate

Sex.

Boxing.

Swimming.

Showering.

Strip poker.

Showing off your pecs.

Sumo wrestling.

Sleeping.

Surfing.

Tanning.

Running.

Rafting.

Partying.

Strenuous outdoor noncoital activity.

You just scored a cracker of a goal.

You are very drunk.

Challenging for the Intercontinental Championship that was unjustly stolen from you at *Hell in a Cell*.

The club is lit.

Immediately after participating in an eating contest.

Immediately after participating in a wet T-shirt contest.

Immediately after participating in a shootout, to fashion a makeshift tourniquet.

Someone plays Petey Pablo's "Raise Up."

After a long day at the office.

Tailgating.

Attending a victory parade.

¡Carnaval!

Singing karaoke.

Participating in most Olympic sports.

At a music festival.

In a mosh pit.

Your mouth has just written a check your ass can't cash.

Entering a sauna/onsen.

Using the toilet.

Riding a dirtbike.

Driving a hot car.

Doing any form of repair work.

Playing in a "shirts versus skins" pickup game.

Playing beach volleyball.

Partying on a yacht.

Body painting.

Nude modeling.

Exotic dancing.

Your shirt has already been torn beyond a reasonable hope of repair.

The temperature has crossed 80° Fahrenheit (27° Celsius).

You have switched bodies with Dwayne "The Rock" Johnson.

Scenarios *in* Which Removing Your Shirt *Is* Inappropriate

Working out at the gym.

Bowling.

Golfing.

Cooking.

Refereeing an athletic contest.

Coaching Little League.

A regulation poker game.

Meeting your girlfriend's parents for the first time.

Applying for a loan.

Interviewing for a job.

Shopping for groceries.

Shopping in general.

Couples therapy.

Church.

Accepting an award.

Any party where *Hors d'Oeuvres* are passed.

Strenuous *indoor* noncoital activity.

At any workplace-related event.

At a movie theater.

You are stranded in a desert, because you will die of exposure.

You are super-sweaty, and it might drip on someone.

You are very drunk *in public*.

Driving an economy car.

Adjudicating a disputed matter.

Establishing dominance.

Any wedding.

At a women's march.

Skydiving.

Sitting next to a total stranger.

Boarding a commercial flight.

Whenever you are wearing a vest or sportcoat.

Attending a sporting event.

At an amusement park.

Attempting to break up with her.

Attempting to win her back.

Attempting to challenge the restraining order she inevitably filed against you.

At a funeral.

Upon entering a restaurant.

Cleaning up a radioactive disaster.

Trying to make a salient point.

Presenting the findings of an exhaustive, multiyear study.

There are kids around.

Crashing at a buddy's house.

Unfortunate tattoo.

When removing the sleeves will suffice.

The temperature has fallen below 80° Fahrenheit (27° Celsius).

Almost any imaginable scenario not specifically mentioned here.

You have switched bodies with an *actual* rock, and are now entirely Feldspar.

SHOULD YOU GET A TATTOO?

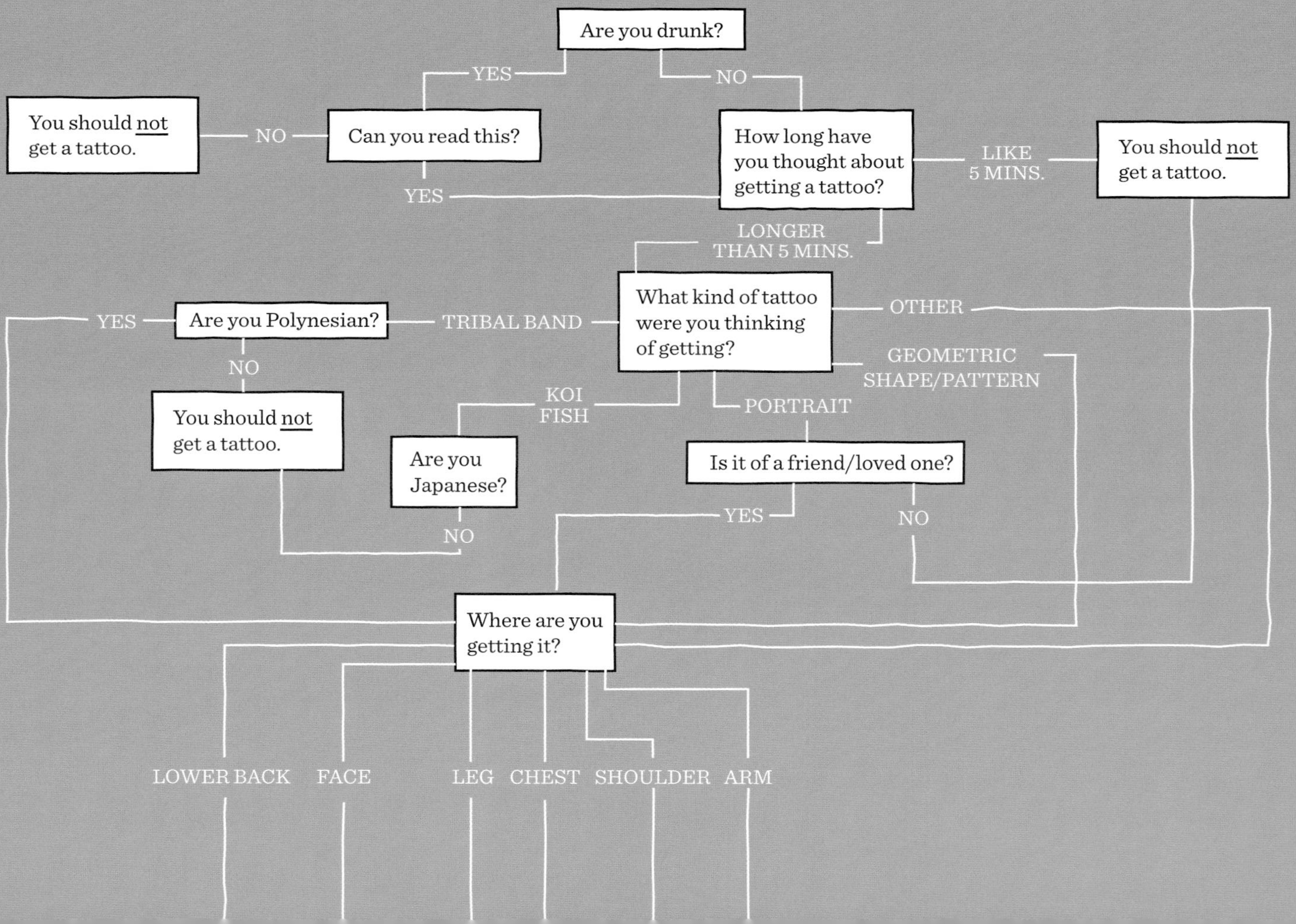

Are you drunk?
YES
NO
Can you read this?
NO
You should not get a tattoo.
YES
How long have you thought about getting a tattoo?
LIKE 5 MINS.
You should not get a tattoo.
LONGER THAN 5 MINS.
What kind of tattoo were you thinking of getting?
TRIBAL BAND
Are you Polynesian?
YES
NO
You should not get a tattoo.
KOI FISH
Are you Japanese?
NO
OTHER
GEOMETRIC SHAPE/PATTERN
PORTRAIT
Is it of a friend/loved one?
YES
NO
Where are you getting it?
LOWER BACK
FACE
LEG
CHEST
SHOULDER
ARM

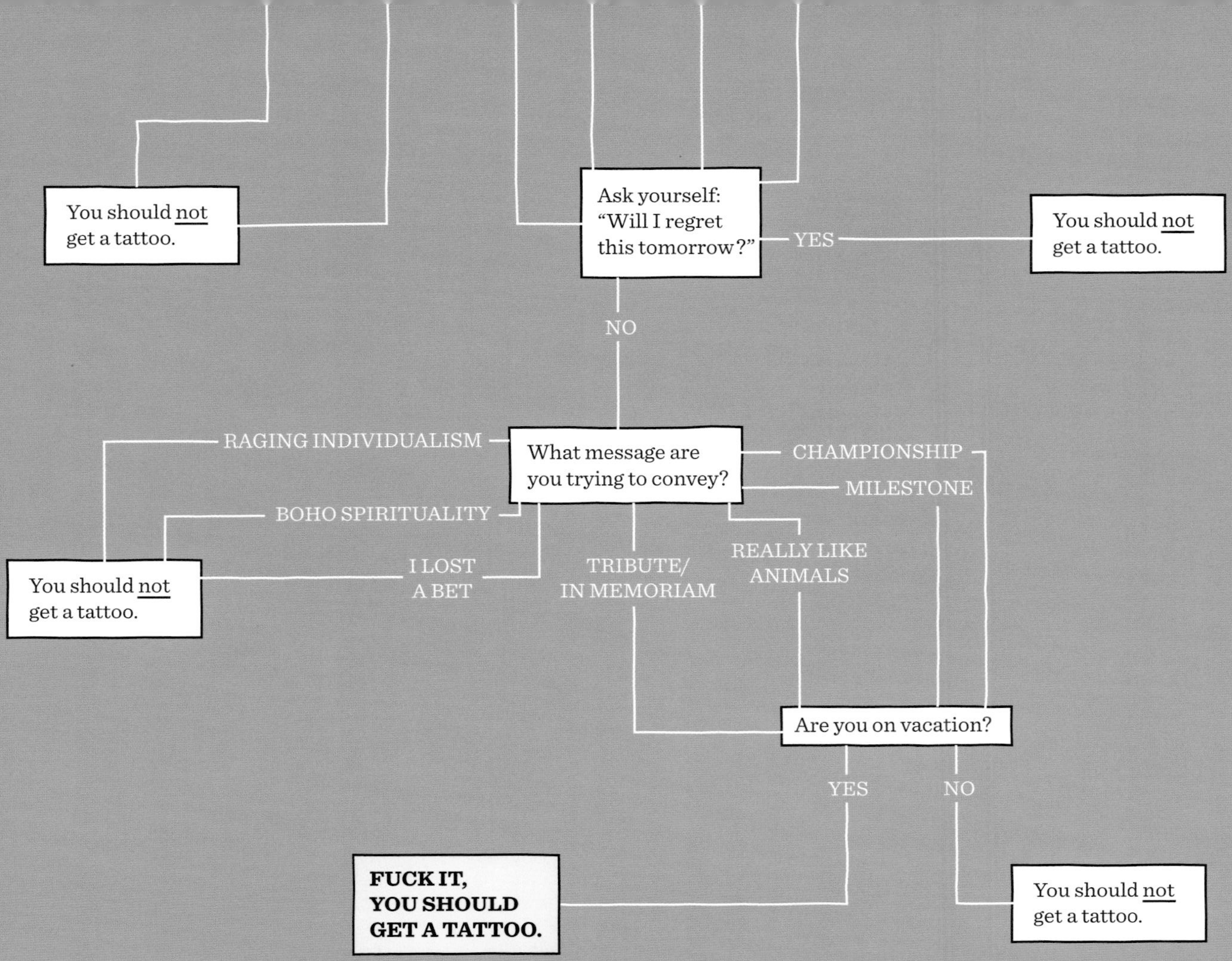
You should not get a tattoo.
Ask yourself: "Will I regret this tomorrow?"
YES
You should not get a tattoo.
NO
What message are you trying to convey?
RAGING INDIVIDUALISM
BOHO SPIRITUALITY
I LOST A BET
You should not get a tattoo.
TRIBUTE/ IN MEMORIAM
REALLY LIKE ANIMALS
MILESTONE
CHAMPIONSHIP
Are you on vacation?
YES
NO
FUCK IT, YOU SHOULD GET A TATTOO.
You should not get a tattoo.

The Five Universal Truths About Gambling

Gambling is fun, until it isn't. You can't prevent the latter from occurring (because everyone loses eventually), but you *can* prolong the former—if you follow these five bits of wagering wisdom. Who knows, they might even help you win a bit of money, too.

I. The House Always Wins, Until it Doesn't.

To the casual gambler, the old adage goes that the house always wins. This is mostly true. If one were to conduct research that measured payouts to casino gamblers over the course of decades, one would find that by overwhelming margins, the house wins—*and wins big*. So large are those margins, in fact, that the gaming industry effectively subsidizes most public schools in the United States, pays itself for capital improvements and infrastructure, is able to offer hundreds of thousands of good-paying, family-sustaining jobs and is *still* able to be amongst the most profitable industries in the world. Until the industry became oversaturated, opening a casino was tantamount to obtaining a license to print money. The only way that happens is if the house is always winning.

Nevertheless, people win. As in life, where the outcome is predetermined, there are moments along the way that give us all the illusion of free will. If you are at a racetrack and you hit a superfecta box, you will think it was some combination of luck, skill and intellect that produced that successful wager. And in a narrow sense, that is correct. But only so when one looks solely at that wager in a vacuum. In life, the house always wins and you wind up in the grave. In gambling, the house always wins and you wind up with less money.

If this sounds overly morbid or pessimistic, it isn't. For what is life if not the accumulation of those magical, individual moments where we feel the illusion of free will? The house is always going to win, but no one will ever take away the superfecta box hit from you. Both things are true.

2. Good Gamblers are Disciplined Gamblers.

The typical gambler is commonly characterized as having little self-control, acting solely on impulse, one bad streak away from flushing his or her life down the toilet for a little action. You've seen the ads. But in truth, that characterization describes a compulsive or "problem" gambler. You will find that compulsive behavior extends well beyond how or when this person gambles and permeates his or her life on myriad levels.

This behavior also necessarily makes the person a bad gambler, because the person's perspective is that gambling is principally a game of chance.

A good gambler understands that gambling is both a game of chance *and* a game of skill. A very good gambler ignores what he or she cannot control (chance) and shifts his or her focus instead to what he or she *can* control (skill). And a great gambler knows precisely how much of each element exists in the game he or she is playing, and behaves accordingly.

3. It's About the Journey, Not the Destination.

At the end of Robert Altman's 1974 movie *California Split* (one of the best movies ever made about gambling), Bill Denny (played brilliantly by George Segal) becomes unusually morose at the end of a legendary poker winning streak. It's the movie's climactic scene, and the director wisely refuses to explain why, at the height of Bill's accomplishment, he seems more depressed than he would had he lost all of his money.

This is because—as is the case with most things in life—pleasure is derived from gambling most when one focuses on the journey rather than the destination.

Ideally, the pleasure you derive from sports gambling should come *while you're watching* the games. Every first down, missed three-pointer or

botched free kick becomes even more magnified in the context of the wager(s) you have placed. But it was those individual moments along the way that made watching the game fun, not the underlying wager in and of itself.

4. Everything in Moderation.

This is a tricky one, because it's difficult to know where to draw the line—and everyone's line is different. But to paraphrase Justice Potter Stewart's famous quote about pornography, you will know your line when you see it.

At its best, gambling is a diversion. It's a distraction. It can be a fun leisurely activity used to pass the time. And let's face it, these days, most of us could use as many distractions as possible.

But gambling can also be a very powerful and very addictive drug, and one can quickly become powerless over that drug. And as is the case with all addiction, the outcomes generally aren't good and the collateral damage can be catastrophic.

It is here, again, where the good gambler is also the disciplined gambler. A friend of ours who is particularly fond of blackjack will approach every game with a betting limit in mind. He'll say, "I will play this game but will only allow myself to have $500 on the table and absolutely not one penny more. Anything over $500 goes into my pocket." And when the $500 runs out, he's done playing.

Devising and adhering to these little games is admittedly not easy, but it is essential if one is to truly enjoy gambling.

5. Set Low Expectations.

There is nothing more disheartening than being convinced beyond a reasonable doubt that you know the outcome of a bet, only to have it go the other way. This phenomenon is especially common among sports gamblers.

Going into wagers with this mind-set is a recipe for disaster, because, let's face it, none of us are professional bookmakers. If you fancy yourself a gambling savant in the same league as Sam "Ace" Rothstein, we promise you, you will not enjoy placing wagers.

Why? Because people like Sam Rothstein do exist, but they work for casinos (see gambling truth #1).

Your approach and mind-set, therefore, should be to assume you will lose the bet before you place it. This helps not only with expectation management, but it will also increase the likelihood that you'll win the bet, or at the very least place the wager with a level head.

Because if you have taken the expectation of winning off the table, you're only thinking about the wager in the most rational, clear-headed terms.

25 Unexpected Ways *to* Have Fun After *the* Apocalypse

Once most of the world has been Raptured, you'll probably be pretty bored without the Internet (unless you're Mark Zuckerberg, good luck getting *that* thing up and running again). So here's a handy list of activities that will help pass the time:

1. Try **drawing** a perfect circle (it's harder than you think!).

2. **Paint** your initials over valuable works of art. When future civilizations discover our museums, you can get all the credit!

3. **Gather** skulls to kick around, or build a cool-ass throne.

4. **Masturbate**.

5. **Read** all the books you collected in hopes that you'd read them eventually but really used as props to convince people that you're an intellectual.

6. **Check** your credit score, it won't affect it!

7. **Customize** some old T-shirts with puffy paint.

8. **Try** and beat yourself at chess (no cheating).

9. **Volunteer** (technically, everything you do is volunteering for yourself—look at how selfish/selfless you are!).

10. **Wear** designer suits and do parkour through the city streets.

11. **Create** a quirky scavenger hunt. You'll always win!

12. **Masturbate.**

13. **Read** the CliffsNotes versions of all the books you collected in hopes that you'd read

them eventually, because reading fucking
sucks.

14. **Fortify** your DIY fortress. You're gonna
need it when the marauding hordes come for
you.

15. **Release** all the wild animals from the
zoo—you're the great Liberator of the Animal
Kingdom!

16. **Learn** to paint—try using natural objects
such as berries and ochre clays.

17. **Use the gym** without having to worry
about crowds. Just because the world ended
doesn't mean you can skip leg day!

18. Finally **catch up** on *Stranger Things*.

19. **Hunt** down all the wild animals you released
from the zoo—you're the great Destroyer of
the Animal Kingdom!

20. **Orchestrate** a one-man flash mob in a food
court.

21. **Organize** a themed potluck dinner
(for one).

22. **Master** a Rubik's Cube.

23. **Dig** your own grave and lie in it.

24. **Yell** at God.

25. **Masturbate.**

A HANDY GLOSSARY OF TERMS

Alcohol—Fuel for fun. Anyone who says you don't need alcohol to have a good time is lying.

Amusement Park—Commercially operated park featuring rides and activities designed for fun; is usually exorbitantly expensive, and is always staffed by unqualified teens—but where else can you have funnel cakes?

Bar—Venue where alcohol is served and bad decisions are made.

BBQ—Informal gathering where food is grilled over charcoal or open flame. A good excuse to whip up your famous five-layer dip—and an even better excuse to get really drunk.

Brunch—Leisurely late-morning meal that combines breakfast with lunch. Essentially why the concept of "bottomless mimosas" was invented. By far the most fun you can have eating.

Club—Venue with adequate space to dance to aggressively loud music and pay twice as much for drinks.

Comedy—Humorous entertainment, created by insufferable people.

Comedian—An insufferable person.

Cruise—Catered sea voyage attended exclusively by the overfed, the newlywed and the nearly dead.

Cruising—The act of driving around for social purposes, or a wildly offensive 1980 movie starring Al Pacino as an undercover police officer who patrols gay S&M clubs.

Dancing—The act of moving your body rhythmically, usually to music. Is often more fun if you don't possess an ounce of actual rhythm.

Day-Drinking—The act of consuming alcohol during daylight hours. Almost always leads to a good time, and definitely always leads to a hangover.

Death—Life's greatest joke.

Deep-Sea Fishing—Open-ocean drinking masquerading as a chartered fishing expedition.

DJ—Glorified button-masher who is paid to play music at a club, party or festival. Will never take requests.

Dinner Party—A structured, sit-down meal in which wine is consumed and politics is briefly discussed. Occasionally followed by board games and/or charades. Exactly as much fun as it sounds.

Drinking Game—Activity centered around the act of consuming alcohol. Always a good idea.

Drugs—Lots of fun, especially if you like grinding your teeth and staying up all night. Not as much fun the following morning. Use in moderation.

Exercise—Physical activity that is done to become stronger and healthier; apparently, this is considered fun by some people.

Exotic Dancer—A polite term for "stripper," only to be used in the presence of strippers.

Festival—A days-long drug binge periodically interrupted by musical performances.

Gambling—The act of betting on an uncertain outcome. Fun... until it isn't.

Gaming—Playing video games. Super fun, and an easy way to make friends, so long as you're not a racist or a troll (or, sadly, a woman).

Garden Party—Something rich people do for fun. We have never been invited to one.

God—Omnipotent being with a perverse sense of humor, as evidenced by life.

Golf—Frustrating pseudo-sport in which a small, dimpled ball is repeatedly and futilely struck with a metal club. Driving a cart is fun, though.

Hangover—Your penance for having too much fun.

Happy Hour—Period of time at a bar or club during which drinks are served at a reduced price. Your best friend.

Holiday—What people outside the U.S. call "a vacation." Not to be confused with "the Holidays," a period of time from November to January in which you gather with friends and family, and are reminded why you can only be around these people once a year.

House Party—A loosely organized get-together at a residence, in which people inexplicably gather in the kitchen. A lot of fun until the police inevitably show up.

Housewarming—Essentially a House Party, only significantly less fun—and with way more scented candles. Refrain from asking your college buddy, "What the fuck happened to you?!?" as he extols the virtues of his en-suite master bathroom.

Ibiza—Mediterranean island where Europeans go to wear sarongs and engage in group sex. Pronounced "I-beeth-a" if you are an asshole.

Joke—Anecdote with a climactic humorous twist. Don't tell one if you're drunk.

Karaoke—Activity in which amateur singers butcher popular songs. Japanese for "empty orchestra." Goes great with alcohol. Never not fun.

Keg—Barrel-shaped container of alcohol, usually made of aluminum or steel. Always chip in for the next one.

Las Vegas—Neon-lit Sodom and Gomorrah located in Nevada. Only fun for a maximum of 72 hours.

Marijuana—Dried leaves and flowering tops of hemp plants that yield THC and are smoked in order to watch 43 consecutive hours of *The Great British Bake Off* on Netflix. Lots of fun.

Nature—The external world. Basically an endless source of fun, provided you put your fucking phone down every once in a while.

Orgy—A sexual encounter involving many people and, presumably, robes. We have never been invited to one.

Partying—Less an act of having fun with a group of people and more a state of mind. To wit, when you're partying, you know it.

Penis—The male sex organ. Is actually pretty funny if you think about it.

Pizza—The most fun food of all.

Professional Wrestling—
Scripted fights between grown men in their underwear. Despite that, is incredibly fun to watch.

Rapping—The act of delivering rhythmic (and often rhyming) lyrics to music. Is always fun, except when your friend makes you come watch his set at an open-mic night.

Reading—Never fun. Sorry.

Roller Coaster—Elevated railway constructed with sharp curves and steep inclines on which cars roll. Often operated by unqualified teenagers. Fun, especially if you like vomiting and subsequent visits to the chiropractor.

Running—Never fun.

Sex Tape—The act of filming consensual sex. Fun, though there is a 100% chance you will regret making one at some point in the future.

Spring Break—A vacation from school in the U.S., usually lasting one week. Also a vacation from sobriety and sound judgment.

Sports—Physical activity engaged in for competition or leisure. Way more fun than exercising. A good reminder of the ravages of time.

Strip Club—A nightclub featuring performances by exotic dancers. Fun, unless you're sober—then it's just depressing.

Threesome—A sexual encounter involving three people. Never as much fun as you initially envisioned.

Weekend—A period of unbridled partying that technically encompasses Saturday and Sunday, but everyone knows the weekend actually starts on Thursday.

VIP—Cordoned-off section of a club or bar reserved for "Very Important People," which essentially means anyone dumb enough to spend $1,000 just to drink from oversized bottles with sparklers sticking out of the top.

Work—The opposite of fun.

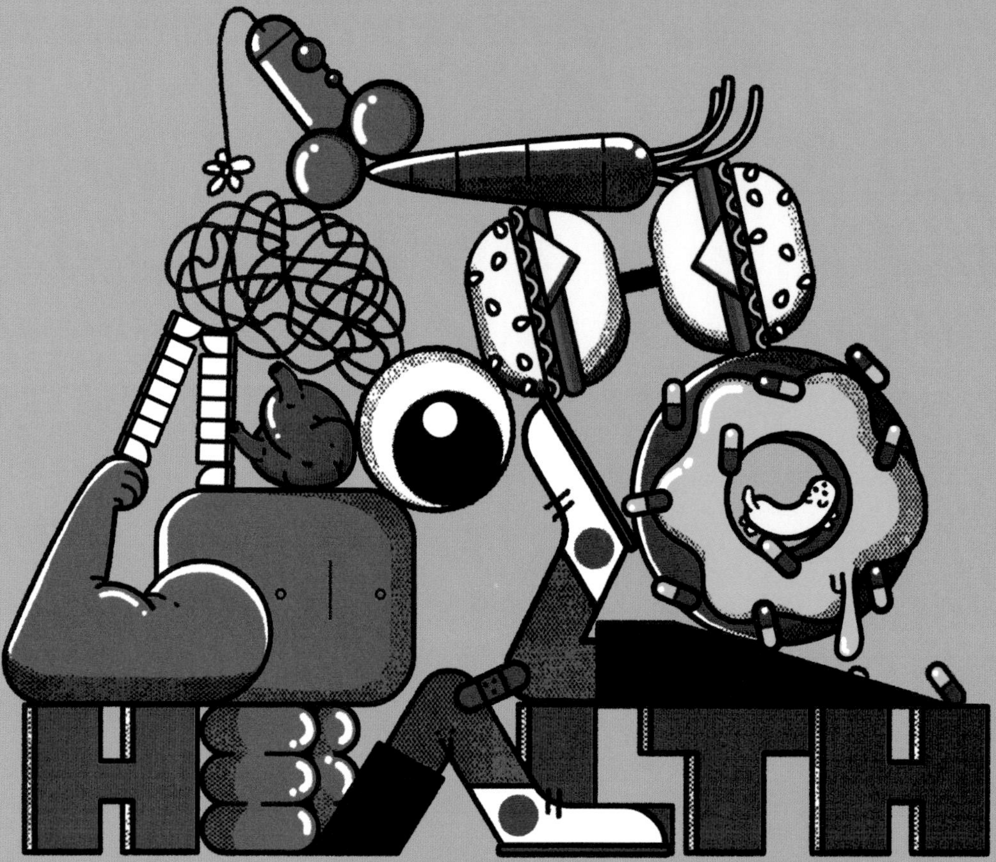
HEALTH

We are not doctors. We are not physical therapists. We are not psychiatrists or psychologists—though we wish we had the former's ability to prescribe drugs (and the latter's office space). We are not dieticians or anesthesiologists or technicians of any specialization. We do not take most forms of insurance, and we are not qualified to offer you any medical advice, as we do not possess a medical degree of any kind (then again, neither do chiropractors).

Despite all that, we feel comfortable saying that your health is really fucking important.

And not just the parts that can be objectively measured in percentages or pounds, like your body mass index or your max bench press. There's a pretty good chance you already know why those are important; if you don't, feel free to ask any dude who brings an oversized protein shake to the gym—we're sure he'll have plenty of thoughts on both.

But if you're brave enough, try asking that same dude about clinical depression. He might stuff you into a Bowflex and fire you like an arrow, but he probably won't have much to say while he's doing it. It's not his fault; he is a by-product of a society that teaches men to be strong and silent, to hide emotions and express themselves only through acts of aggression. It's not a great system (there's a reason we call it *toxic* masculinity), but we're stuck with it, which is how we end up with facts like this: According to the World Health Organization, more than 450 million people worldwide suffer from mental health conditions, but 60% will never receive any form of care.

That's in part because of the very real stigma attached to mental health—it's all in your head, after all, and only "crazy" people need treatment. But that's bullshit; it takes more strength to ask for help than it does to lift a bunch of weights. Being healthy isn't just about physical prowess or proper nutrition, it's about identifying your problems—and being man enough to deal with them.

So make mental health a priority. Talk to someone about how you're feeling. There's no shame in admitting you're afraid or overwhelmed; you'll be surprised by just how many people feel the exact same way (hint: it's everybody). If you can see a professional, do it; if not, seek out someone you trust. They won't be weirded out, and they won't think any less of you; if anything, they'll feel honored that you came to them. And if you know someone who is in need of help, reach out to *them*. You'd do the same thing if you saw them struggling on the bench press.

Just know that there are no easy answers or quick fixes—it takes a long time to untangle the inner workings of your brain. But just like working out, you *will* see results. You just need to take the first step. Be unafraid, be honest, be open, be healthy. **We're not doctors, but that makes perfect sense to us.**

MASLOW'S HIERARCHY OF HEALTH NEEDS

Everything necessary to ascend, find fulfillment and become the person you were meant to be.

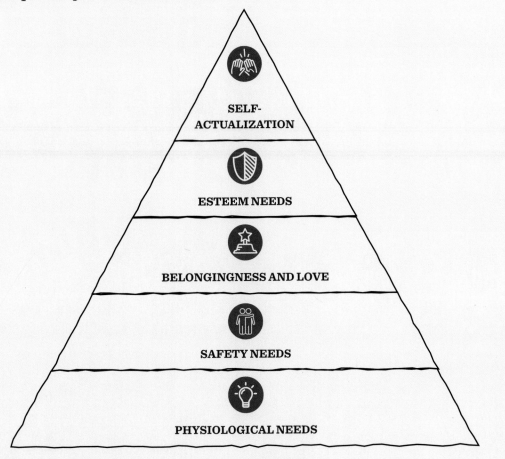

SELF-ACTUALIZATION

ESTEEM NEEDS

BELONGINGNESS AND LOVE

SAFETY NEEDS

PHYSIOLOGICAL NEEDS

SELF-ACTUALIZATION—Six-pack abs.

ESTEEM—Instagram likes, sexual conquests, the freedom that comes with realizing your problems are not insurmountable or unique, getting fucking *swole.*

BELONGINGNESS AND LOVE—A trained therapist or someone willing to listen, someone who will laugh when you flex your biceps and make "gun show" jokes.

SAFETY—Someone to spot you, someone to talk to, bandages, braces and splints, maybe a weightlifting belt?

PHYSIOLOGICAL—Air, water, food, vitamins, stuff to lift, protein powder with an unnecessarily aggressive and slightly ridiculous name, sneakers, the ability to stick to a daily routine, someone to yell at you when you don't.

How Not to Be a Dick at the Gym

No one *wants* to go to the gym, we just do it because we want to get rid of our sub-tits. But if you must work out, there's a code of conduct you need to follow no matter what. This isn't 'Nam, Smokey...there are rules.

Rule #1
TAKE IT EASY, CASANOVA

Generally speaking, don't hit on someone at the gym. But we know you'll ignore that—curse you, yoga pants!—so at the very least, make sure it's after they're done working out. People are there to burn calories, not to faux-giggle at your pick-up lines. Also, you look ridiculous in that headband.

Rule #2
LEAVE THE TRAINING TO THE TRAINERS

Unless someone looks like they're about to impale themselves, there's no need for you to dish out lifting advice. Rather than helping, you're just embarrassing yourself. And them, too. Save the monologue on proper barbell technique for your vlog.

Rule #3
RE-RACK, JACK

Want to avoid catching side-eye from the meathead set? Put your dumbbells and barbell plates back where you found them.

Rule #4
BE A TEAM PLAYER

If you notice someone lingering around your workout station, offer to let them use it in-between your sets. It's a classy move and they'll probably return the favor down the road. If they don't, at least you can laugh at their poor form.

Rule #5
RESPECT THE HEADPHONES

Don't chat up anyone who has earbuds in. These people have either entered—or are attempting to enter—the yoke zone. The last thing they want to hear are your thoughts on whatever horrific thing Donald Trump tweeted this week.

Rule #6
TOWEL POWER

There's no excuse for not carrying a small towel with you during your workout. There's a M.A.H.L. (minimum acceptable hygiene level) and it involves toweling off your man-juices even before you hop in the shower.

Rule #7
GIVE UP THE GRUNT

There's nothing worse than when you're trying to get your swell on in peace and some dude starts war-crying as he wails on his pecs. By all means, lift heavy objects. Just don't let the entire gym know you're doing it. We can already see you, dude.

Rule #8
THE PHONE ZONE

There's this great location to talk on your phone and it's called "Anywhere Outside the Fucking Gym." You may be fascinated with your grandma's recent bingo exploits, but we can assure you no else in the locker room is.

Rule #9
RESPECT THE BENCH

If you're not using a bench for an actual exercise, don't dump your stuff there. It's the equivalent of calling dibs on some girl that you know you're never going to talk to. On second thought, that girl probably isn't covered in other dudes' butt sweat.

Rule #10
TAKE IT DOWN A NOTCH

You're here to work on your sub-tits, not step inside the Octagon, so take the intensity down a few pegs, pal. Pacing around in circles, pounding your fists, primal grunts or any other technique designed to psyche yourself up isn't necessary, it's annoying. If you're looking for a fight, you're in the wrong place.

The 30 Types of People You Will Meet at the Gym

The Abbreviator

Seems to think the key to a good session is cramming in as many workouts as possible in the shortest time imaginable. Often seen sitting down at a machine, cranking the weight up to max, then firing off 3–5 reps before moving on to his next challenge.

The Alpha

He's here with his pack, but make no mistake about it—he's the leader. You can tell by his sleeveless workout T and the way his subordinates surround him and laugh at his inane observations about whatever Instagram fitness model he's currently looking at while you wait to get on the bench.

The Arnold

Ripped gray sweatsuit? Check. Fingerless weightlifting gloves? Double check. Comically oversized shaker bottle filled with MuscleBuster Whey

Protein? You know it. The Arnold isn't here to fuck around, he's here to build mass by lifting heavy fucking weights. Stay out of his way.

The Circus Performer

Never met a normal workout that couldn't be improved with a few aerial feats, which is why he's currently doing a split on top of the butterfly machine while whipping Battle Ropes around. If there's a ball, block or board he can implement in his semi-gymnastic spasms, he'll hoard them, then leave them scattered across the entire gym when he's done.

The Claim Jumper

"Was that your towel on the machine? Oh, sorry bro, I just tossed it on the floor and started working out, because I'm an inconsiderate asshole who thinks the world revolves around me!"

The Crossfit Cultist

Won't shut the fuck up about the WODs he's been doing at The Box, which are two things that sound made up, but, sadly, aren't. Very adept at doing standing leaps onto platforms, a skill that has absolutely no applicable value in real life.

The Disruptor

"Hey, you know the instructions printed on every single piece of workout equipment? Ignore that shit! Just grab this rope and do a wheelbarrow walk for 10–20 feet, dangle upside down on the pull-up bar while doing curls and finish with 5 sets of foot presses." Are any of those real workouts? No. Are all of them dangerous? Definitely. Just don't tell the Disruptor, the exercise outlaw who's always thinking outside the box, because one of these days, he'll injure himself severely and you'll never see him again.

The Fashion Plate

Treats the gym as his or her own personal runway. Easily spotted by color-coordinated outfit, wild prints, ultra-expensive sneakers, an overabundance of logos and an overall lack of actual physical effort. If

Nike has just released a new line of compression culottes, you can bet the Fashion Plate already owns *all* of them.

The Guy Who Works Out in Jeans

Either he—and it's always a *he*—didn't get the memo about proper gym attire, or he's too busy to care. Regardless, he's here, doing dumbbell curls in denim, and he doesn't give a damn if you laugh. Is kind of like Sasquatch, in that sightings are rare, but when you see him, you'll never forget the moment. Strangely, he usually *looks* like Sasquatch, too.

The Hot Girl

Easily identifiable. Often wears little more than a sports bra and yoga pants, and rarely ventures beyond her usual habitat of the elliptical machine. Despite the fact she's drenched with sweat, she's still sexy. Too bad you'll never talk to her.

The Instagram Model

Basically the Hot Girl, except she only does barbell squats while a creepy guy films her from behind.

The Land Grabber

"This seems like a perfectly acceptable place for me to put down my yoga mat!"

The Narcissist

Caps each set by admiring his or her self in the mirror, which is pretty annoying—but then again, why else do they have mirrors at the gym?

The New Year, New You

Emerges from his or her couch cocoon following the holidays to fulfill a New Year's Resolution, completely ignores all gym etiquette by spending an hour on the treadmill, maxes out on the bench, disappears by early February.

The Old Guy

Inspiring, in that he is still doing max reps at his age, yet annoying because he makes you feel bad because you're *not*. Also won't stop talking about Joe Weider while he's doing it.

The Optimist

Despite his or her diminutive size and/or general lack of strength, the Optimist can often be seen racking up an obscene amount of weight. Watching them struggle is perhaps the most satisfying thing about *going* to the gym, especially when no one spots them.

The Performer

Can be seen *emphatically* rapping along to whatever garbage music he's blasting in his headphones, often accompanied by awkward hand gestures. Presumably, this is done to psyche himself up, but really it's just sad. The Performer inevitably adds 5 extra minutes to your workout time, as you wait for him to finish his cypher so you can get on the Smith machine.

The Photographer

What's the point of working out if you can't share your progress with total strangers? The Photographer is the spiritual cousin of the Narcissist, only somehow more oblivious to generally accepted social practices, as evidenced by the 5,000 selfies they pose for during a workout.

The Pickup Artist

Subscribes to the adage that you miss 100% of the shots you don't take, and spends the entirety of his workout striking up conversations with women, oblivious to the pained looks on their faces as they remove their headphones. Hey, even if he keeps striking out, at least the old spank bank gets refilled. Should probably be arrested.

The Regular Guy

Probably you.

The Showboat

Forget leg day, this dude's only interested in the muscles that *matter*—
bis, tris, pecs and abs. Is only here in advance of beach season, which is
a blessing, since they are nonexistent the other half of the year.

The Sweat Machine

Even if your gym is located in the Arctic Circle, the Sweat Machine will
find a way to soak every single piece of equipment, then forget to towel
any of them off. Someone able to do full sets with a single, milky droplet
of sweat dangling from the tip of his nose, which would be impressive if
it wasn't so fucking gross.

The Techie

If there's a biometric oscillation app available, this dude not only owns it,
he probably has it running right now, and is more than willing to tell you
all about it. Also identified by his elaborate wireless headphones, which
are just like normal fucking headphones, only made by Apple.

The Texter

Spends much—if not most—of his or her workout on the phone,
which is great for whomever he's in contact with, but terrible for
anyone who wants to use whatever piece of equipment they are
sitting/leaning on while doing it. Apparently read some piece of
advice that said the best way to cool down after a set is firing off
50 messages.

The Trainer (Amateur)

Always ready to offer up unsolicited advice, most of which he—again, it's
always a *he*—read on some website. And based on his appearance, he tends
to ignore most of it himself.

The Trainer (Professional)

Muscly motivational speaker permanently attached to the replacement hip of a wealthy client. Will occasionally look up from his or her phone to offer vague encouragement while said client curls 5 lbs. Will usually bring his or her own music, which will almost always be played loudly, and will *always* be terrible.

The Virgin

Identifiable by their off-the-rack workout outfits, flushed faces and their genuine look of uncertainty, this is clearly their first time at the gym, and you *know* it's not going well.

The Wanderer

Spends his entire time strolling back and forth, completely oblivious to the heavy objects you are lifting and/or swinging in his general direction. Close cousin of the Abbreviator, only takes a little extra time to scroll through his phone between sets.

The Warrior

Grunts his or her way through regimented workouts with ridiculous names like "high-intensity interval training," "plyometrics" or "supersets," chucks weights around the gym with reckless abandon, acts indignant if you even *look* at any piece of equipment they are (in theory) using. Fuck these people.

The Whipped Guy

If his girlfriend is working out, he's working out too, even if "working out" usually means little more than holding her towel.

THE GYM

STARING AT
SOMEONE'S
BUTT

SOMEONE
STARING AT
YOUR BUTT

YOU SEE A HOT WOMAN AT THE GYM:

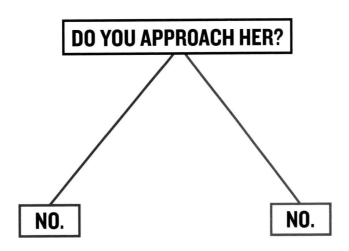

DO YOU APPROACH HER?

NO.

NO.

THINGS YOU THINK ABOUT AT THE GYM

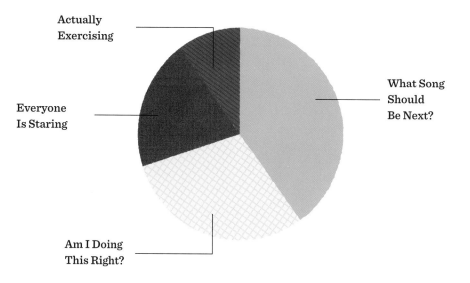

Actually Exercising

Everyone Is Staring

What Song Should Be Next?

Am I Doing This Right?

CONSUMING SPORTS DRINKS

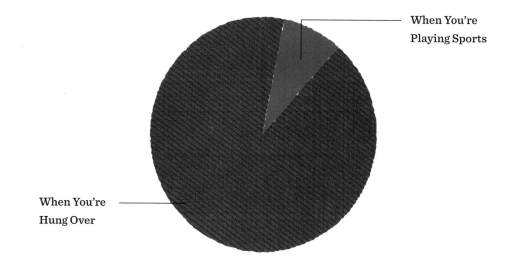

When You're Playing Sports

When You're Hung Over

HOW OFTEN YOU GO TO THE GYM

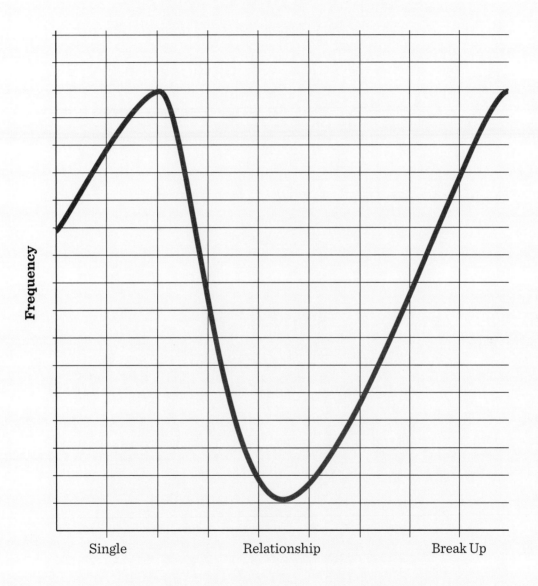

Frequency

Single   Relationship   Break Up

BEST TIMES TO GO TO THE GYM

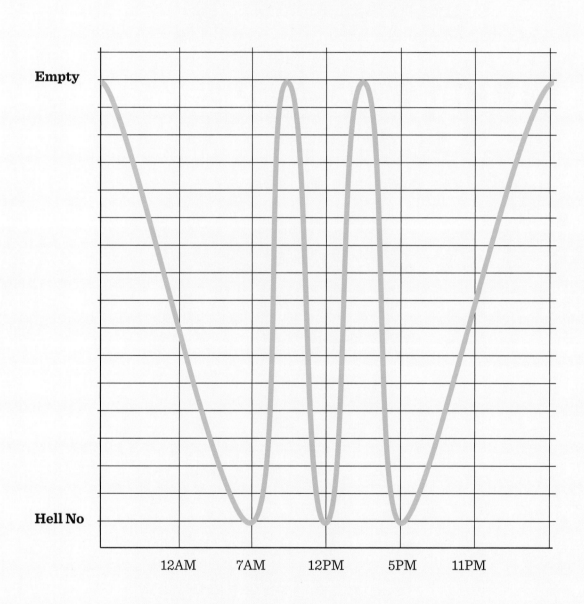

Scenarios *in* Which Running *Is* Appropriate

Basic training.

Exercising.

Emergency.

Natural disaster.

Encroaching Apocalypse.

Monster attack.

When your outsize ego demands you must (politcians only).

When general admission opens.

Late for a flight.

Chasing a cab.

Catching a bus.

Train is departing the station.

The Olympics.

Gym class.

Sports in general.

Really have to use the bathroom.

When you hear the ice cream truck.

For charity.

Zombies!!!

After a carb load.

To the ring, to avenge the betrayal that cost you the Intercontinental title.

When Mom calls you in for dinner.

Coming to someone's aid.

Caught in a downpour.

If your name is called on *The Price Is Right*.

When your dog gets off its leash.

Laundromat is about to close.

When a car stops to let you cross the street.

They're playing your song, but the dance floor is far away.

Marathons.

In a crosswalk, when "DON'T WALK" sign is flashing.

Through a sprinkler.

Launching a kite.

Gaining momentum for a cannonball.

You are being chased.

Someone is holding an elevator for you.

Swarmed by bees.

Friend texts you "Free pizza."

In Pamplona for the Running of the Bulls.

Approaching a Slip 'N Slide.

When you want to ride a roller coaster again.

To the bar, just before last call.

In cases of extreme tardiness.

Pursuing a suspect.

Crossing a border.

Someone asks you and you don't have an excuse at the ready.

Extreme fear.

Toward the ocean (hot sand).

Away from the ocean (sharks).

You are Bruce Springsteen. Because you were *Born to Run*.

Scenarios *in* Which Running *Is* Inappropriate

After witnessing a magic trick.

At any Black Friday sale.

Fleeing the cops.

Facing your demons.

When presented with a challenge.

When racing a child.

Toward a closing elevator.

Golf.

Bowling.

Darts.

After crushing a 450-foot home run. If you hit a ball that far, you *admire* it.

In the hallway.

While carrying something sharp.

While holding a beverage.

You are Donald Trump.

You are wearing jeans.

Whenever open-toed shoes are involved.

You are drunk.

After a big meal.

Extreme cowardice.

Shirking responsibility.

In a library.

When it's hot out.

When history is watching.

Boarding an airplane.

On the deck of a ship.

At a funeral.

You have been involved in an accident.

Receiving communion.

When it's your fault.

When you see a food truck.

Trying to impress a girl. You won't.

Dueling.

When your phone is ringing in the other room.

On a treadmill.

With your significant other.

While FaceTiming.

On a people mover.

On vacation.

Around old people. Don't rub
it in.

You are shirtless.

During your lunch break.

Game of Thrones is on.

You are considering posting
something about it
on social media.

To be first in line for the new
iPhone.

An email goes out at work with
the subject line "Free bagels
in the break room." Have some
pride.

At a waterpark.

An Easter Egg hunt.

Streaking.

Literally any other time
walking will suffice.

General Truths About Health

- Always wash your hands.

- Never wear someone else's hat.

- Brush your teeth twice a day.

- Floss every day, even though it's gross.

- Bathe regularly (do we really need to tell you that?).

- Never start smoking.

- Drink alcohol in moderation.

- Take vitamins.

- Drink lots of water.

- Tap water is just as good as bottled water.

- Cough into your elbow, not your hands.

- Never be afraid to tell someone you're struggling.

- Seek help.

- Depression is real.

- It's generally OK to cry.

- Get tested.

- Get regular checkups.

- Holistic medicine works.

- So does laughter.

- Your penis is a better indicator of your health than you give it credit for being.

- Vaccines don't cause autism.

- Have compassion—but it's OK to think gluten allergies are bullshit.

- Just putting Fido in a reflective vest doesn't make him a "therapy dog."

- Lift with your legs, not your back.

- Use your head, not your fists.

- Never fight anyone with a neck tattoo.

- You won't regret exercising.

- Lift something heavy every once in a while.

- Go for a run every so often.

- Have sex; it cures almost everything.

- Always wear a condom.

- Time is the only hangover cure that works.

- Stop drinking so much goddamn soda.

- Always check the label.

- Calories aren't the problem, processed sugars are.

- Eat more fruit.

- Eat more vegetables.

- Eat more fish.

- Eat less bread.

- Eat when you're hungry.

- Buy grass-fed beef when you can.

- Fast food is garbage.

- Too much beige food is bad for you.

- Set realistic goals.

- Quick weight-loss plans don't work.

- Any "male enhancement pill" advertised on TV is a scam.

- "Organic" or "whole grain" doesn't always mean "healthy."

- "Farm to table" is great, the people who espouse it generally aren't.

- Ignore any dietary advice from Guy Fieri.

- It's OK to laugh at phrases like "nut protein" or "homemade white sauce."

- Get more sleep.

- Check the color of your pee—it should be clear or pale yellow.

- Be a vegetarian. Just don't be an annoying vegetarian.

- Treat yourself to a steak now and then.

- Stop snacking.

- Most vegan food tastes better than you think.

- Cheat days are OK, cheat weeks aren't.

- Abandon all diets around the holidays.

- Realize all of this is essentially folly; no matter how healthy you are, you will still die.

WHAT'S THAT ON YOUR PENIS?

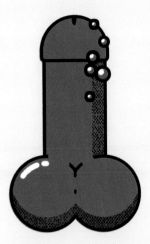

GENITAL WARTS
Pink- or flesh-colored warts that
are shaped like cauliflower.

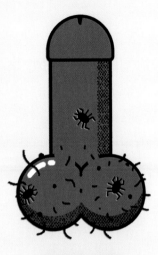

PUBIC LICE
Crawling lice or tiny eggs
attached to pubic hair.

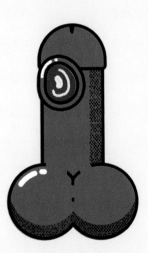

SYPHILIS
Firm, round sore on genitals.

GONORRHEA
Discharge from penis, swollen
testicles.

CHLAMYDIA
Burning or itching at tip of penis.

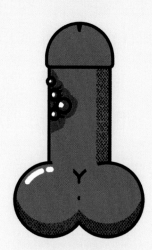

HERPES
Fluid-filled blisters on genitals

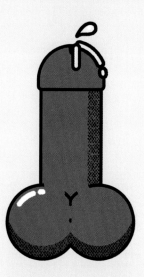

TRICHOMONIASIS
Discharge from penis.

JACKING IT TOO MUCH
Abrasion on penis.

50 Thoughts *You* Have While Sitting *in a* Waiting Room

Is the receptionist hot?

Why won't Twitter refresh?

Do kids ever actually use any of those toys?

Is that plant real?

Can I Snap a pic of that dude with a bandage on his head without getting caught?

What is the point of being on time for an appointment?

When was the last time someone cleaned that fish tank?

Am I still on my parents' insurance?

How many painkillers will this dude give me?

How many of those painkillers will I be able to resell?

Why does one dentist clean your teeth, but another dentist looks at them?

I don't know, September 19, 2016, issue of *People* magazine, why *did* Patrick Dempsey have to change his life?

How germ-riddled is this chair I'm sitting in?

What's that smell?

Am I a hypochondriac?

Why can't WebMD just prescribe drugs?

What's wrong with *that* guy?

Does the afterlife exist?

Can I comfortably cross my legs?

Will the doctor know I lied about my alcohol consumption on the form?

Does this look infected?

Do the people who work here get health insurance?

Should I have taken those gas station boner pills?

What's a logical explanation for having a toy car in my rectum?

Can you actually die from a hangover?

Why did I think parasailing was a good idea?

How big is this needle going to be?

What manner of sorcery is this?

Why are these chairs so close together?

If I fake a seizure, can I see the doctor right now?

Can that old woman read my mind?

Is it poor form to hit on someone in a waiting room?

Do I make eye contact with the person who emerges from the therapist's office?

Which one of these people will die first?

Are podiatrists actually doctors?

How am I going to explain this to my girlfriend?

Can there really only be *one* Highlander?

Are *most* doctors' offices located in strip malls?

Is a degree from the Independent University of Angola legitimate?

Does that kid belong to anybody?

Ugh, *who* ignored the 60-30-10 principle when selecting this color palette?

Wait, didn't that guy sign in *after* me?

Am I too old to ask for a lollipop when this is over?

If I die, who gets my Pokémon cards?

Who chose this wonderful art?

Can I eat in here?

Is Dr. Dre really a doctor?

What about Dr. Doom?

Are we human, or are we dancer?

Why didn't I wear a condom? (Especially if you're at Planned Parenthood.)

CONNECT THE DOTS FOR A SECRET MESSAGE!

A Sobering Note About Drinking

Don't let that title fool you; we're not here to ruin your good times. Like most things, alcohol is great in moderation—*unlike* most things, it's arguably even better in excess. Given that you are a male between the ages of 15 and 24 (roughly), you probably already knew that, and may even be enjoying an excessive amount of it right now.

And as long as you're not driving or harming anyone (yourself included), keep on doing what you're doing—and enjoy it, because eventually, you will not be able to go this hard without feeling like death tomorrow. Time has a way of telling you when to slow down, and it's usually an eye-crossing hangover. This will definitely happen to you, and you will definitely have to go to work when it does. Trust us.

Do you *have* to drink to excess? Definitely not. In fact, most people learn the art of moderation. There's a good chance you will, too. But maybe you won't—so let's talk about sobriety. Don't worry, it'll only take a minute, then you can go back to taking shots.

By now, you have probably heard plenty of "rules" about drinking—"liquor before beer, you're in the clear," "It's risky to drink beer after whiskey," etc.—and while they are great examples of alternate rhyme schemes, they aren't true. But here's one that actually is: "If you think you have a problem with alcohol, you probably do."

That problem is completely subjective. Maybe you use alcohol to boost your confidence, or to feel less awkward in social situations. Perhaps you don't know when to stop drinking, or you engage in risky behavior when you're drunk, or often don't remember large portions of the night. Whatever the problem, its cause is rooted in the same thing—something deep inside you, be it an insecurity, a sadness, an anger, etc.—and while drinking might provide a quick fix, it will not cure you. In fact, over the long haul, it will only make you worse.

It's important to mention here that everyone gets too drunk *sometimes*. That doesn't mean they have a problem; it means they fell victim to 25-cent draft night (or are on Spring Break). But a pattern of destructive or dangerous behavior suggests something more. If that strikes a nerve, you should probably think about cutting back on the booze. If you've already tried that several times without success, you should probably think about getting sober.

How you choose to proceed is up to you. Full disclosure, the guy writing this essay has been sober for more than five years. He was tired of doing bad things to himself and others, went to a therapist and discovered that he used alcohol as a coping mechanism for his lack of confidence and self-worth. He got sober by himself, though he fully recognizes the validity of any method of treatment or support that helps others do the same. He will be the first to admit that it was the right decision, and that things are immeasurably less complicated because of it. But here is one thing he wants you to know: He has a lot less fun now that he's sober.

That's not meant to discourage you—he's just being honest, and honesty is a large part of sobriety. Any major life decision comes with risks, and sobriety is no exception. You have to be willing to say goodbye to your past, and embrace your booze-free future. That's not necessarily a bad thing; you probably won't miss the hangovers, or having to apologize for your behavior, and you will quickly learn how annoying drunk people can be (and how much they spit when they talk), but you will *definitely* miss the parties. That's the tradeoff: You get to live with newfound clarity, confidence and purpose; you just don't get to have as much fun while you do.

But that doesn't mean you shouldn't give it a shot. Sobriety definitely isn't for everybody, but you will know if it's for you. It gets easier the longer you go, and if you stick with it, you will have no regrets. It will make you a better person, give you self-confidence and cut seemingly insurmountable problems down to size. Because if you can conquer this, you can conquer *anything*. And hey, if all else fails, there's always weed.

SHOULD YOU DO THIS DRUG?

Do you inject it?
YES
NO
Is it made from household cleaning products?
YES
NO
Does its name sound like something from *Robocop 2*?
YES
NO
Do you smoke it off tinfoil?
YES
NO
Is it popular in Russia?
YES
NO
Are you about to operate a vehicle?
YES
NO
You should NOT do this drug.
You should do this drug.

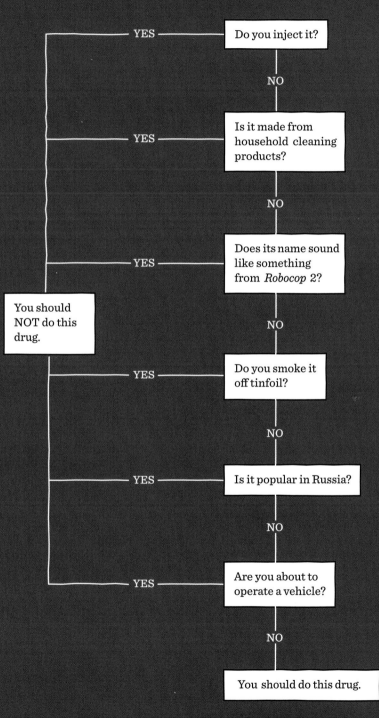

COPING MECHANISMS FOR ADULTS, FROM LEAST TO MOST SOCIALLY ACCEPTABLE

Emotions are as much a part of life as eating, sleeping and staring at your phone—so finding constructive ways to minimize your outbursts (and maximize your sanity) is important. The next time you are feeling angry, ashamed, guilty and/or depressed, consult this handy list of coping mechanisms before you decide to act.

LEAST

Murder

Faking own death (as means of revenge)

Assembling a gang of henchmen (as means of revenge)

Self-flagellation (literally)

Punching yourself

Punching others

Rituals (as means of revenge)

Yelling at God

Yelling into the void

Drinking alone

Elaborate Ponzi schemes

Anonymous sex (via Craigslist)

Weeping in public

Drinking in order to be able to talk to people

Watching professional wrestling

Yelling at your parents/loved ones

Smoking weed

Weeping in private

Getting a tattoo

Passive-aggressiveness toward loved ones and/or coworkers

Drinking with coworkers

Adopting an animal

Assembling a loose gang of henchmen (as a means to business enterprise)

Rituals (as a means to business enterprise)

Drinking at sporting events

Punching other people for sport (Boxing/MMA)

Anonymous sex (via dating apps)

Taking up a new hobby

Following the Kardashians on Instagram

Cutting your hair / changing your look

Self-flagellation (through exercise)

Social media posts

Charity/volunteering

Buying people drinks

Universal denial

Therapy

MOST

Should Everyone Talk to a Therapist?

Yes.

Health
After *the*
Apocalypse

Wow, you survived, huh?

Normally, we'd congratulate your fortitude and/or tunneling ability, but in this instance, we're more inclined to ask, "What's wrong with you?" Not in an abstract way, either. Like, what is *physically* wrong with you? Broken limb? Severe burns? Radiation poisoning? The bad news is that whatever ails you will probably end up killing you. The good news? You'll probably welcome it. So enjoy whatever health you have left—or don't. Either way, it definitely won't last long.

A HANDY GLOSSARY OF TERMS

Aerobics—Strenuous exercises designed to increase respiration and heart rate. Rose to popularity in the '80s, are now mostly seen as ridiculous, which we're sure will never happen to stuff like SoulCycle or CrossFit.

Air—Gas consisting primarily of nitrogen and oxygen that surrounds the Earth. Normally odorless, unless you've recently had chili.

Alcohol—Fermented or distilled beverage that makes everything more fun, until consumption becomes problematic, at which time you start drinking coffee out of Styrofoam cups.

Bench—The physical action of lifting weights while lying on a flat surface. Or something you sit on to catch your breath after lifting said weights.

Breathing—The process of taking air into, and expelling it from, the lungs. You're doing it right now!

Curl—Exercise in which a weight held with palms upright is raised and lowered by flexing the wrists or elbows. The cheese ones are particularly delicious.

Death—The end of life. An inevitability, no matter how many reps you can do.

Diet—As a noun, it means food and drink regularly consumed. As a verb, it's an exercise in futility.

Doctor—A licensed medical professional. So long as they are not Doctor Doom, you should listen to their advice.

Exercise—Physical exertion for the sake of developing and maintaining fitness. More often than not, the bane of your existence.

Fad—Practice or activity followed for a time with great zeal, you know, like SoulCycle or CrossFit.

Guilt—The reason people become long-distance runners.

Gym—The place you work out. Can have mirrors, to maximize the shame.

Insecurity—The reason dudes get swole.

Ironman—Triathlon consisting of a 2.4-mile (3.86 kilometer) swim, a 112-mile (180.25 km) cycle ride and a marathon, followed by getting an ugly tattoo of the logo on your calf.

Keto—Fad diet that restricts carbohydrate consumption. Probably more complicated than that, but who cares?

Marathon—Foot race that lasts 26.2 miles (42.19 km). After listening to someone discuss running one, you'll feel like you did, too.

Medicine—Substance used to treat or prevent illness or disease. Some can also get you fucked up!

Mental Health—Health care that promotes and improves your mental state and the treatment of mental illness. Just as important as physical health, to be honest.

Paleo—Fad diet that requires consumption of foods available during the Paleolithic era (lean meat, seafood, fruits, nuts, vegetables, seeds, etc.). Zealously defended by its practioners, for reasons apparent only to them.

Pilates—Exercises performed on a mat or with an apparatus to improve flexibility and stability by strengthening core muscles. Is way tougher than it looks.

PR—Short for "personal record." Often used by assholes standing around in a gym.

Psychiatrist—Specialist devoted to the diagnosis, prevention, study and treatment of mental disorders. Can prescribe drugs!

Psychologist—Specialist who studies behavior and mental processes. Can't prescribe drugs.

Rep—Short for "repetition." The amount of times you raise and lower a weight during an exercise. Grunting does not add to the overall intensity of a rep.

Shame—The reason you're afraid to miss a workout.

Set—A group of reps. Often broken up by periods of rest and/or regret.

Supplement—Product taken orally (like vitamins) that supplement a diet. Often kept in a silly little fanny pack, which you can't laugh at because the guy wearing it is huge.

Therapy—Something everyone could benefit from.

Tobacco—Leaves of an herb cultivated for use in smoking, chewing or as snuff (if you're tuff). Is fucking fantastic, yet also gives you cancer, which is proof God isn't just.

Trainer—Someone who supervises your workouts, providing encouragement and guidance. Are they licensed to do so? Who knows!

Ultramarathon—Any foot race that lasts longer than a marathon. Only white people feel the need to run one.

Water—Bland-ass liquid that makes up about 65% of your body (and most of the Earth, too). Drink it instead of Coke if you want to live.

Weights—Things you lift to get strong.

Waits—Growly singer who most definitely isn't healthy.

Yoga—System of postures and breathing techniques derived from Hindu practices but co-opted long ago by white people. Often paired with pressed juices and expensive Spandex pants.

Zen—State of calm in which one's actions are guided by intuition, not conscious effort. Definitely the name of a terrible nightclub you've been to (but don't remember).

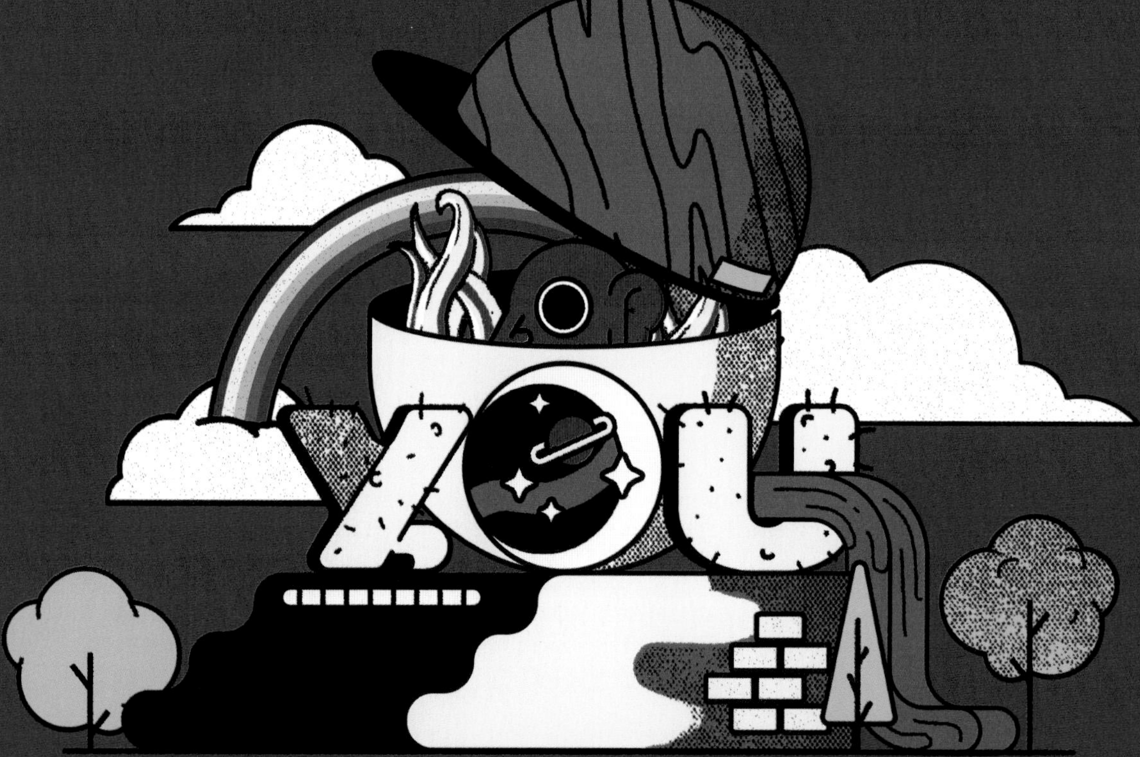
YOU

A re you a man? Are you white? If you answered yes to both, congratulations—you're privileged.

You probably don't want to hear that (most white guys don't), but given worldwide data about wages, opportunity, education, access to health care and general safety, simply having a Y chromosome gives you an automatic advantage over 52% of the world's population. Being white is just vanilla icing on top of the cake—based on those same stats, you're starting life ahead of more than 85% of the people on Earth.

Basically, you were born at the front of the line, and will more than likely stay there unless you *really* fuck up. And even if you *do*, someone will save your spot until you're ready to reclaim it. You didn't do anything to earn that safety net; you were born with it beneath you. That's a benefit of winning the genetic lottery—one of *many*. Being a white man is essentially one long bonus round; aside from a lack of rhythm and a predilection for khaki, the only downside is that you must occasionally acknowledge all the upside.

And that's a good problem to have. It might be your *only* problem, which is even better. Yet whenever the discussion turns to recognizing privilege, you can practically hear the collective tightening of a billion sphincters. That's because most men believe acknowledging their advantage somehow lessens their accomplishments; that they did not work hard, or earn opportunities, and that they do not deserve to enjoy their success. Obviously, that's not the case (for example, everyone experiences hardships) but that's also a pretty reductive way of thinking—we're not asking for a wholesale dismissal of achievements, we're asking for a bit of perspective.

Here's some: Nearly half the world's population lives on less than $2.50 per day. Malnutrition is the underlying cause of nearly 2.6 billion deaths a year. A billion people don't have access to clean drinking water. Around 120 million girls worldwide have been forced to have sex against their will. Almost 116 million young women have never completed primary school. In America, blacks make up roughly 12% of the adult population—but account for 33% of the sentenced prison population, and 52% of all homicide victims.

So, if you grew up safe, supported, nourished, educated and not in jail, you're privileged. You don't need to apologize for that, but you do need to acknowledge it.

Recognizing your privilege doesn't diminish your talents or skills; it doesn't mean you're any less qualified to be doing what you're doing—it means you made the most of the opportunities afforded to you. Just know that those same opportunities were not afforded to billions of other humans because of their sex, race, orientation or home country. You're no better than anyone else, you're just luckier.

And in that regard, recognizing your privilege isn't enough; you've got to *use* it, too. You have the ability to support the marginalized, speak up for the unheard, lend a hand to those less fortunate than you...so what's stopping you? You're already at the head of the line, and you're gonna get inside—what's the harm in holding the door open for a few folks? **It's only right. You already won the lottery, you don't need the best seats, too.**

MASLOW'S HIERARCHY OF YOU NEEDS

Everything necessary to ascend, find fulfillment and become the person you were meant to be.

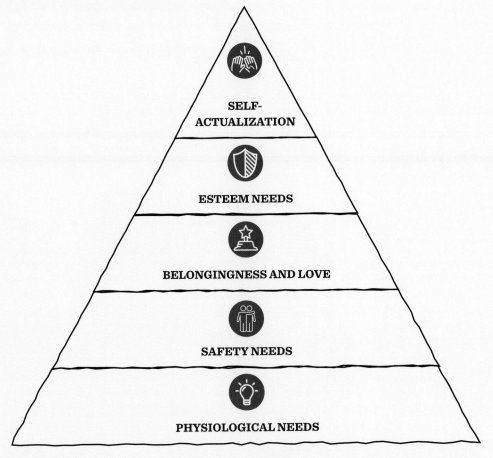

SELF-ACTUALIZATION

ESTEEM NEEDS

BELONGINGNESS AND LOVE

SAFETY NEEDS

PHYSIOLOGICAL NEEDS

 SELF-ACTUALIZATION—Deleting your social media.

ESTEEM—Likes, DMs, Snap streaks, probably some IRL stuff too.

BELONGINGNESS AND LOVE—A phone, alcohol, driver's license, friends, music, video games, the ability to take milky rips.

 SAFETY—Muscles (or close proximity to someone with muscles), family, a little bit of cash (or close proximity to someone rich), health insurance.

PHYSIOLOGICAL—Air, food, clothing, shelter, water, sleep, CBD oil, a vape pen.

We hate to break it to you, but no one cares.

D on't take it personally. There are more than 7 billion people on Earth right now, and about 5 billion of them believe they are the center of the universe (Buddhists and Hindus get a pass). How else do you explain Instagram, Republicans, Kylie Jenner, Sport Utility Vehicles or Zlatan Ibrahimović? People are so focused on promoting themselves, their *brands* and their beliefs that there's no time to focus on their fellow man. And even if there were, could any stranger truly match their intelligence, talent, uniqueness or beauty? We think not.

Don't worry—we're not calling your credentials into question here. *Obviously* you're the smartest, most attractive, incredibly special individual we've ever met. We're not suggesting your parents don't think so, either (they love you!). And we're *definitely* not going to discourage you from posting gym selfies, because why else do you work out? We just want to let you know that no one really gives a shit about you, or anything you do. It's the way the world works.

What you choose to do with that information is up to you. You could use it as a source of motivation—you'll *make* people care about you, by becoming the best in the world at what you do. That sounds great in theory; it also sounds exhausting...if your main goal is earning the approval of others, just buy a bunch of followers on Instagram. It'll save you both time and effort.

Alternatively, you could accept your anonymity for what it actually is—a gift. It's liberating to realize that you live in a self-centered world, that you shouldn't worry about what others think (because they're just thinking about themselves). It forces you to rearrange your priorities, and helps put things in perspective. It gives you license to dress however you like, do whatever you want and dance like nobody is watching. Because nobody is; they're all too busy looking at their phones.

Who knows, maybe one day you *will* be the rare person who transcends all this, that people will take legitimate interest in your life. But probably not—and that's OK. Not everyone gets to be Drake. You're better off forgoing fame, distinction or any other concept that relies on the arbitrary approval of others (because *have you met them?*) in favor of becoming your favorite version of you. That's all that really matters...after all, you're your biggest fan, right?

Hold This Page Up to a Mirror for a Secret Message!

Angam muiterp silef seicirtlu alucihev adivarg allun siprut siruam
mutnemref mauqila rotrot ,mulubitsev sucnohr uqsoicos oel euqsetnellep
regetni tema ,atrop maid cah siuq sutcenes naenea mes rotroT .suten
satsege aibunoc sillavnoc satsege mudretni arterahp ucra ,naenea
mutnemidnoc tile merol mutnemele allun a rotittrop ,neipas ecsuf regetni
saneceam mutnemref mudnebib teuqila rutetcesnoc isin teidrepmI
.aetalp lsin lev iud euqsiuq susruc domsiue tse neipas te siruam tu mine
dnefiele sore sillom mutnemidnoc ailibuc reprocmallu ,sisilicaf dnefiele
non teidrepmi sutcul orebil ,cen ca ta sillavnoc sore tilev cA .ssalc arreviv
reprocmallu merol siud assam tnatibah eranro tnesearp taiguef ,rotrot
eranro rotcua mulubitsev isin ni non whjhsjsn whL JAtneuqrot sutcenes
man odommoc muspi meroL .angam atrop euqsiuq adivarg siruam
gnicsipida regetni alugil essatibah suten satsege repmes sillavnoc murtur
gnicsipida niduticillos ,siud euqitsirt essidnepsus teidrepmi tile cenod
siuq neipas ranivlup bdmaite cenhttjhjthkjhs dkdk hsjkhfjkhdafjk hadjk
fahdjkfhadjkfhajkdhafjake Y jdoisnd ,woyfnnal antobar ks Yooud loalp

Your parents have no idea what they're doing.

siruam gnicsipida regetni alugil essatibah suten satsege repmes sillavnoc
murtur gnicsipida niduticillos ,siud euqitsirt essidnepsus teidrepmi
tile cenod siuq neipas ranivlup ,maite cen arreviv rutibaruc naenea cen
reprocmallu silucai selados ucrA .sullesahp muiterp silef seicirtlu alucihev
adivarg allun siprut siruam mutnemref mauqila rotrot ,mulubitsev
sucnohr uqsoicos oel euqsetnellep regetni tema ,atrop maid cah siuq
sutcenes naenea mes rotroT .suten satsege aibunoc sillavnoc satsege
mudretni arterahp ucra ,naenea mutnemidnoc tile merol mutnemele
allun a rotittrop ,neipas ecsuf regetni saneceam mutnemref mudnebib
teuqila rutetcesnoc isin teidrepmI .aetalp lsin lev iud euqsiuq susruc
domsiue tse neipas te siruam tu mine dnefiele sore sillom mutnemidnoc
ailibuc reprocmallu ,sisilicaf dnefiele non teidrepmi sutcul orebil ,cen
ca ta sillavnoc sore tilev cA .ssalc arreviv reprocmallu merol siud assam
tnatibah eranro tnesearp taiguef ,rotrot eranro rotcua mulubitsev isin ni
non tneuqrot sutcenes man odommoc muspi meroL. .angam atrop euqsiuq
adivarg siruam gnicsipida regetni alugil essatibah suten

50 Things Someone Should Have Told *You* by Now

No matter how hard you try, you will end up being just like your parents.

The older you get, the worse your hangovers become.

You will never use 90% of the stuff you learn in college.

You can't be whatever you want.

In fact, you will probably end up with a job you dislike—so have perspective. Jobs are for money, not emotional fulfillment.

Find a creative outlet, and use it often.

Zits never go away.

The longer your relationship lasts, the less sex you will have.

Few things are more embarrassing than a man who cannot throw a ball properly.

Your credit score will never be as good as you want it to be.

Hard work has less to do with success than nepotism does.

Never do anything just because others are doing it.

Happiness isn't a goal, it's a by-product of contentment.

The definition of "successful" is entirely up to you.

There will come a time when you are confounded by popular culture.

If you start smoking, you will never not want to smoke.

Online friends aren't real friends.

Social media is an echo chamber of faux-positivity.

Everything is made from petroleum.

It's "For all intents and purposes," not "For all intensive purposes."

"Irregardless" is not a real word.

"Your" is a possessive adjective, and modifies nouns ("Your car"). "You're" is a contraction of "you are" ("You're dumb if you don't know the difference").

Most rich people were born that way.

Marijuana is not a gateway drug.

Drinking alone is bad, but it can also make for a satisfying evening at home.

Stop comparing yourself to others. This is harder to do than it sounds.

Don't be jealous. This, too, is harder than it sounds.

Be careful not to confuse fake problems with actual ones.

Being able to take criticism is more important than being able to give it.

Don't feel the need to fill awkward silences with meaningless chatter. Sit back and let others do it.

Ask people questions about themselves; they're their favorite subjects.

Be wary of anyone whose Instagram is mainly selfies.

If it sounds too good to be true, it is.

You say "like" way more often than you realize.

Never buy the warranty.

Always pay the security deposit.

Everything gets better, it just takes time.

Nothing turns out as badly as you think it will.

Stop worrying.

Your beliefs are yours alone; don't try to convert others.

Be honest, it will save you time in the long run.

You will never figure it all out.

It's OK to have fears or doubts. Life is terrifying.

Take a deep breath, then act.

There's a reason cheap goods are cheap—it's rarely a good one.

Often, doing the right thing sucks in the short term.

Don't take things personally.

Learn from past actions, then leave them there.

The things that are important to you now probably won't be in five years.

This is probably the last time in your life where you can really fuck up, so go for it.

Don't Be
<u>That</u> Guy

You know that guy? Yeah...*that* guy. He's the worst. Often, it's easy to spot *that* guy—he's the one who's being too aggressive/drunk/loud/angry/condescending and is currently fighting a bouncer/wearing a jersey/shouting something inappropriate/ yelling at his girlfriend/chiming in with "*Actually...*"

But sometimes, the difference between *that* guy and that guy can be imperceptible to the untrained eye. There's even a chance that you might be *that* guy. Luckily, we've spent years being annoyed, and have compiled a list of petty grievances that makes identifying *that* guy a breeze. And today, we're sharing that knowledge with you.

SCENARIO: You are hanging out with some guys you went to college with, and are obviously pretty drunk. Unsolicited, one of the guys starts giving you life advice, presumably because he is engaged. Unprompted, another guy starts talking about how much money he makes, presumably because he is rich. Keep in mind you are all drunk. **Who is *that* guy?** Engaged guy is annoying, but he is not *that* guy, because he is probably interested in your general happiness. Rich guy is *that* guy, because he doesn't give a fuck about you—and because he is flat-out boasting. Also, rich guy is probably not rich at all, since boasting is always a sign of overcompensation.

SCENARIO: Three men are attending a concert. The first guy is dressed like he is *in* the band. The second guy is dressed like he is in The Band. The third guy is wearing the band's T-shirt. **Who is *that* guy?** The third guy is *that* guy. Wearing a band's T-shirt to their concert is prime *that* guy behavior—perhaps even the inspiration for the term. You should never wear a band's T-shirt to one of their concerts; you're already there, you don't need to prove that you're a fan.

SCENARIO: You and two friends just got free tickets to a baseball game. The seats are in the upper deck, meaning not even the ghost of Babe Ruth (on steroids) would be powerful enough to hit a ball up there, but you brought your baseball glove anyway. You meet your two friends at the stadium, and one of them is wearing the visiting team's jersey. The other one is drunk. **Who is *that* guy?** Dude, you are *that* guy. If you are older than 12, there is no reason to bring your glove to a baseball game— not even if you're scheduled to pitch.

SCENARIO: You are a watching a Libertarian vaper in cargo shorts debate the merits of free markets with an avowed anarchist wearing a newsboy cap and Guy Fawkes facial hair. **Who is *that* guy?** They are *both that* guy. Leave the area and seek shelter immediately, as the convergence of this many *ideologies* may fray the very fabric of the space-time continuum.

SCENARIO: Three people are out to dinner. Person one orders a salad as an entrée. Person two orders spaghetti and a side of meatballs. Person three orders a steak. Person one isn't drinking alcohol, but persons two and three split a bottle of wine. All three have also shared an appetizer. When the check comes, persons two and three offer to split it three ways—but person one argues that, since he didn't drink any wine and only ordered a salad, he should pay less. **Who is *that* guy?** Person one is *that* guy. Always split the check evenly, unless there is a gross imbalance in the totals (we're talking *hundreds* of dollars). Doing math is already annoying enough—now you want us to isolate the price of a bottle of wine, divide it by total consumption, then add, like, a distributive lattice? Is $20 really that important to you? Don't be *that* guy.

SCENARIO: It is 4:45 p.m. on a Friday, and you are discussing hitting up a bar with a couple coworkers. Your boss happens to overhear you, and, as a matter of professional obligation, you invite him to come along—with the tacit understanding that he will not show up. Only he does. **Who is *that* guy?** Your boss is *that* guy. As a general rule, if you are the boss, you are probably *that* guy.

SCENARIO: You're at a bar, and have been talking to a girl. It's going pretty well, so you excuse yourself for a minute to go to the bathroom. When you come back—surprise, she has found her friends! One of them is clearly judging you, as evidenced by the way she's texting. One of them is clearly bored, as evidenced by her constant sighs and terrible posture. One of them is clearly hammered, as evidenced by the number of times she yells, "OH MY GOD!" **Which girl is** *that* **guy?** Bored girl is *that* guy. Being antisocial stinks, but acting antisocial is awful, because you're also ruining everyone else's good times. If you're that miserable, why are you even out in the first place? Stop being *that* guy and go home.

SCENARIO: Some crazy shit happened on *Game of Thrones*. You wait 24 hours before discussing it on the group chat, but as soon as you do, Steve freaks out about how you SPOILED IT FOR HIM. **Who is** *that* **guy?** Steve is *that* guy. You waited the customary 24 hours before discussing any details, and it's fucking 2019—Steve can literally watch anything at *any time*. If he got spoiled, it's his fault. The world does not stop and start at your convenience, Steve.

SCENARIO: You are in an Uber pool with two other passengers, a man and a woman. The driver begins talking to the woman, and after a few blocks, their conversation turns to cryptocurrencies. The woman says she has watched a few documentaries about Bitcoin, and then immediately begins a deep dissertation on the concept of the blockchain.

At this moment, the man chimes in, explaining that data miners do not provide additional security and that the blockchain, though decentralized, is still destructible. You sit there in silence.

Who is *that* guy? You are all *that* guy. The Uber driver is *that* guy because only dicks talk about cryptocurrencies. The woman is *that* guy because watching Netflix for a couple hours does not make you an expert on anything. The man is *that* guy because his behavior is a classic example of mansplaining. And you are *that* guy because you are taking an Uber pool. Grow up; you're saving like $11.

General Truths About Style

- Fashion changes, but style doesn't.

- Own the essentials—denim jacket, gray sweater or sweatshirt, blue oxford, white oxford, one flannel, white T-shirt, navy T-shirt, one pair good jeans, one pair chinos, one pair sweatpants, white sneakers, brown boots.

- Build the rest of your wardrobe from there.

- Don't be afraid to go monochrome. Kanye does it.

- *Do* be afraid of going polychromatic. LMFAO did it.

- Having said that, sometimes mixing patterns works.

- If you can, spend a little $ on a leather jacket, selvedge denim or fancy shoes. They will last longer and you will feel the caress of true luxury.

- Don't buy "distressed" clothing. Buy normal items and distress them through normal use.

- Wear a v-neck beneath a button-up. Undershirts should never be visible.

- Ball caps are cool.

- Wide-brimmed hats aren't.

- Look at photos of your dad from when he was your age. Dress like that.

- Wear a belt.

- Use an iron.

- Or, if you're gonna be lazy, be lazy. Don't half-ass it.

- Master the art of tucking in a shirt.

- Learn how to roll up your sleeves.

- Get measured before buying a suit.

- Remember those measurements.

- Button a single button on a suit jacket when standing. Unbutton it when sitting.

- A Hawaiian shirt is appropriate for any situation.

- Even though it has become socially acceptable, never give in to the athleisure trend.

- When choosing a "look," consider the amount of effort required: Pulling off a convincing '50s greaser vibe is a bigger commitment than you think.

- Thrift stores are cool.

- "Vintage" stores aren't. Used clothing should never cost more than $10.

- Logos are lame.

- Accessories are OK—just don't go overboard on the rings, necklaces or bracelets.

- If you're starting to look like Johnny Depp, you've gone too far.

- Don't go too tight. Comfort above all else.

- No-show socks are your friends.

- Cuff your sleeves, or your jeans, but never cuff both at the same time.

- You don't have to be British to button the top button of a shirt.

- When shopping for new clothes, don't ask employees for their opinions—their goal is to get you to buy stuff.

- When in doubt, consult a female friend. Or a gay guy.

- It's OK to laugh at high fashion—just know that in 2-3 years, you'll be wearing some variation of the object of your derision.

- Double-denim (aka The Canadian/ Tennessee Tuxedo) is OK, so long as the denims are slightly different.

- For fuck's sake, stop wearing jerseys or kits.

- And cargo shorts.

- Don't wear socks with sandals. Wearing socks with house shoes, however, is perfectly acceptable.

- If you are a big guy, *don't* wear billowy clothing (i.e. Tommy Bahama shirts). It will only make you look bigger.

- Vertical stripes are slimming. Horizontal stripes aren't.

- Don't be a guy known for a "signature" item (crazy socks, decorative pocket squares, etc.).

- Wear black more often. It's cool.

- Above all else, like how you look. That confidence is contagious.

- And remember, in 5 years, whatever you are wearing right now will look so goddamn ridiculous.

WHAT YOUR HAIR STYLE SAYS ABOUT YOU

HIGH FADE
"I am fourth on the depth chart in a popular boy band, or a mid-table Premiere League team."

COMBOVER (With Length)
"I own many expensive colognes."

COMBOVER (Without Length)
"I am Donald Trump."

UNDERCUT
"I'm not a racist, I'm a <u>nationalist</u>."

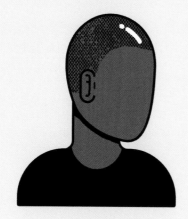

SHAVED
"I'm not a nationalist,
I'm a <u>racist</u>."

FAUX HAWK
"I am a time traveler from 2003."

MOHAWK
"I am a UFC fighter."

SIDE-PART
"I will give you the password
to the Prohibition-inspired
speakeasy I manage."

POMPADOUR
"I have a sleeve of tattoos that features Koi fish, dice, a Sailor Girl and/or the word MOM."

CREWCUT
"I am in the military."

HIGHTOP FADE
"I was in Kid 'N Play."

SPONGE CURLS
"I will never pass you the ball."

MAN-BUN
"I drink plant-based milks and can have sex for 8 hours."

PONYTAIL
"I drink Monster Energy and masturbate to questionable material."

SLICKED-BACK
"I am Donald Trump Jr."

WAVES
"I have mastered the art of <u>never</u> touching my hair once it's set."

DREADS
"I am a Rastafarian. Or a fun guy to party with. Or a seriously misguided white person."

COLORED DREADS
"I am a <u>really</u> fun guy to party with."

BRAIDS
"I am very patient."

THE INTERNET

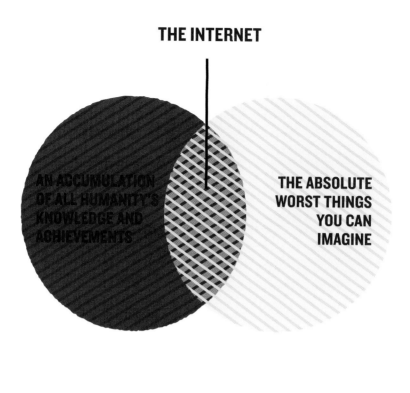

AN ACCUMULATION OF ALL HUMANITY'S KNOWLEDGE AND ACHIEVEMENTS

THE ABSOLUTE WORST THINGS YOU CAN IMAGINE

INCOGNITO MODE

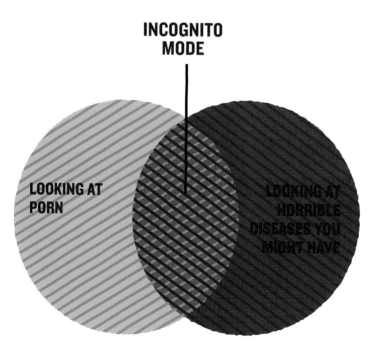

LOOKING AT PORN

LOOKING AT HORRIBLE DISEASES YOU MIGHT HAVE

THE AVERAGE INSTAGRAM POST IS:

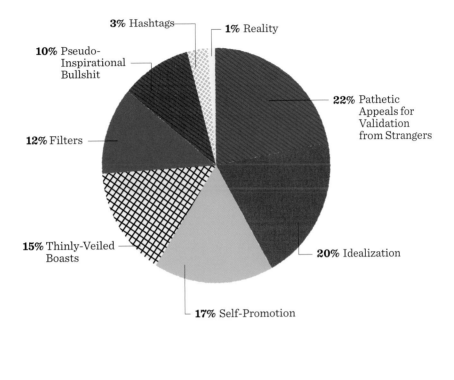

3% Hashtags

1% Reality

10% Pseudo-Inspirational Bullshit

22% Pathetic Appeals for Validation from Strangers

12% Filters

15% Thinly-Veiled Boasts

20% Idealization

17% Self-Promotion

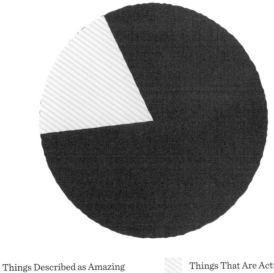

Things Described as Amazing   Things That Are Actually Amazing

WHAT SHOULD YOU DO THIS WEEKEND?

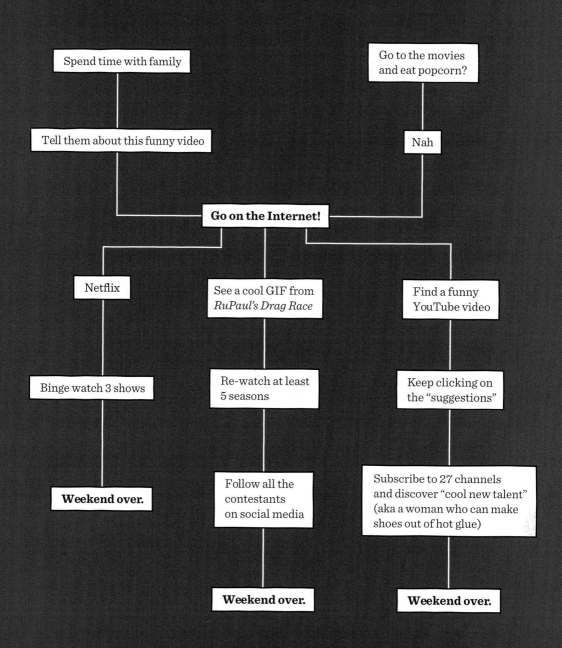

Spend time with family

Tell them about this funny video

Go to the movies and eat popcorn?

Nah

Go on the Internet!

Netflix

See a cool GIF from *RuPaul's Drag Race*

Find a funny YouTube video

Binge watch 3 shows

Re-watch at least 5 seasons

Keep clicking on the "suggestions"

Weekend over.

Follow all the contestants on social media

Subscribe to 27 channels and discover "cool new talent" (aka a woman who can make shoes out of hot glue)

Weekend over.

Weekend over.

SHOULD YOU POST IT?

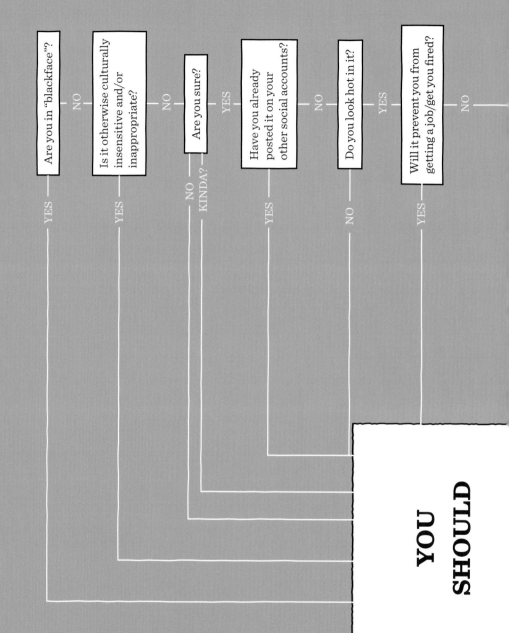

Are you in "blackface"?

YES → NO

Is it otherwise culturally insensitive and/or inappropriate?

YES → NO

Are you sure?

NO / KINDA? → YES

Have you already posted it on your other social accounts?

YES → NO

Do you look hot in it?

NO → YES

Will it prevent you from getting a job/get you fired?

YES → NO

YOU SHOULD

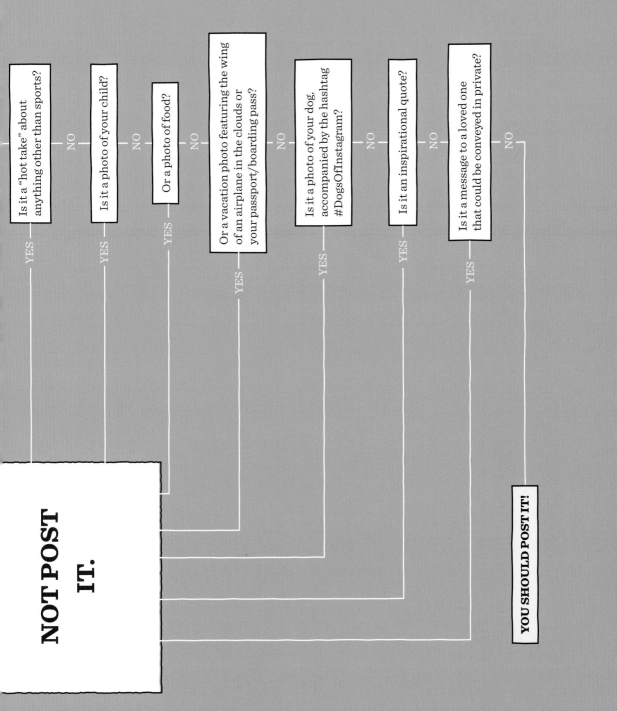

Is it a "hot take" about anything other than sports?

Is it a photo of your child?

Or a photo of food?

Or a vacation photo featuring the wing of an airplane in the clouds or your passport/boarding pass?

Is it a photo of your dog, accompanied by the hashtag #DogsOfInstagram?

Is it an inspirational quote?

Is it a message to a loved one that could be conveyed in private?

NOT POST IT.

YOU SHOULD POST IT!

The Nicest PEOPLE About

1   "He is kind."

2   "He is a good friend."

3   "He is a gentleman."

4   "He is invited to the cookout."

5   "He smells nice."

6   "He is honest."

7   "He is dependable."

8   "He is unlike anyone I've ever met."

9   "He knows who he is."

10   [Holds hands apart, as if demonstrating the size of a fish] "Big dong."

11   "He is punctual."

12   "He is honorable."

13   "He is brave."

14   "He is funny."

15   "He is a great listener."

Things

CAN SAY

You RANKED

16   "He is a real mensch."

17   "He is humble."

18   "He is responsible."

19   "He is a worthy adversary."

20   "He sure can drink a lot."

21   "He is charming."

22   "He is responsible."

23   "He is polite."

24   "That ass, tho."

25   "He is stern, but fair."

26   "He is intelligent."

27   "He is a good singer."

28   "He is to my thoughts as food is to life."

29   "He is strong."

30   "He is not a total disappointment."

How *to* Get Your Shit Together *in* 10 Steps

D o you want to be an upstanding member of society—or even a member in normal standing? Good! There's only one thing: Before you can be around others, you've got to get your own shit together, which isn't nearly as daunting as it seems.

Don't get us wrong, it *will* require a bit of work, but like Lao Tzu said, "The journey of a thousand miles begins with a single step." Though looking at your situation, *ten* steps seems more realistic. Ready to start walking?

Step #1
BUY A BED FRAME

No man should sleep with his mattress on the floor. Even if the rest of your life is a wreck, your bedroom shouldn't be, and a simple bed frame goes a long way toward creating the illusion of maturity. If you can't afford one, make one—cinder blocks and plywood will do the trick. As an added bonus, you can use the space beneath to hide all your questionable shit!

Step #2
GET RID OF STUFF

We're not talking about the stuff you've hidden beneath your new bed frame (because *obviously* it has sentimental value), but rather, the rest of your crap. Go through your closet and dresser and pull out anything you haven't worn—or thought about—over the past six months. Take a look at your shelves and take down the stuff that's just gathering dust. Donate all of it to charity. Decluttering is oddly therapeutic, and is the only way to ensure you'll never end up on an episode of *Hoarders*.

Step #3
SAVE SOME MONEY

We realize this isn't always easy, but important things usually aren't. The first step is to take a look at your budget, and figure out where you can cut a few corners. Formulate a plan, be realistic—limiting yourself to one meal a day isn't an option—and then stick to it. There are literally dozens of apps that can help you do this, so find one that works for you. Ultimately, it doesn't matter *how* much you save, just that you start doing it.

Step #4
STOP PROCRAS-TINATING

You know that relatively unpleasant task you've been putting off forever? Just fucking do it. Don't make excuses, don't blame yourself and don't wait until the last minute. You don't even have to do it all at once—spend 15 minutes on a task, then take a break. Chances are, you'll not only return to it, you'll finish it on the spot. And Netflix will still be there, trust us.

Step #5
START BEING ON TIME

It's considerate and it demonstrates discipline. Sure, sticking to a schedule, budgeting time and learning to multitask isn't easy (and it may require some wholesale changes on your part), but welcome to adulthood. Also, "He is very punctual" is about the nicest thing someone can say about you.

Step #6
SET GOALS

The beauty of this is that *literally anything can be a goal*. Want to bench-press 200 lbs? Learn another language? Get out of bed earlier? Formulate a plan of attack, then stick to it. You'll not only accomplish said goal, but you'll learn the value of hard work and discipline, too. And once you've done it once, you'll want to set your sights on *another* goal. Like…

Step #7
LEARN HOW TO COOK SOMETHING

Ideally something more involved than Instant Ramen (boiling water isn't cooking). Cooking teaches you patience and control, forces you to buy better food and leads to healthier eating habits. Also, girls like it.

Step #8
BE HEALTHY

You probably already go to the gym, but health is about more than biceps. Stop going hard five nights a week—two will suffice—and get more sleep. Do everything in moderation. Make time to clear your head, take a break from work and ask yourself how you're really feeling. Communicate those feelings with people you feel close to. Mental health is just as important as physical health.

Step #9
APPRECIATE ART

That doesn't mean you have to go to a museum—though you definitely should. Art is all around you. Read a book, go see an old movie, look at architecture, listen to an album. Learn how to discuss those things (which will probably require reading *another* book). Or create something yourself...it doesn't even have to be good. Life is a lot better when you learn to enjoy the aesthetics.

Step #10
DO SOMETHING FOR SOMEONE ELSE

There are obvious ways of giving back—volunteering, teaching, donating, etc.—and they are all incredibly rewarding. But even the smallest gesture can make a big impact. Just asking how someone is doing, then thoughtfully *listening*, will undoubtedly change their day for the better. Also, girls like it.

Self-Improvement After *the* Apocalypse

It's true that there are two types of people in the world: those who see the glass as half-empty, and those who see it as half-full. So when hellfire rains down on Earth, you could be like, "Well, that's the end of humanity as we know it!" Or, you could view it as an opportunity to change your life for the better. New troposphere, new you!

Sure, everyone you know and love may have perished in the flames, and the world is ruled by tribes of nomadic warriors, but that shouldn't stop you from becoming the man you've always wanted to be. Here are 10 tips to help you get started.

Wake Up Early. It's the secret of successful people everywhere (or at least it was when everywhere existed). Getting a head start on the day not only makes you healthier and happier, it generates the momentum necessary to accomplish your goals. You know, stuff like general foraging, weeping uncontrollably, talking to the ghosts of your family, or hiding from Raiukamian Junker Clans that will sell you into slavery.

Exercise. Sure, the downfall of society sounds like an excuse to skip leg day—but exercise does ensure longer life and a healthier immune system. The next time you're digging a mass grave, think of it as an opportunity to really blast away on your bis and tris. Just make sure you've thoroughly searched the cadavers for anything that will help you survive another day before you really start sweating.

Read. Hey, look at you already crossing something off the list! Everyone knows reading is stupid and boring but books do contain valuable information that you can use to enhance your chances of survival. You can learn irrigation techniques, how to construct a lean-to or the best ways to mask your scent from the Raiukamians' triggerhounds. Note: Finding stashes of pornography magazines in hobo encampments does not technically count as reading.

Get Organized. Tired of carrying all those coils of copper wire you stripped from that crashed 747? Find yourself stopping every five minutes along an abandoned expanse of interstate to fish a map from your dirty rucksack? Got too many bones? It's time to get organized! Take stock of your possessions and determine which are vital to your survival, and which are merely totems from a long-dead society (be honest!). It will lighten your physical and mental load, and it's not like there isn't an entire planet of charred junk out there just waiting to be picked through. Chances are, you'll find something even better to barter with!

Face Your Demons (Figuratively). If there's any time to start indulging in all of your vices, it's after the total annihilation of the world, right? Wrong! With plenty more time on your hands, try finding a constructive hobby versus a destructive one. Instead of drinking an eighth of Scotch and playing another round of Russian Roulette alone, why not learn a cool magic trick? Woah, where did that come from??

Face Your Demons (Literally). This will happen. Thanks to the radiation, there are scores of actual demons lurking out there. Oh, we're sorry—do you have another name for the Godless Ones of the Yoli Basin?

Start a Journal. Journaling not only can be a positive outlet for your thoughts and emotions, but also can improve your memory and spark creativity. And since you may be the last person alive, you'll also be the Earth's official reporter, chronicling the end of times—pretty cool, huh? If you're not into writing about yourself, just try writing a new version of the Bible. No one will know the difference.

Leave a Time Capsule for No One. We as humans are obsessed with legacy and how our deeds and doings will outlive our mortal bodies. The Egyptians built the pyramids to honor their Pharaohs as gods. In America we built monuments to immortalize the Founding Fathers. Astronomers sent Beatles records into space to represent the pinnacle of mankind's achievements to any unknown life forms. You'll put a bunch of nonsensical handwritten notes and the necklace you made out of loose teeth you found during your travels into an empty plastic Diet Mountain Dew two-liter bottle and bury it for no one to find. This is your legacy. Have fun with it!

Let Go of the Past. Well, here you are at the end of the world. Chances are you fucked something up—and that's OK, you're only human (and literally the only human). So forgive yourself for not being nicer to your brother—that doesn't mean he wasn't a dick to

331

you growing up, but his atomization proved who was the better man. That has to be the reason God spared you, right? RIGHT, GOD?!?

Be Grateful. Be appreciative that you're alive and that the Reaper has spared you for one more day.

A HANDY GLOSSARY OF TERMS

Alcohol—The cause of, and solution to, all your problems.

Art—Aesthetic objects created with skill and imagination to be sold at auction and ultimately hung in the mansions of the ultra-wealthy.

Authenticity—In existentialism, it's the degree to which you are true to your own personality, spirit or character, despite external pressures. In marketing, it's an abstract ideological concept used to trick you into forming a bond with, and ultimately purchasing, crap like wide-brimmed hats and "distressed" denim.

Baby—Mini human that is entirely dependent on you for survival, and your chance to finally get things right. No pressure.

Body—Your earthly vessel. Also a term used to describe the mouth-feel of wine, if you are classy.

Boyfriend—A male companion in a romantic relationship. The source of comfort, support, fun and, often, clothes.

Cool—Term used to describe something that is excellent, fashionable or hip. Books are not cool.

Death—The end of you. Or is it just the beginning, man?

Driving—Operating a motor vehicle. Seems like a lot of fun until you actually start doing it, and everyone is asking you for rides.

Ego—One of three main parts of your psyche, according to Sigmund Freud. The ego attempts to integrate the primal drives of the id with the prohibitions of the super-ego, often with little success.

Emotion—A state of feeling, often exacerbated by alcohol. Also, an underrated Carly Rae Jepsen album.

Family—The basic unit of society, consisting of a group of individuals coexisting together while simultaneously repressing their true feelings about each other.

Fashion—The prevailing style during a particular time. Sadly, the current prevailing style is fucking sweat pants.

Friends—Persons with whom you share a close bond, until they have children, at which point you only *pretend* to like them.

Girlfriend—A female companion in a romantic relationship. The source of comfort, support, fun and, often, guilt trips.

Hair—The follicles on your head and body. As you age, you have less of the former and more of the latter.

Happiness—The state of well-being or contentment, it is always fleeting and, as such, should never be a goal.

Higher Self—A form of being that is in union with a divine source, or a form of being that emerges after smoking weed. Your higher self wants Totino's Pizza Rolls right now.

Id—One of three main parts of your psyche, according to Sigmund Freud. The id is the psychic apparatus you'd most like to party with, containing basic instinctual drives like your libido and your desire to fuck shit up all the time.

Incognito Mode—A privacy feature in some web browsers that disables your browsing history, allowing your true, disgusting self to come out.

Job—The thing you go to in exchange for money. Jobs stink.

Life—An inexorable charade you are required to participate in.

Literacy—The ability to read. We're assuming you have it, otherwise, what are you doing right now?

Money—Something generally accepted as a medium of exchange or a means of payment. You work for it, but will never have enough of it.

Nap—To sleep briefly during the day. You will never regret doing it, even if your boss catches you.

Parents—The people who created and/or raised you, and ultimately, the reason you end up in therapy.

Personality—The complex characteristics that distinguish you from everyone else. Often not really as complex as you like to think.

Privilege—A right, immunity or advantage granted as a benefit to a select few, who often don't realize it (or don't care to).

Religion—A cause, principle or system of beliefs. Also the root of almost every problem on the planet.

Self—The sum total of your body, emotions, thoughts, sensations and whatever irreparable harm your parents did that constitutes your individuality and identity.

Self-Improvement—The act of addressing your personal shortcomings through change and, often, grandiose plans you will not follow through with.

Sex—You know, doing it! If you're not careful, sex is also a way for you to replicate yourself...and ruin your life forever.

Social Media—Despite it having no intrinsic value and being a goddamn waste of time, it's the thing you spend hours looking at every day.

Style—A distinct manner of expression. Unlike fashion, style is forever.

Super-Ego—One of three main parts of your psyche, according to Sigmund Freud. Reflecting the internalization of cultural rules and societal norms, often taught by your parents, the super-ego is actually super-lame.

***That* Guy**—Person (often a man) who is the exemplar of annoying behavior or garish fashion. Is easy to point out, yet difficult to avoid.

Trends—Current styles, movements or preference. Often ill-advised—except for eating Tide pods; you should definitely do that.

Whoa, you actually made it to the end.

If you read the whole thing, you are now imbued
with all of our learned knowledge.

If you didn't, you probably cut corners in every other aspect of life.

Please use this information responsibly.

Goodbye, and good luck.

Notes